The Greek Way

Edith Hamilton (1867–1963) was born in Dresden, Germany, to American parents and relocated to Indiana shortly after. She was an educator at the Bryn Mawr School, Baltimore, Maryland, and began her writing career at the age of sixty-two with the release of her debut novel, *The Greek Way* (1930). Her other works include, *The Roman Way* (1932), *The Prophets of Israel* (1936), *Three Greek Plays* (1937) and her magnum opus, *Mythology* (1942). She received honorary degrees from the University of Rochester, University of Pennsylvania and Yale University. She was also elected to the American Institute of Arts and the American Academy of Letters. She was awarded the Golden Cross of the Order of Benefaction, which is Greece's highest honor, and was also given the status of an honorary citizen of Athens in 1957.

"An authoritative knowledge of the world of antiquity and ancient legends..."

—Emily Wilson, *The Nation*

"At once a reference book and a book which may be read for stimulation and pleasure."

—John Cournos, *New York Times*

"Hamilton's writing, unencumbered by scholarly apparatus, seems to rise spontaneously from deep knowledge and love of her subject."

—Mary Norris, *The New Yorker*

Introducing the Hachette BlackJackets

After the revival of the yellowbacks, Hachette India is pleased to announce the revival of another great series for India from the Hachette stable. Hodder & Stoughton launched the Black Jacket series as an imprint in 1937. The series included about 50 titles, with an emphasis on exploration and travel traversing mainly non-fiction though they did include some fiction too. With works by over 50 authors, such as J.M. Barrie, Reginald Campbell, Janet Beith and Katherine Parker, the series brought the best of both fiction and non-fiction to readers.

This current reissue rebadged as the **Hachette BlackJackets** will pay tribute to the legacy of the series and will focus on a carefully curated collection of classic non-fiction with a few classics of offbeat (non-commercial, literary crossover) fiction also featuring every now and then. The original logo of the series was an extension of the Hodder & Stoughton logo at the time. The new series logo, in a nod to the original, has reconceptualised its elements into a new graphic representation that in thematic continuity with the original colophon depicts an Atlas like figure carrying a BlackJacket book on his shoulders, keeping it aloft.

For more details visit: https://www.hachetteindia.com/Home/blackjackets

THE ROMAN WAY

Edith Hamilton

Hachette Blackjackets

hachette INDIA

The Greek Way
First published by W. W. Norton & Company, Inc., 1930

This edition published in 2025 by Hachette India
(Registered name: Hachette Book Publishing India Pvt. Ltd)
An Hachette UK company
www.hachetteindia.com

1

Text as written by Edith Hamilton

The text in this edition in most cases has been reprinted as is, with minimal editorial changes and by and large no bowdlerizing for political correctness; though in some cases, a few words and phrases considered archaic, or those considered offensive now, along with archaic punctuation may have been modified to make the text more accessible to today's readers. The narratives, language, beliefs, social mores and/or cultural depictions in this edition are a reflection of its times and must be viewed as such. It may also contain certain cultural, racial and gender prejudices and stereotypes that may be outdated or clearly wrong then and wrong today; but their removal would be tantamount to claiming these prejudices never existed. The Publisher does not endorse or support those depictions or stereotypes; and this book has been made available for a discerning audience that will read it for entertainment value and a chronicle/record of popular fiction of past times.

ISBN: 978-93-5731-948-5

Hachette Book Publishing India Pvt. Ltd
4th & 5th Floors, Corporate Centre
Plot No. 94, Sector 44, Gurugram – 122003, India

Typeset by InoSoft Systems, Noida

Printed and bound in India
by Thomson Press India Ltd.

MIX
Paper | Supporting responsible forestry
FSC® C010615
FSC www.fsc.org

To

DORIS FIELDING REID

Κοινὰ τὰ τῶν φίλων

CONTENTS

Preface ix

I. East and West 1
II. Mind and Spirit 14
III. The Way of the East and the West in Art 31
IV. The Greek Way of Writing 44
V. Pindar: The Last Greek Aristocrat 56
VI. The Athenians as Plato Saw Them 72
VII. Aristophanes and the Old Comedy 90
VIII. Herodotus: The First Sight-seer 117
IX. Thucydides: The Thing That Hath Been Is That Which Shall Be 136
X. Xenophon: The Ordinary Athenian Gentleman 154
XI. The Idea of Tragedy 172
XII. Æschylus: The First Dramatist 181

XIII.	Sophocles: Quintessence of the Greek	198
XIV.	Euripides: The Modern Mind	210
XV.	The Religion of the Greeks	221
XVI.	The Way of the Greeks	236
XVII.	The Way of the Modern World	260
	Image Copyright Information	266

PREFACE

The first edition of *The Greek Way* was an incomplete work. A number of the writers of the great age of Greece were discussed in it, but others quite as notable and important were omitted. The result was a picture of Greek thought and art at the time of their highest achievement with some of the very greatest thought and art left out; the poet Pindar, for instance, put by the Greeks themselves in the same class with Æschylus; the two historians, Herodotus and Thucydides, still foremost among the historians of the world. There cannot, indeed, be any real perception of the breadth and depth and splendor of the intellectual life in fifth-century Athens without some knowledge of Herodotus with his keen curiosity and warm humanity, and the profundity of thought and somber magnificence of Thucydides.

The present volume has made good the former omissions. All the writers of the Periclean age are considered.

I have felt while writing these new chapters a fresh realization of the refuge and strength the past can be to us in the troubled present. "Let us keep our silent sanctuaries," Sénancour wrote, "for in them the eternal perspectives are preserved." Religion is the great stronghold for the untroubled vision of the eternal; but there are others too. We have many silent sanctuaries in which we can find a breathing space to free ourselves from the personal, to rise above our harassed and perplexed minds and catch sight of values that are stable, which no selfish and timorous preoccupations can make waver, because they are the hard-won and permanent possession of humanity. "Excellence," said Aristotle, "much labored for by the race of men."

When the world is storm-driven and the bad that happens and the worse that threatens are so urgent as to shut out everything else from view, then we need to know all the strong fortresses of the spirit which men have built through the ages. The eternal perspectives are being blotted out, and our judgment of immediate issues will go wrong unless we bring them back. We can do so only, Socrates said in the last talk before his death, "when we seek the region of purity and eternity and unchangeableness, where when the spirit enters, it is not hampered or hindered, but ceases to wander in error, beholding the true and divine (which is not matter of opinion.)"

A great French scholar of the last century said to his class at the Collège de France shortly after Sedan and the triumphant occupation of Paris by the German army:

> *Gentlemen, as we meet here today we are in a free country, the republic of letters, a country which has no national boundaries, where there is neither Frenchman nor German, which knows no prejudice nor intolerance, where one thing alone is valued, truth in all her manifold aspects. I propose to study with you this year the works of the great poet and thinker, Goethe.*

How noble and how tranquilizing. The eternal perspectives open out, clear and calm. Intolerance, hatred—how false they look and how petty.

"Beyond the last peaks and all seas of the world" stands the serene republic of what Plato calls "the fair and immortal children of the mind." We need to seek that silent sanctuary today. In it there is one place distinguished even above the others for sanity and balance of thought—the literature of ancient Greece.

Greece and her foundations are
Built below the tide of war,
Based on the crystalline sea
Of thought and its eternity.

EAST AND WEST

Five hundred years before Christ in a little town on the far western border of the settled and civilized world, a strange new power was at work. Something had awakened in the minds and spirits of the men there which was so to influence the world that the slow passage of long time, of century upon century and the shattering changes they brought, would be powerless to wear away that deep impress. Athens had entered upon her brief and magnificent flowering of genius which so molded the world of mind and of spirit that our mind and spirit today are different. We think and feel differently because of what a little Greek town did during a century or two, twenty-four hundred years ago. What was then produced of art and of thought has never been surpassed and very rarely equalled, and the stamp of it is upon all the art and all the thought of the Western world. And yet this full stature of greatness came to pass at a time when the mighty civilizations of the ancient world had perished and the shadow of "effortless barbarism" was dark upon the earth. In that black and fierce world a little centre of white-hot spiritual energy was at work. A new civilization had arisen in Athens, unlike all that had gone before.

What brought this new development to pass, how the Greeks were able to achieve all they did, has significance for us today. It is not merely that Greece has a claim upon our attention because we are by our spiritual and mental inheritance partly Greek and cannot escape if we would that deep influence which worked with power through the centuries, touching with light of reason and grace of beauty the wild Northern savages. She has a direct contribution for us as well. The actual Greek remains are so few and so far away, so separated from us by space and a strange, difficult language, they are felt to be matters for the travellers and the scholars and no more. But in truth what the Greeks discovered, or rather how they made their discoveries and how they brought a new world to birth out of the dark confusions of an old world that had crumbled away, is full of meaning for us today who have seen an old world swept away in the space of a decade or two. It is worth our while in the confusions and bewilderments of the present to consider the way by which the Greeks arrived at the clarity of their thought and the affirmation of their art. Very different conditions of life confronted them from those we face, but it is ever to be borne in mind that though the outside of human life changes much, the inside changes little, and the lesson-book we cannot graduate from is human experience. Great literature, past or present, is the expression of great knowledge of the human heart; great art is the expression of a solution of the conflict between the demands of the world without and that within; and in the wisdom of either there would seem to be small progress.

Of all that the Greeks did only a very small part has come down to us and we have no means of knowing if we have their best. It would be strange if we had. In the convulsions of that world of long ago there was no law that guaranteed to art the survival of the fittest. But this little remnant preserved by the haphazard of chance shows the high-water mark reached in every region of thought and beauty the Greeks entered. No sculpture comparable to theirs; no buildings ever more beautiful; no writings superior. Prose, always late of development, they had time only to touch upon, but they left masterpieces. History has yet to find a greater exponent than Thucydides; outside of the Bible there is no poetical prose that can touch Plato. In poetry they are all but supreme; no epic is to be mentioned with Homer; no odes to be set beside Pindar; of the four masters of the tragic stage three are Greek. Little is left of all this wealth of great art: the sculptures, defaced and broken into bits, have crumbled away; the buildings are fallen; the paintings gone forever; of the writings, all lost but a very few. We have only the ruin of what was; the world has had no more than that for well on to two thousand years; yet these few remains of the mighty structure have been a challenge and an incitement to men ever since and they are among our possessions today which we value as most precious. There is no danger now that the world will not give the Greek genius full recognition. Greek achievement is a fact universally acknowledged.

The causes responsible for this achievement, however, are not so generally understood. Rather is it the fashion nowadays to speak of the Greek miracle, to consider the radiant bloom of Greek genius as having no root in any soil that we can give an account of. The anthropologists are busy, indeed, and ready to transport us back into the savage forest where all human things, the Greek things, too, had their beginnings; but the seed never explains the flower. Between those strange rites they point us to through the dim vistas of faraway ages, and a Greek tragedy, there lies a gap they cannot help us over. The easy way out is to refuse to bridge it and dismiss the need to explain by calling the tragedy a miracle, but in truth the way across is not impassable; some reasons appear for the mental and spiritual activity which made those few years in Athens productive as no other age in history has been.

By universal consent the Greeks belong to the ancient world. Wherever the line is drawn by this or that historian between the old and the new the Greeks' unquestioned position is in the old. But they are in it as a matter of centuries only; they have not the hallmarks that give title to a place there. The ancient world, in so far as we can reconstruct it, bears everywhere the same stamp. In Egypt, in Crete, in Mesopotamia, wherever we can read bits of the story, we find the same conditions: a despot enthroned, whose whims and passions are the determining factor in the state; a wretched, subjugated populace; a great priestly organization to which is handed over the domain of the intellect. This is what we know as the Oriental state today. It has persisted down from the ancient world through thousands of years, never changing in any essential. Only in the last hundred years—less than that—it has shown a semblance of change, made a gesture of outward conformity with the demands of the modern world. But the spirit that informs it is the spirit of the East that never changes. It has remained the same through all the ages down from the antique world, forever aloof from all that is modern. This state and this spirit were alien to the Greeks. None of the great civilizations that preceded them and surrounded them served them as model. With them something completely new came into the world. They were the first Westerners; the spirit of the West, the modern spirit, is a Greek discovery and the place of the Greeks is in the modern world.

The same cannot be said of Rome. Many things there pointed back to the old world and away to the East, and with the emperors who were gods and fed a brutalized people full of horrors as their dearest form of amusement, the ancient and the Oriental state had a true revival. Not that the spirit of Rome was of the Eastern stamp. Commonsense men of affairs were its product to whom the cogitations of Eastern sages ever seemed the idlest nonsense. "What is truth?" said Pilate scornfully. But it was equally far removed from the Greek spirit. Greek thought, science, mathematics, philosophy, the eager investigation into the nature of the world and the ways of the world which was the distinguishing mark of Greece, came to an end for many a century when the leadership passed from Greece to Rome. The classical world is a myth in so far as it is conceived of as marked by the same characteristics. Athens and Rome had little in common. That which distinguishes the modern world from the ancient, and that which divides the West from the East, is the supremacy of mind in the affairs of men, and this came to birth in Greece and lived in Greece alone of all the ancient world. The Greeks were the first intellectualists. In a world where the irrational had played the chief role, they came forward as the protagonists of the mind.

The novelty and the importance of this position are difficult for us to realize. The world we live in seems to us a reasonable and comprehensible place. It is a world of definite facts which we know a good deal about. We have found out a number of rules by which the dark and tremendous forces of nature can be made to move so as to further our own purposes, and our main effort is devoted to increasing our power over the outside material of the world. We do not dream of questioning the importance of what acts, on the whole, in ways we can explain and turn to our advantage. What brings about this attitude is the fact that, of all the powers we are endowed with, we are making use pre-eminently of the reason. We are not soaring above the world on the wings of the imagination or searching into the depths of the world within each one of us by the illumination of the spirit. We are observing what goes on in the world around us and we are reasoning upon our observations. Our chief and characteristic activity is that of the mind. The society we are born into is built upon the idea of the reasonable, and emotional experience and intuitive perception are accorded a place in it only if some rational account can be given of them.

When we find that the Greeks, too, lived in a reasonable world as a result of using their reason upon it, we accept the achievement as the natural thing that needs no comment. But the truth is that even today our point of view obtains only within strict limits. It does not belong to the immense expanse and the multitudinous populations of the East. There what goes on outside of a man is comparatively unimportant and completely undeserving of the attention of the truly wise. The observing reason which works on what we of the West call the facts of the real world, is not esteemed in the East. This conception of human values has come down from antiquity. The world in which Greece came to life was one in which the reason had played the smallest role; all that was important in it belonged to the realm of the unseen, known only to the spirit.

That is a realm in which outside fact, everything that makes up this visible, sensible, audible world, plays only an indirect part. The facts of the spirit are not seen or felt or heard; they are experienced; they are peculiarly a man's own, something that he can share with no one else. An artist can express them in some sort, partially at best. The saint and the hero who are most at home in them can put them into words—or pictures or music—only if they are artists, too. The greatest intellect cannot do that through the intellect. And yet every human being has a share in the experiences of the spirit.

Mind and spirit together make up that which separates us from the rest of the animal world, that which enables a man to know the truth and that which enables him to die for the truth. A hard and fast distinction between the two can hardly be made; both belong to the part of us which, in Platonic phraseology, draws us up from that which is ever dragging down or, in the figure Plato is fondest of, that which gives form to the formless. But yet they are distinct. When St. Paul in his great definition says that the things that are seen are temporal and the things that are not seen are eternal, he is defining the realm of the mind, the reason that works from the visible world, and the realm of the spirit that lives by the invisible.

In the ancient world before Greece the things that are not seen had become more and more the only things of great importance. The new power of mind that marked Greece arose in a world facing toward the way of the spirit. For a brief period in Greece East and West met; the bias toward the rational that was to distinguish the West, and the deep spiritual inheritance of the East, were united. The full effect of this meeting, the immense stimulus to creative activity given when clarity of mind is added to spiritual power, can be best realized by considering what had happened before Greece, what happens, that is, when there is great spiritual force with the mind held in abeyance. This is to be seen most clearly in Egypt where the records are fullest and far more is known than about any other nation of antiquity. It is materially to the point, therefore, to leave Greece for a moment and look at the country which had had the greatest civilization of all the ancient world.

In Egypt the centre of interest was the dead. The ruling world-power, a splendid empire—and death a foremost preoccupation. Countless numbers of human beings for countless numbers of centuries thought of death as that which was nearest and most familiar to them. It is an extraordinary circumstance which could be made credible by nothing less considerable than the immense mass of Egyptian art centred in the dead. To the Egyptian the enduring world of reality was not the one he walked in along the paths of everyday life but the one he should presently go to by the way of death.

There were two causes working in Egypt to bring about this condition. The first was human misery. The state of the common man in the ancient world must have been wretched in the extreme. Those tremendous works that have survived through thousands of years were achieved at a cost in human suffering and death which was never conceived of as a cost in anything of value. Nothing so cheap as human life in Egypt and in Nineveh, as nothing more cheap in India and China today. Even the well-to-do, the nobles and the men of affairs, lived with a very narrow margin of safety. An epitaph extant of a great Egyptian noble holds him up to admiration in that he was never beaten with whips before the magistrate. The lives and fortunes of all were completely dependent upon the whims of a monarch whose only law was his own wish. One has but to read the account Tacitus gives of what happened under the irresponsible despotism of the early Roman emperors to realize that in the ancient world security must have been the rarest of goods.

In such conditions men, seeing little hope for happiness in this world, turned instinctively to find comfort in another. Only in the world of the dead could there be found security and peace and pleasure which a man, by taking thought all his life for, might attain. No concern of earthly living could count to him in comparison or be esteemed as real in comparison. Little profit for him there to use his mind, his reasoning powers. They could do nothing for him in the one matter of overwhelming importance, his status in the world to come. They could not give him hope when life was hopeless or strength to endure the unendurable. People who are terrified and hard pressed by misery do not turn to the mind for their help. This instinctive recoil from the world of outside fact was enormously reinforced by the other great influence at work upon the side of death and against the use of the mind, the Egyptian priesthood.

Before Greece the domain of the intellect belonged to the priests. They were the intellectual class of Egypt. Their power was tremendous. Kings were subject to it. Great men must have built up that mighty organization, great minds, keen intellects, but what they learned of old truth and what they discovered of new truth was valued as it increased the prestige of the organization. And since Truth is a jealous mistress and will reveal herself not a whit to any but a disinterested seeker, as the power of the priesthood grew and any idea that tended to weaken it met with

Aristotle and Plato in the center of a fresco

a cold reception, the priests must fairly soon have become sorry intellectualists, guardians only of what seekers of old had found, never using their own minds with freedom.

There was another result no less inevitable: all they knew must be kept jealously within the organization. To teach the people so that they would begin to think for themselves, would be to destroy the surest prop of their power. No one except themselves must have knowledge, for to be ignorant is to be afraid, and in the dark mystery of the unknown a man cannot find his way alone. He must have guides to speak to him with authority. Ignorance was the foundation upon which the priest-power rested. In truth, the two, the mystery and those who dealt in it, reinforced each other in such sort that each appears both the cause and the effect of the other. The power of the priest depended upon the darkness of the mystery; his effort must ever be directed toward increasing it and opposing any attempt to throw light upon it. The humble role played by the reason in the ancient world was assigned by an authority there was no appeal against. It determined the scope of thought and the scope of art as well, with an absolutism never questioned.

We know of one man, to be sure, who set himself against it. For a few years the power of the Pharaoh was pitted against the power of the priests and the Pharaoh won out. The familiar story of Akhenaton, who dared to think for himself and who built a city to enshrine and propagate the worship of the one and only God, might appear to point to a weakness in the great priestly body, but the proof is, in point of fact, rather the other way about. The priests were men deeply learned and experienced in human nature. They waited. The man of independent thought had only a very brief reign—did his contests with the priests wear him out, one wonders?—and after his death nothing of what he had stood for was allowed to remain. The priests took possession of his successor. They erased his very name from the monuments. He had never really touched their power.

But whatever their attitude to this autocrat or that, autocratic government never failed to command the priests' allegiance. They were ever the support of the throne as well as the power above it. Their instinct was sure: the misery of the people was the opportunity of the priest. Not only an ignorant populace but one subjugated and wretched was their guarantee. With men's thoughts directed more and more toward the unseen world, and with the keys to it firmly in their own grasp, their terrific power was assured.

When Egypt ended, the East went on ever farther in the direction Egypt had pointed. The miseries of Asia are a fearful page of history. Her people found strength to endure by denying any meaning and any importance to what they could not escape. The Egyptian world where dead men walked and slept and feasted was transmuted into what had always been implicit in its symbolism, the world of the spirit. In India, for centuries the leader of thought to the East, ages long since, the world of the reason and the world of the spirit were divorced and the universe handed over to the latter. Reality—that which we have heard, which we have seen with our eyes and our hands have handled, of the Word of life—was dismissed as a fiction that had no bearing upon the Word. All that was seen and heard and handled was vague and unsubstantial and forever passing, the shadow of a dream; only that was real which was of the spirit. This is always man's way out when the facts of life are too bitter and too black to be borne. When conditions are such that life offers no earthly hope, somewhere, somehow, men must find a refuge. Then they fly from the terror without to the citadel within, which famine and pestilence and fire and sword cannot shake. What Goethe calls the inner universe, can live by its own laws, create its own security, be sufficient unto itself, when once reality is denied to the turmoil of the world without.

So the East found a way to endure the intolerable, and she pursued it undeviatingly through the centuries, following it to its farthest implications. In India the idea of truth became completely separated from outside fact; all outside was illusion; truth was an inner disposition. In such a world there is little scope for the observing reason or the seeing eye. Where all except the spirit is unreal, it is manifest folly to be concerned with an exterior that is less than a shadow.

It is easy to understand how in these conditions the one department of the intellect that flourished was mathematics. Nothing is less likely to react practically upon life or to intrude into the domain of theology than the world of the ideal revealed to the mathematical imagination. Pure mathematics soars into a region far removed from human wretchedness and no priest ever troubled himself about the effects of free inquiry along mathematical lines. There the mind could go where it pleased. "Compared with the Egyptians we are childish mathematicians," observes Plato. India, too, made notable contributions in this field. But, sooner or later, if the activity of the mind is restricted anywhere it will cease to function even where it is allowed to be free. Today in India the triumph of the spirit over the mind is complete, and wherever Buddhism, the great product of the Indian spirit, has prevailed, the illusoriness of all that is of this earth and the vanity of all research into its nature is the centre of the faith.

As in Egypt, the priests saw their opportunity. The power of the Brahmans, the priestly caste, and of the great Buddhist hierarchy, is nothing less than stupendous. The circle is complete: a wretched populace with no hope save in the invisible, and a priesthood whose power is bound up with the belief in the unimportance of the visible so that they must forever strive to keep it an article of faith. The circle is complete in another sense as well: the wayfarer sheltering for the night in an abandoned house does not care to mend the roof the rain drips through, and a people living in such wretchedness that their one comfort is to deny the importance of the facts of earthly life, will not try to better them. India has gone the way of the things that are not seen until the things that are seen have become invisible.

That is what happens when one course is followed undeviatingly for ages. We are composite creatures, made up of soul and body, mind and spirit. When men's attention is fixed upon one to the disregard of the others, human beings result who are only partially developed, their eyes blinded to half of what life offers and the great world holds. But in that antique world of Egypt and the early Asiatic civilizations, that world where the pendulum was swinging ever farther and farther away from all fact, something completely new happened. The Greeks came into being and the world, as we know it, began.

MIND AND SPIRIT

Egypt is a fertile valley of rich river soil, low-lying, warm, monotonous, a slow-flowing river, and beyond, the limitless desert. Greece is a country of sparse fertility and keen, cold winters, all hills and mountains sharp cut in stone, where strong men must work hard to get their bread. And while Egypt submitted and suffered and turned her face toward death, Greece resisted and rejoiced and turned full-face to life. For somewhere among those steep stone mountains, in little sheltered valleys where the great hills were ramparts to defend and men could have security for peace and happy living, something quite new came into the world; the joy of life found expression. Perhaps it was born there, among the shepherds pasturing their flocks where the wild flowers made a glory on the hillside; among the sailors on a sapphire sea washing enchanted islands purple in a luminous air. At any rate it has left no trace anywhere else in the world of antiquity. In Greece nothing is more in evidence. The Greeks were the first people in the world to play, and they played on a great scale. All over Greece there were games, all sorts of games; athletic contests of every description: races—horse-, boat-, foot-, torch-races; contests in music, where one side out-sung the other; in dancing—on greased skins sometimes to display a nice skill of foot and balance of body; games where men leaped in and out of flying chariots; games so many one grows weary with the list of them. They are embodied in the statues familiar to all, the disc thrower, the charioteer, the wrestling boys, the dancing flute players. The great games—there were four that came at stated seasons—were so important, when one was held, a truce of God was proclaimed so that all Greece might come in safety without fear. There "glorious-limbed youth"—the phrase is Pindar's, the athlete's poet—strove for an honor so coveted as hardly anything else in Greece. An Olympic victor—triumphing generals would give place to him. His crown of wild olives was set beside the prize of the tragedian. Splendor attended him, processions, sacrifices, banquets, songs the greatest poets were glad to write. Thucydides, the brief, the severe, the historian of that bitter time, the fall of Athens, pauses, when one of his personages has conquered in the games, to give the fact full place of honor. If we had no other knowledge of what the Greeks were like, if nothing were left of Greek art and literature, the fact that they were in love with play and played magnificently would be proof enough of how they lived and how they looked at life. Wretched people, toiling people, do not play. Nothing like the Greek games is conceivable in Egypt or Mesopotamia. The life of the Egyptian lies spread out in the mural paintings down to the minutest detail. If fun and sport had played any real part they would be there in some form for us to see. But the Egyptian did not play. "Solon, Solon, you Greeks are all children," said the Egyptian priest to the great Athenian. At any rate, children or not, they enjoyed themselves. They had physical vigor and high spirits and time, too, for fun. The witness of the games is conclusive. And when Greece died and her reading of the great enigma was buried with her statues, play, too, died out of the world. The brutal, bloody Roman games had nothing to do with the spirit of play. They were fathered by the Orient, not by Greece. Play died when Greece died and many and many a century passed before it was resurrected.

To rejoice in life, to find the world beautiful and delightful to live in, was a mark of the Greek spirit which distinguished it from all that had gone before. It is a vital distinction. The joy of life is written upon everything the Greeks left behind and they who leave it out of account fail to reckon with something that is of first importance in understanding how the Greek achievement came to pass in the world of antiquity. It is not a fact that jumps to the eye for the reason that their literature is marked as strongly by sorrow. The Greeks knew to the full how bitter life is as well as how sweet. Joy and sorrow, exultation and tragedy, stand hand in hand in Greek literature, but there is no contradiction involved thereby. Those who do not know the one do not really know the other either. It is the depressed, the gray-minded people, who cannot rejoice just as they cannot agonize. The Greeks were not the victims of depression. Greek literature is not done in gray or with a low palette. It is all black and shining white or black and scarlet and gold. The Greeks were keenly aware, terribly aware, of life's uncertainty and the imminence of death. Over and over again they emphasize the brevity and the failure of all human endeavor, the swift passing of all that is beautiful and joyful. To Pindar, even as he glorifies the victor in the games, life is "a shadow's dream." But never, not in their darkest moments, do they lose their taste for life. It is always a wonder and a delight, the world a place of beauty, and they themselves rejoicing to be alive in it.

Quotations to illustrate this attitude are so numerous, it is hard to make a choice. One might quote all the Greek poems there are, even when they are tragedies. Every one of them shows the fire of life burning high. Never a Greek poet that did not warm both hands at that flame. Often in the midst of a tragedy a choral song of joy breaks forth. So Sophocles, of the three tragedians the soberest, the most severe, sings in the *Antigone* of the wine-god, "with whom the stars rejoice as they move, the stars whose breath is fire." Or in the *Ajax* where "thrilling with rapture, soaring on wings of sudden joy," he calls to "Pan, O Pan, come, sea-rover, down from the snow-beaten mountain crag. Lord of the dance the gods delight in, come, for now I, too, would dance. O joy!" Or in the Œdipus Coloneus, where tragedy is suddenly put aside by the poet's love of the out-of-door world, of the nightingale's clear trilling note and the stainless tide of pure waters and the glory of the narcissus and the bright-shining crocus, "which the quire of the muses love and Aphrodite of the golden rein." Passages like these come again and again, lifting the black curtain of tragedy to the full joy of life. They are no artifice or trick to heighten by contrast. They are the natural expression of men who were tragedians indeed but Greeks first, and so thrillingly aware of the wonder and beauty of life, they could not but give it place.

The little pleasures, too, that daily living holds, were felt as such keen enjoyment: "Dear to us ever," says Homer, "is the banquet and the harp and the dance and changes of raiment and the warm bath and love and sleep." Eating and drinking have never again seemed so delightful as in the early Greek lyrics, nor a meeting with friends, nor a warm fire of a winter's night—"the stormy season of winter, a soft couch after dinner by the fire, honey-sweet wine in your glass and nuts and beans at your elbow"—nor a run in the springtime "amid a fragrance of woodbine and leisure and white poplar, when the plane-tree and the elm whisper together," nor a banqueting hour, "moving among feasting and giving up the soul to be young, carrying a bright harp and touching it in peace among the wise of the citizens." It is a matter of course that comedy should be their invention, the mad, rollicking, irresponsible fun of the Old Comedy, its verve and vitality and exuberant, overflowing energy of life. A tomb in Egypt and a theatre in Greece. The one comes to the mind as naturally as the other. So was the world changing by the time the fifth century before Christ began in Athens.

"The exercise of vital powers along lines of excellence in a life affording them scope" is an old Greek definition of happiness. It is a conception permeated with energy of life. Through all Greek history that spirit of life abounding moves. It led along many an untried way. Authoritarianism and submissiveness were not the direction it pointed to. A high-spirited people full of physical vigor do not obey easily, and indeed the strong air of the mountains has never been wholesome for despots. The absolute monarch-submissive slave theory of life flourishes best where there are no hills to give a rebel refuge and no mountain heights to summon a man to live dangerously. When history begins in Greece there is no trace of the ancient state. The awful, unapproachable sacred potentate, Pharaoh of Egypt, priest-king of Mesopotamia, whose absolute power none had questioned for thousands of years, is nowhere in the scene. There is nothing that remotely resembles him in Greece. Something we know of the Age of the Tyrants in Greek history but what we know most clearly is that it was put a stop to. Abject submission to the power on the throne which had been the rule of life in the ancient world since kings began, and was to be the rule of life in Asia for centuries to come, was cast off by the Greeks so easily, so lightly, hardly more than an echo of the contest has come down to us.

In the *Persians* of Æschylus, a play written to celebrate the defeat of the Persians at Salamis, there is many an allusion to the difference between the Greek way and the Oriental way. The Greeks, the Persian queen is told, fight as free men to defend what is precious to them. Have they no master? she asks. No, she is told. No man calls Greeks slaves or vassals. Herodotus in his account adds, "They obey only the law." Something completely new is here. The idea of freedom has been born. The conception of the entire unimportance of the individual to the state, which had persisted down from earliest tribal days and was universally accepted in all the ancient world, has given place in Greece to the conception of the liberty of the individual in a state which he defends of his own free will. That is a change not worked by high spirit and abounding vigor alone. Something more was at work in Greece. Men were thinking for themselves.

One of the earlier Greek philosophic sayings is that of Anaxagoras: "All things were in chaos when Mind arose and made order." In the ancient world ruled by the irrational, by dreadful unknown powers, where a man was utterly at the mercy of what he must not try to understand, the Greeks arose and the rule of reason began. The fundamental fact about the Greek was that he had to use his mind. The ancient priests had said, "Thus far and no farther. We set the limits to thought." The Greeks said, "All things are to be examined and called into question. There are no limits set to thought." It is an extraordinary fact that by the time we have actual, documentary knowledge of the Greeks there is not a trace to be found of that domination over the mind by the priests which played such a decisive part in the ancient world. The priest plays no real part in either the history or the literature of Greece. In the *Iliad* he orders a captive taken back to appease an angry god and stop a pestilence, and is given a grudging obedience—with the backing of the pestilence, but that is his sole appearance on the scene. The Trojan War is fought out by gods and men with no intermediaries. A prophet or two appears in the tragedies but for evil oftener than for good. In the *Agamemnon* of Æschylus, a hundred years before Plato, there is a criticism of the dark powers exercised by the ministers of religion which goes with precision to the heart of the matter:

And, truly, what of good
ever have prophets brought to men?
Craft of many words,
only through
evil your message speaks.
Seers bring aye
terror, so to keep
men afraid.

The conclusion might be drawn from the words that something of that sort of power was in fact wielded then by priest and prophet, but what is certainly true is that the poet who spoke them to a great audience, with the most important priests sitting in the front-row seats, won for himself not disapproval but the highest mark of favor the people could give. There is nothing clearer and nothing more astonishing than the strict limits the Greeks set to the power of the priests. Priests in numbers there were and altars and temples, and at a time of public danger, disrespect shown to the forms of religion would arouse even in Athens superstition and popular fury, but the place of the priest in Greece was in the background. The temple was his and the temple rites, and nothing else.

The Greek kept his formal religion in one compartment and everything that really mattered to him in another. He never went to a priest for guidance or advice. Did he want to know how to bring up his children or what Truth was, he went to Socrates, or to the great sophist Protagoras, or to a learned grammarian. The idea of consulting a priest would never have occurred to him. The priests could tell him the proper times and the proper forms for sacrifices. That was their business and only that. In the *Laws*, written in Plato's old age and on the whole in a spirit of reaction against his earlier revolts, the entire subject of religion is discussed without a single reference to a priest. The *Laws*, it should perhaps be pointed out, is not written for the ideal state, the heavenly pattern of the *Republic*, but is addressed to the ideas and feelings of the Greeks of that day. The Athenian, who is the chief speaker, often meets with criticism from the two other personages of the dialogue when he proposes an innovation, but they accept without a word of surprise or dissent a statement that those who talk loosely about the gods and sacrifices and oracles, should be admonished by—members of the governing Council! These are to "converse with them touching the improvement of their soul's health." There is not a suggestion from any of the three that a priest might be of use here. Furthermore, "Before a man is prosecuted for impiety the guardians of the law shall determine if the deed has been done in earnest or only from childish levity." It was clearly not the idea that in matters touching the life and liberty of a Greek citizen the priest should have a voice. At the end of the argument the priest's proper domain is briefly indicated: "When a man is disposed to sacrifice, let him place his offerings in the hands of the priests and priestesses who have under their care the holy rite." That is the sum total of what the speakers hold to be the priest's part in religion, and he has no part in anything except religion. Even more noteworthy as illustrating the Greek point of view is the Athenian's characterization as "monstrous natures" of those "who say they can conjure the dead and bribe the gods with sacrifices and prayers"—in other words, those who used magic and tried to obtain favors from heaven by practices not unknown in the most civilized lands today.

No doubt the oracles, at Delphi notably, played a prominent role in Greece, but none of the oracular sayings that have come down to us bear the familiar priestly stamp. Athens seeking guidance from the Delphic priestess at the time of the Persian invasion is not told to sacrifice hecatombs to the god and offer precious treasure to the oracle, but merely to defend herself with wooden walls, a piece of acute worldly wisdom, at least as interpreted by Themistocles. When Crœsus the rich, the king of Lydia, sent to Delphi to find out if he would succeed in a war against Persia and paved his way by magnificent gifts, any priests in the world except the Greeks would have made their profit for their church by an intimation that the costlier the offering the surer his success, but the only answer the Greek holy of holies gave him was that by going to war he would destroy a great empire. It happened to be his own, but, as the priestess pointed out, she was not responsible for his lack of wit, and certainly there was no intimation that if he had given more, things would have turned out better. The sentences which Plato says were inscribed in the shrine at Delphi are singularly unlike those to be found in holy places outside of Greece. *Know thyself* was the first, and *Nothing in excess* the second, both marked by a total absence of the idiom of priestly formulas all the world over.

Something new was moving in the world, the most disturbing force there is. "All things are at odds when God lets a thinker loose on this planet." They were let loose in Greece. The Greeks were intellectualists; they had a passion for using their minds. The fact shines through even their use of language. Our word for school comes from the Greek word for leisure. Of course, reasoned the Greek, given leisure a man will employ it in thinking and finding out about things. Leisure and the pursuit of knowledge, the connection was inevitable—to a Greek. In our ears Philosophy has an austere if not a dreary sound. The word is Greek but it had not that sound in the original. The Greeks meant by it the endeavor to understand everything there is, and they called it what they felt it to be, the *love* of knowledge:

> *How charming is divine philosophy—*

In the world of antiquity those who practiced the healing art were magicians, priests versed in special magic rites. The Greeks called their healers physicians, which means those versed in the ways of nature. Here in brief is an exemplification of the whole trend of the Greek mind, its swing away from antiquity and toward modernity. To be versed in the ways of nature means that a man has observed outside facts and reasoned about them. He has used his powers not to escape from the world but to think himself more deeply into it. To the Greeks the outside world was real and something more, it was interesting. They looked at it attentively and their minds worked upon what they saw. This is essentially the scientific method. The Greeks were the first scientists and all science goes back to them.

In nearly every field of thought "they took the first indispensable steps." The statement means more than is apparent on the surface.

The reason that antiquity did not give birth to science was not only because fact tended to grow more and more unreal and unimportant. There was an even more cogent cause: the ancient world was a place of fear. Magical forces ruled it and magic is absolutely terrifying because it is absolutely incalculable. The minds of those who might have been scientists had been held fast-bound in the prison of that terror. Nothing of all the Greeks did is more astonishing than their daring to look it in the face and use their minds about it. They dared nothing less than to throw the light of reason upon dreadful powers taken completely on trust everywhere else, and by the exercise of the intelligence to banish them. Galileo, the humanists of the Renaissance, are glorified for the courage in venturing beyond the limits set by a power that could damn their souls eternally, and in demanding to know for themselves what the universe was like. No doubt it was high courage, great and admirable, but it was altogether beneath that shown by the Greeks. The humanists ventured upon the fearful ocean of free thought under guidance. The Greeks had preceded them there. They chanced that great adventure all alone.

High spirit and the energy of great vital powers had worked in them to assert themselves against despotic rule and to refuse to submit to priestly rule. They would have no man to dictate to them and being free from masters they used their freedom to think. For the first time in the world the mind was free, free as it hardly is today. Both the state and religion left the Athenian free to think as he pleased.

During World War I, a play would have had short shrift here which showed up General Pershing for a coward; ridiculed the Allies' cause; brought in Uncle Sam as a blustering bully; glorified the peace party. But when Athens was fighting for her life, Aristophanes did the exact equivalent of all these things many times over and the Athenians, pro-and anti-war alike, flocked to the theatre. The right of a man to say what he pleased was fundamental in Athens. "A slave is he who cannot speak his thought," said Euripides. Socrates drinking the hemlock in his prison on the charge of introducing new gods and corrupting the youth is but the exception that proves the rule. He was an old man and all his life he had said what he would. Athens had just gone through a bitter time of crushing defeat, of rapid changes of government, of gross mismanagement. It is a reasonable conjecture that he was condemned in one of those sudden panics all nations know, when the people's fears for their own safety have been worked upon and they turn cruel. Even so, he was condemned by a small majority and his pupil Plato went straight on teaching in his name, never molested but honored and sought after. Socrates was the only man in Athens who suffered death for his opinions. Three others were forced to leave the country. That is the entire list and to compare it with the endless list of those tortured and killed in Europe during even the last five hundred years is to see clearly what Athenian liberty was.

The Greek mind was free to think about the world as it pleased, to reject all traditional explanations, to disregard all the priests taught, to search unhampered by any outside authority for the truth. The Greeks had free scope for their scientific genius and they laid the foundations of our science today.

Homer's hero who cried for more light even if it were but light to die in, was a true Greek. They could never leave anything obscure. Neither could they leave anything unrelated. System, order, connection, they were impelled to seek for. An unanalyzed whole was an impossible conception for them. Their very poetry is built on clarity of ideas, with plan and logical sequence. Great artists though they were, they would never give over trying to understand beauty as well as to express it. Plato is speaking as a typical Greek when he says that there are men who have an intuitive insight, an inspiration, which causes them to do good and beautiful things. They themselves do not know why they do as they do and therefore they are unable to explain to others. It is so with poets and, in a sense, with all good men. But if one could be found who was able to add to his instinct for the right or the beautiful, a clear idea of the reason for its rightness or beauty, he would be among men what a living man would be in the dead world of flitting shades. That statement is completely Greek in its conception of values. There never were people farther from the idea of the contemplation of beauty as a rest to the mind. They were not in the world to find rest for their mind in anything. They must analyze and reflect upon everything. Any general term they found themselves using must be precisely realized and the language of all philosophy is their creation.

But to leave the intellectuality of the Greeks here would be to give only half of the picture. Even in Greece Science and Philosophy wore a sober look, but the Greeks did not think soberly about the exercise of the intellect. "Thoughts and ideas, the fair and immortal children of the mind," as a Greek writer calls them, were a delight to them. Never, not in the brightest days of the Renaissance, has learning appeared in such a radiant light as it did to the gay young men of imperial Athens. Listen to one of them talking to Socrates, just waked up in the early dawn by a persistent hammering at his door: "What's here?" he cries out, still half asleep. "O Socrates," and the voice is that of a lad he knows well, "Good news, good news!" "It ought to be at this unearthly hour. Well, out with it." The young fellow is in the house now. "O Socrates, Protagoras has come. I heard it yesterday evening. And I was going to you at once but it was so late—" "What's it all about—Protagoras? Has he stolen something of yours?" The boy bursts out laughing. "Yes, yes, that's just it. He's robbing me of wisdom. He has it—wisdom, and he can give it to me. Oh, come and go with me to him. Start now." That eager, delightful boy in love with learning can be duplicated in nearly every dialogue of Plato. Socrates has but to enter a gymnasium; exercise, games, are forgotten. A crowd of ardent young men surround him. Tell us this. Teach us that, they clamor. What is Friendship? What is Justice? We will not let you off, Socrates. The truth—we want the truth. "What delight," they say to each other, "to hear wise men talk!" "Egypt and Phœnicia love money," Plato remarks in a discussion on how nations differ. "The special characteristic of our part of the world is the love of knowledge." "The Athenians," said St. Luke, "and the strangers sojourning there spend their time in nothing else but to tell or to hear some new thing." Even the foreigners caught the flame. That intense desire to know, that burning curiosity about everything in the world—they could not come into daily contact with it and not be fired. Up and down the coast of Asia Minor St. Paul was mobbed and imprisoned and beaten. In Athens "they brought him unto the Areopagus, saying, 'May we know what this new teaching is?'"

Aristotle, the model scientist, the man of cool head and detached observation, unbiased, impersonal, does not display any dispassionate aloofness in his consideration of reason. He so loves it and delights in it that when it is the theme of discourse he cannot be held within the sober bounds of the scientific spirit. His words must be quoted, they are so characteristically Greek:

> *Since then reason is divine in comparison with man's whole nature, the life according to reason must be divine in comparison with (usual) human life. Nor ought we to pay regard to those who exhort us that as men we ought to think human things and keep our eyes upon mortality: nay, as far as may be, we should endeavor to rise to that which is immortal, and live in conformity with that which is best, in us. Now, what is characteristic of any nature is that which is best for it and gives most joy. Such to man is the life according to reason, since it is this that makes him man.*

Love of reason and of life, delight in the use of the mind and the body, distinguished the Greek way. The Egyptian way and the way of the East had led through suffering and by the abnegation of the intellect to the supremacy of the spirit. That goal the

Greeks could never come within sight of. Their own nature and the conditions of their life alike, shut them off from it, but they knew the way of the spirit no less. The all-sufficing proof that the world of the spirit was where the flame of their genius burned highest is their art. Indeed their intellectuality has been obscured to us precisely by virtue of that transcendent achievement. Greece means Greek art to us and that is a field in which the reason does not rule. The extraordinary flowering of the human spirit which resulted in Greek art shows the spiritual power there was in Greece. What marked the Greeks off from Egypt and India was not an inferior degree of spirituality but a superior degree of mentality. Great mind and great spirit combined in them. The spiritual world was not to them another world from the natural world. It was the same world as that known to the mind. Beauty and rationality were both manifested in it. They did not see the conclusions reached by the spirit and those reached by the mind as opposed to each other. Reason and feeling were not antagonistic. The truth of poetry and the truth of science were both true.

It is difficult to illustrate this conception of reality by isolated quotations, but the attitude of the greatest of Greek scientists may serve as an example. Aristotle was in one sense the typical scientist, a man endowed with extraordinary powers of observation and of reasoning upon his data, preoccupied with what he could see and what he could know. Anywhere else and at any other time he would have been the man of pure reason, viewing with condescension if not contempt conclusions reached in any way except that of the mind. But to Aristotle the Greek the way of the spirit was also important, and the scientific method sometimes to be abandoned in favor of the poetic method. In his well-known statement in the *Poetics* that poetry has a higher truth than history since it expresses truth of general application whereas that of history is partial and limited, he is not speaking as a scientist nor would the statement commend itself to the scientific mind outside of Greece. There is no evidence, again, of the scientist's point of view in the great passage where he sets forth the reason for the work of his life, his search into the nature of all living things:

> *The glory, doubtless, of the heavenly bodies fills us with more delight than the contemplation of these lowly things, but the heavens are high and far off, and the knowledge of celestial things that our senses give us, is scanty and dim. Living creatures, on the contrary, are at our door, and if we so desire we may gain full and certain knowledge of each and all. We take pleasure in a statue's beauty; should not then the living fill us with delight? And all the more if in the spirit of the love of knowledge we search for causes and bring to light evidences of meaning. Then will nature's purpose and her deep-seated laws be revealed in all things, all tending in her multitudinous work to one form or another of the beautiful.*

Did ever scientist outside of Greece so state the object of scientific research? To Aristotle, being a Greek, it was apparent that the full purpose of that high enterprise could not be expressed in any way except the way of poetry, and, being a Greek, he was able so to express it.

Spirituality inevitably brings to our mind religion. Greek religion is known to us chiefly or only as a collection of fairy tales, by no means always edifying. This is to belie the immense hold the Greeks had on things spiritual. It would have been impossible for the nation that produced the art and the poetry of Greece to have a permanently superficial view of religion, just as it would have been impossible for them not to use their minds on Homer's gods and goddesses. Those charming stories which came down from a time when men had a first-hand knowledge of nature now forever lost, were never, it is true, anathematized with book and bell and public recantation. That was not the Greek way. They loved them and their fancy played with them, but they found their way through them to what underlies all religion, East or

West. Æschylus will speak like a prophet of Israel, and the Zeus he praises Isaiah would have understood:

Father, Creator, mighty God,
great craftsman, with his hand he fashioned man.
Ancient in wisdom, working through all things,
into safe harbor guiding all at last...
With whom the deed and word are one,
to execute with swiftness all the ends
conceived in the deep counsels of his mind.

"Ye men of Athens," said St. Paul on the Areopagus, "I perceive that in all things ye are too superstitious"—so the Bible version runs, but the last word could quite as accurately be translated "in dread of the divine power," a meaning borne out by the reason St. Paul gives for his use of it: "For as I passed by and beheld your devotions I found an altar with this inscription, *To the Unknown God.*" The words carry us far away from the gay company of the Olympians. They go back to the poet who had written, "Through thick and shadowed forests stretch the pathways of his purpose, beyond our power to search out." That altar to the Unknown God who is past our power to search out, could have been raised only by men who had gone beneath the pleasant surface of comfortable orthodoxies and easy certainties. A single sentence of Socrates, spoken when he was condemned to death, shows how the Greek could use his mind upon religion, and by means of human wisdom joined to spiritual insight could sweep aside all the superficialities and see through to the thing that is ultimate in religion: "Think this certain, that to a good man no evil can happen, either in life or in death." These words are the final expression of faith.

There is a passage in Socrates' last talk with his friends before his death, which exemplifies with perfect fidelity that control of the feelings by the reason, and that balance between the spirit and the mind, which belonged to the Greek. It is the last hour of his life and his friends who have come to be with him to the end have turned the talk upon the immortality of the soul. In such a moment it would be natural to seek only for comfort and support and let calm judgment and cool reason loosen their hold. The Greek in Socrates could not do that. His words are:

> *At this moment I am sensible that I have not the temper of a seeker after knowledge; like the vulgar, I am only a partisan. For the partisan, when he is engaged in a dispute, cares nothing about the rights of the question, but is anxious only to convince his hearers. And the difference between him and me at the present moment is only this—that while he seeks to convince his hearers that what he says is true, I am seeking to convince myself; to convince my hearers is a secondary matter with me. And do but see how much I have to gain by this. For if what I say is true, then I do well to believe it; and if there be nothing after death, still, I shall save my friends from grief during the short time that is left me, and my ignorance will do me no harm. This is the state of mind in which I approach the argument. And I would ask you to be thinking of the truth and not of Socrates. Agree with me if I seem to you to speak the truth; or, if not, withstand me might and main that I may not deceive you as well as myself in my desire, and like the bee leave my sting in you before I die. And now let us proceed.*

Thus in Greece the mind and the spirit met on equal terms.

THE WAY OF THE EAST AND THE WEST IN ART

The way a nation goes, whether that of the mind or that of the spirit, is decisive in its effect upon art. A brief consideration will show that it must be so. The spirit has not essentially anything to do with what is outside of itself. It is mind that keeps hold of reality. The way of the spirit is by withdrawal from the world of objects to contemplation of the world within and there is no need of any correspondence between what goes on without and what goes on within. Not the mind but the spirit is its own place, and can make a Hell of Heaven, a Heaven of Hell. When the mind withdraws into itself and dispenses with facts it makes only chaos.

In the early days of the Restoration a great discussion was held by the learned men in the presence of the king on why, if a live fish were put into a brimming pail, the water would not overflow, while if the fish were dead, it would. Many elevating reasons that had to do with the inner significance of life and death were adduced for this spiritually suggestive property of water—or fish, until the king asked that two such pails be brought in and the fish added to them before his eyes. When it turned out that the water reacted in the same way to the fish alive or dead, the scientists received a lesson that had far-reaching results on the advisability of the mind's not going the way of the spirit and withdrawing into itself to exercise the pure reason free and unhampered, but of remaining strictly within the limits of the outside world. Abide by the facts, is the dictum of the mind; a sense for fact is its salient characteristic.

In proportion as the spirit predominates, this sense disappears. So in the Middle Ages when the West was turning more and more to the way of the spirit, the foremost intellects could employ their great powers in questioning how many angels could stand on a needle's point, and the like. Carry this attitude toward the world of fact a few steps farther and the result is the Buddhist devotee swaying before the altar and repeating *Amida* a thousand, thousand times until he loses all consciousness of altar, *Amida*, and himself as well. The activity of the mind has been lulled to rest and the spirit, absorbed, is seeking the truth within itself. "Let a man," say the *Upanishads*, the great Brahman document, "meditate on the syllable Om. This is the imperishable syllable and he who knowing this, loudly repeats that syllable, enters into it and becomes immortal." "God offers to everyone," says Emerson, "his choice between truth and repose. Take which you please—you can never have both." That is the West speaking and the way of the mind. Truth means, from this point of view, finding out about things—very active exercise.

The practical effect of the divergence is of course immediately apparent in the intellectual realm. Those whose aim is to be completely independent of "this muddy vesture of decay" do not become scientists or archæologists or anything that has to do with actualities past or present. In art the result, though less immediately apparent, is no less decisive. In proportion as the spirit predominates, the real shapes and looks of things become unimportant and when the spirit is supreme, they are of no importance at all.

In Egypt, as has been said, the reality of the unseen world slowly overshadowed that of the seen, but invisible though it was, it remained substantial. The dead bodies must be preserved from returning to dust; they must be placed in tombs that were underground fortresses safe from disturbance; they must be surrounded by all the furnishings they had made use of in life. The body was enormously important and there was no idea that the abundance of the things a man possessed was not eternally important too. The art of such a people would keep a firm hold on reality. The pyramids are as real as the hills. They look to be nothing made by hands but a part of the basic structure of the earth. Where the wind lifts the sand into shapes of a gigantic geometry—triangles which, as one watches, pass into curves and break again into sharp-pointed outlines, a cycle of endless change as fixed as the movement of the stars, against the immensity of the desert which never changes—the pyramids, immutable, immovable, are the spirit of the desert incased in granite. All the tremendous art of Egyptian sculpture has something of this unity with the physical world. The colossal statues have only just emerged from the rocks of the hills. They keep the marks of their origin as securely as the marks of the artist's tools that shaped them from their background.

This hold on reality is something completely different from that grasped by the mind. It has nothing to do with the action of the mind; it is a profound intuition on the part of people whose consciousness has not yet divided them from the ways of nature. This intuitive feeling is as different from the conception of reality which the mind attains to as an Egyptian tomb, where life and death are hardly differentiated, is from that prison in which Socrates sat, trying to think out what was true in the hope of immortality.

What Egyptian art would have resulted in if it had been allowed a free development, is one of those questions that forever engage the attention through the realization of an immense loss to the world. But the priests stepped in, and that direct experience of nature which was being illumined more and more by the experience of the spirit was arrested at a certain point and held fast. The priests set a fixed pattern for art all must conform to. Art can work in chains for a long time as the mind cannot, and it was centuries before the full effect appeared of the control of the artist's spirit by the priest's dogma; but by the time it was apparent, Egyptian art was ended. Plato's comment is to all intents and purposes its funeral oration:

> *In Egypt the forms of excellence were long since fixed and patterns of them displayed in the temples. No painter or artist is allowed to innovate on the traditional forms or invent new ones. To this day, no alteration is allowed—none at all. Their works of art are painted or molded in the same forms which they had 10,000 years ago.*

But in the East there was no arrested development. There the spirit was free—it alone was free—to work unhampered. Hindoo art was produced by men who had been trained from earliest youth to look at all outside them as illusion. The belief in a solid, durable stuff which the senses induce, was the fundamental falsehood men must clear themselves from. That which appears solid and durable is only a perpetually shifting appearance, a kaleidoscope always moving, where each pattern is forever dissolving into another and all are no more significant than a spectacle for a child. Reality, permanence, importance, belong alone to the world within where truth is absolutely known because it is experienced and where the man who wills can achieve complete mastery. This is the fundamental dogma of the *Upanishads*:

The infinite is the Self. He who perceives this, is lord and master of all the world. Air, fire, water, food, appearances, disappearances—all spring from the Self. He who sees this sees everything and obtains everything.

It is difficult for us to associate this idea with the production of art. Art is to us of the West the unifier of what is without and what is within. It is as firmly rooted in the one as in the other. And it is quite true that the complete mystic, if such a one could be, would never even desire to put into any concrete form the beatific vision. He would remain in utter quiescence, desiring nothing:

When to a man who understands, the Self has become all things, what sorrow, what seeking, can there be, to him who once beholds that unity?

But mystical rapture even in the East is for the few. To all the rest, reality, however illusory it is conceived of as being, remains to be reckoned with. The great Hindoo artists were not prevented from expressing themselves through it as all artists will forever, but their conception of it shaped the mold of their art. The procedure laid down for a Buddhist artist before beginning his work is applicable in what it aims at to all Hindoo art. He was to proceed to a place of solitude. There he must prepare himself, first, by performing "the Sevenfold Office" and offering to the hosts of Buddhas "real or imaginary flowers." (It is clear that the first had no superiority over the second.) Next, he must realize "the four infinite moods" and meditate upon the emptiness and non-existence of all things, until "by the fire of the idea of the abyss" he lost all consciousness of self and was able to identify himself with the divinity he desired to portray. Then, at last, calling upon him he would behold him. There would come to him visibly the very image of the god, "like a bright reflection," to serve him for his model. It would appear in no human shape, we may be sure. The whole procedure was designed to make that impossible. The conviction had been bred within the artist that the truth of his art was above and apart from all reality. In his solitary watch he had sought to purify it from all that had to do with the flesh, to banish earthly memories and through the spirit undefiled find the manifestation of the eternal. The prerequisite of the statue would be its non-humanity. Scrolls of bright blue hair must mark it off from a mere man, or many heads or arms; or an impression of inhuman force, given by a woman brandishing a human head torn from a mangled body underfoot.

It is said of Polygnotus that when he wished to paint Helen of Troy, he went to Crotona, famed for the beauty of its women, and asked to see all those who were thought to be the most beautiful. These he studied long before painting his picture, and yet when it was done it was not a representation of any one of those lovely faces he had seen but fairer by far than the fairest of them all. The Greek artist, the story would tell us, was not a photographer, any more than his Buddhist confrère; he too in the end withdrew from the visible forms of the women before him and created within himself his own form of beauty; but the story points the difference between the two as well. The studio of the Greek was not a lonely cave of meditation, but the world of moving life. His picture was based on the women he had studied; it was conditioned by their actual bodily shapes; it was super-individual but not supernatural.

The Hindoo artist was subject to no conditions; of all artists he was the freest. The Egyptian was submissive to the ways of nature and the dogma of the priest; the Greek was limited by his mind that would not let him lose sight of the things that are seen; the Hindoo was unhampered by anything outside of himself except the material he worked in, and even there he often refused to recognize a limitation. The art of India and of all the nations of the East she influenced shows again and again sculpture that seems to struggle to be free of the marble. No artists have ever made bronze and stone move as these did. There was nothing fixed and rigid for them; nothing in the world of the spirit is fixed and rigid. Hindu art is the result of unchecked spiritual force, a flood held back by no restraints save those the artist chose to impose upon himself.

But, even though the visible world had no hold upon his conscious attention, he could not, of course—no human being can—create purely within the depths of the spirit what had no connection with facts, no semblance of anything he had seen. His artistic vision was conditioned by actualities, but only indirectly since his aim was to detach himself from them. Reality and probability appeal to the mind alone and to that appeal he was completely indifferent; he was concentrated upon spiritual significance. To him the multitudinous hands and arms of the god who appeared to him in his trance were symbolic; they stood for a truth of the spirit and expressed the only kind of reality worth an artist's while.

Presuppose a complete lack of significance in the visible world and there is only one way out for the artist, the way of symbolism. He of all men is least capable of complete abstraction. The mathematician and the philosopher can deal with pure concepts; to the artist the world of abstract ideas offers nothing at all. In symbolism he can hold to something solid and concrete even while affirming that the real has nothing to do with that which the senses perceive. Symbols are always real things invested with unreality. They are the reflection in the mirror through which we in the flesh can see, if darkly. In symbolism realities are important, even if their only importance is that they stand for something other than what they are. The mystical artist is free to make use of reality and to dispense with it as he pleases. He is at liberty also to improvise his own symbolism which can be of the simplest: many arms to express multi-form power; many breasts to show spiritual nourishment; a sublimated pictorial writing. His only restraint comes from within his own self, but, despising as he does the outside world, predisposed against seeing real things as beautiful, the artist within him, who must find spiritual significance somewhere, is irresistibly impelled toward the pattern which he can make symbolic and, so, significant.

The mystical artist always sees patterns. The symbol, never quite real, tends to be expressed less and less realistically, and as the reality becomes abstracted the pattern comes forward.

The wings on Blake's angels do not look like real wings, nor are they there because wings belong to angels. They have been flattened, stylized, to provide a curving pointed frame, the setting required by the pattern of the composition. In Hindoo art and its branches, stylization reaches its height. Human figures are stylized far beyond the point of becoming a type; they too are made into patterns, schematic designs of the human body, an abstraction of humanity. In the case of an Eastern rug all desire to express any semblance of reality has gone. Such a work of art is pure decoration. It is the expression of the artist's final withdrawal from the visible world, essentially his denial of the intellect.

Dismiss the real world, see it as hateful and hopeless, and the effect upon art is fundamentally the same whether the result is a Fra Angelico angel or a monster-god. Winged angels radiant against a golden background, a many-handed god, both belong to the same conception of the world. The artist has turned his back upon the things that are seen. He has shut the eyes of his mind. The art of the West, after Rome fell and the influence of Greece was lost, went the way of the East as all else did. Pictures grew more and more decorative. The flat unreality of the primitive developed into the flat unreality of the stylized, until at the Renaissance the visible world was re-discovered with the re-discovery of Greece.

Two thousand years after the golden days of Phidias and Praxiteles, of Zeuxis and Apelles, when their statues were defaced and broken and all but irretrievably lost, and their paintings were completely gone forever, men's minds were suddenly directed to what was left of the literature of Greece and Rome. A passion for learning like that of Plato's time swept Italy. To study the literature of Greece was to discover the idea of the freedom of the mind and to use the mind as it had not been used since the days of Greece. Once again there was a fusion of rational and spiritual power. In the Italian Renaissance a great artistic development coincided with a great intellectual awakening and the art that resulted is in its essence more like that of Greece than any other before or since. In Florence, where great painters had great minds, the beauty of the real world was discovered and men painted what they saw with their eyes. Italian painters found the laws of perspective—of course. Not because Signorelli was greater than Simone Martini but only because he and his like were looking at real things and desiring to paint realities, not heavenly visions.

Whether the Greek artists used perspective or not can never be known; not a trace is left of their work; but what they felt about painting things as they are can be known without the possibility of a doubt. Their attitude is revealed in many an allusion.

A famous Greek painter exhibited a picture of a boy holding a bunch of grapes so lifelike, the birds flew down to peck at them, and the people acclaimed him as the master-artist. "If I were," he answered, "the boy would have kept the birds away." The little tale with its delightful assumption of intelligent birds is completely Greek in its fundamental assumption. Grapes were to be painted to look like grapes and boys to look like boys, and the reason was that nothing could be imagined so beautiful and so significant as the real. "Say not, who shall ascend unto Heaven or who shall descend into Hell: for lo, the Word is very nigh thee, in thy mouth and in thy heart." The Greek artist thought neither of Heaven nor of Hell; the word was very nigh unto him; he felt the real world completely sufficient for the demands of the spirit. He had no wish to mark the images of his gods with strange, unearthly attributes to lift them away from earth. He had no wish to alter them at all from what he saw as most beautiful, the shapes of the human beings around him.

A Brahman bronze of Shiva stands poised in the dance, arrested for a moment in an irresistible movement. Many arms and hands curving outward from his body add to the sense of an endless rhythmic motion. The shape, light, slim-waisted, is refined away from the human. Strange symbolic things surround him, deck him, a weaving cobra, a skull, a mermaid creature, long pendants waving from hair and ears, a writhing monster beneath his feet. His beauty is like nothing beautiful ever seen upon the earth.

The Olympic Hermes is a perfectly beautiful human being, no more, no less. Every detail of his body was shaped from a consummate knowledge of actual bodies. Nothing is added to mark his deity, no aureole around his head, no mystic staff, no hint that here is he who guides the soul to death. The significance of the statue to the Greek artist, the mark of the divinity, was its beauty, only that. His art had taken form within him as he walked the streets, watched the games, noted perpetually the people he lived among. To him what he saw in those human beings was enough for all his art; he had never an impulse to fashion something different, something truer than this truth of nature. In his eyes the Word had become flesh; he made his image of the eternal what men could be. The Winged Victory is later Greek; the temple on the Acropolis was built to the Wingless Victory.

The endless struggle between the flesh and the spirit found an end in Greek art. The Greek artists were unaware of it. They were spiritual materialists, never denying the importance of the body and ever seeing in the body a spiritual significance. Mysticism on the whole was alien to the Greeks, thinkers as they were. Thought and mysticism never go well together and there is little symbolism in Greek art. Athena was not a symbol of wisdom but an embodiment of it and her statues were beautiful grave women, whose seriousness might mark them as wise, but who were marked in no other way. The Apollo Belvedere is not a symbol of the sun, nor the Versailles Artemis of the moon. There could be nothing less akin to the ways of symbolism than their beautiful, normal humanity. Nor did decoration really interest the Greeks. In all their art they were preoccupied with what they wanted to express, not with ways of expressing it, and lovely expression, merely as lovely expression, did not appeal to them at all.

Greek art is intellectual art, the art of men who were clear and lucid thinkers, and it is therefore plain art. Artists than whom the world has never seen greater, men endowed with the spirit's best gift, found their natural method of expression in the simplicity and clarity which are the endowment of the unclouded reason. "Nothing in excess," the Greek axiom of art, is the dictum of men who would brush aside all obscuring, entangling superfluity, and see clearly, plainly, unadorned, what they wished to express. Structure belongs in an especial degree to the province of the mind in art, and architectonics were pre-eminently a mark of the Greek. The power that made a unified whole of the trilogy of a Greek tragedy, that envisioned the sure, precise, decisive scheme of the Greek statue, found its most conspicuous expression in Greek architecture. The Greek temple is the creation, *par excellence*, of mind and spirit in equilibrium.

A Hindoo temple is a conglomeration of adornment. The lines of the building are completely hidden by the decorations. Sculptured figures and ornaments crowd its surface, stand out from it in thick masses, break it up into a bewildering series of irregular tiers. It is not a unity but a collection, rich, confused. It looks like something not planned but built this way and that as the ornament required. The conviction underlying it can be perceived: each bit of the exquisitely wrought detail had a mystical meaning and the temple's exterior was important only as a means for the artist to inscribe thereon the symbols of the truth. It is decoration, not architecture.

Again, the gigantic temples of Egypt, those massive immensities of granite which look as if only the power that moves in the earthquake were mighty enough to bring them into existence, are something other than the creation of geometry balanced by beauty. The science and the spirit are there, but what is there most of all is force, unhuman force, calm but tremendous, overwhelming. It reduces to nothingness all that belongs to man. He is annihilated. The Egyptian architects were possessed by the consciousness of the awful, irresistible domination of the ways of nature; they had no thought to give to the insignificant atom that was man.

Greek architecture of the great age is the expression of men who were, first of all, intellectual artists, kept firmly within the visible world by their mind, but, only second to that, lovers of the human world. The Greek temple is the perfect expression of the pure intellect illumined by the spirit. No other great buildings anywhere approach its simplicity. In the Parthenon straight columns rise to plain capitals; a pediment is sculptured in bold relief; there is nothing more. And yet—here is the Greek miracle—this absolute simplicity of structure is alone in majesty of beauty among all the temples and cathedrals and palaces of the world. Majestic but human, truly Greek. No superhuman force as in Egypt; no strange supernatural shapes as in India; the Parthenon is the home of humanity at ease, calm, ordered, sure of itself and the world. The Greeks flung a challenge to nature in the fullness of their joyous strength. They set their temples on the summit of a hill overlooking the wide sea, outlined against the circle of the sky. They would build what was more beautiful than hill and sea and sky and greater than all these. It matters not at all if the temple is large or small; one never thinks of the size. It matters not—really—how much it is in ruins. A few white columns dominate the lofty height at Sunion as securely as the great mass of the Parthenon dominates all the sweep of sea and land around Athens. To the Greek architect man was master of the world. His mind could understand its laws; his spirit could discover its beauty.

The Gothic cathedral was raised in awe and reverence to Almighty God, the expression of the aspiration of the lowly:

We praise thee, O God, we who are as nothing save in our power to praise thee.

The Parthenon was raised in triumph, to express the beauty and the power and the splendor of man:

Wonders are there many—none more wonderful than man.
His the might that crosses seas swept white by storm winds...
He the master of the beast lurking in the wild hills...
His is speech and wind-swift thought—

Divinity was seen incarnate; through perfected mortality man was immortal.

THE GREEK WAY OF WRITING

The art of the Greek sculptors of the great age is known to us by long familiarity. None of the Greek statues upon first sight appear strange in any respect. There is no need to look long, to orient mind and eye, before we can understand them. We feel ourselves immediately at home. Our own sculptors learned their art from them, filled our galleries with reminiscences of them. Plaster casts more or less like them are our commonest form of inappropriate decoration. Our idea of a statue is a composite of Greek statues, and nothing speaks more for the vitality of the originals than their survival in spite of all we have done to them.

The same is true of the Greek temple. No architecture is more familiar to us. That pointed pediment supported by fluted columns—we are satiated with it. Endless replicas of it decorate the public buildings of all our cities and the sight of it anywhere is an assurance of something official within. Greece has been copied by sculptors and builders from the days of Rome on.

The art of the literature of Greece stands in singular contrast to these, isolated, apart. The thought of the Greeks has penetrated everywhere; their style, the way they write, has remained peculiar to them alone. In that one respect they have had no copyists and no followers. The fact is hardly surprising. One must know a foreign language very well to have one's way of writing actually altered by it; one must, in truth, have entered into the genius of that language to such a degree as is hardly possible to a foreigner. And Greek is a very subtle language, full of delicately modifying words, capable of the finest distinctions of meaning. Years of study are needed to read it even tolerably. Small wonder that the writers of other countries left it alone and, unlike their brother artists in stone, never imitated Greek methods. English poetry has gone an altogether different way from the Greek, as has all the art that is not copied but is native to Europe.

This art, the art natural to us, has always been an art of rich detail. In a Gothic cathedral not an inch is left unelaborated in a thousand marvelous patterns of delicate tracery worked in the stone. In a great Renaissance portrait minutest distinctions of form and color are dwelt upon with loving care, frost-work of lace, patterned brocade, the finely wrought links of a chain, a jewelled ring, wreathed pearls in the hair, the sheen of silk and satin and fur-bordered velvet, beauty of detail both sumptuous and exquisite. It is eminently probable that if the temples and the statues of Greece had only just been discovered, we would look at them dismayed at the lack of any of the elaboration of beauty we are used to. To turn from St. Mark's or Chartres to the Parthenon for the first time, or from a Titian to the Venus of Milo never seen before, would undoubtedly be a chilling experience. The statue in her straight, plain folds, her hair caught back simply in a knot, no ornament of any description to set her off, placed beside the lady of the Renaissance or the European lady of any period, is a contrast so great, only our long familiarity with her enables us not to feel her too austere to enjoy. She shows us how unlike what the Greeks wanted in beauty was from what the world after them has wanted.

So the lover of great literature when he is confronted all unprepared with the Greek way of writing, feels chilled at first, almost estranged. The Greeks wrote on the same lines as they did everything else. Greek writing depends no more on ornament than the Greek statue does. It is plain writing, direct, matter-of-fact. It often seems, when translated with any degree of literalness, bare, so unlike what we are used to as even to repel. All the scholars who have essayed translation have felt this difficulty and have tried to win an audience for what they loved and knew as so great by rewriting, not translating, when the Greek way seemed too different from the English. The most distinguished of them, Professor Gilbert Murray, has expressly stated this to be his method:

> *I have often used a more elaborate diction than Euripides did because I found that, Greek being a very simple and austere language and English an ornate one, a direct translation produced an effect of baldness which was quite unlike the original.*

The difficulty is there, no doubt, and yet if we are unable to get enjoyment from a direct translation, we shall never know what Greek writing is like, for the Greek and the English ways are so different, when the Greek is dressed in English fashion, it is no longer Greek. Familiarity has made their statues and their temples beautiful to us as none are more. It is possible that even through the poor medium of translation we might acquire a taste for their writings as well, if, in addition to the easily perceived beauty of such translations as Professor Murray's Euripides, we were willing to accustom ourselves to translations as brief and little adorned as the original, and try to discover what the art that resulted in the Parthenon and the Venus has produced in literature. To be willing to learn from the Greeks in this matter also and to be enabled not only to feel the simple majesty of the Greek temple along with the splendor of St. Mark's and the soaring immensity of Bourges, but to love the truth stated with simplicity as well as the truth set off by every adornment the imagination can devise, to care for the Greek way of writing as well as the English way, is to be immensely the richer; it is to have our entire conception of poetry widened and purified.

Plain writing is not the English genius. English poetry is the Gothic cathedral, the Renaissance portrait. It is adorned by all that beautiful elaboration of detail can do. The words are like rich embroideries. Our poets may draw upon what they will to deck their poems. They are not held down to facts. Greek poets were. "The Greeks soar but keep their feet on the ground," said Landor. Our poets leave earth far behind them, freed by what the Greeks had small use and no name for, poetic license. Our minds are full of pictures of "caverns measureless to man, down to a sunless sea," of "flowers so sweet the sense faints picturing them," of "sermons in stones, books in the running brooks," of "magic casements opening on the foam of perilous seas," of "the floor of heaven thick inlaid with patines of bright gold... still quiring to the young ey'd cherubins." When Homer says, "The stars about the bright moon shine clear to see, for no wind stirs the air and all the mountain peaks appear and the high headlands," when Sophocles describes "White Colonus where the nightingale sings her clear note deep in green glades ivy-grown, sheltered alike from sunshine and from wind," when Euripides writes, "At high-tide the sea, they say, leaves a deep pool below the rockshelf; in that clear place where the women dip their water jars—" the words so literal, so grave, so unemphatic, hardly arrest our attention to see the beauty in them. Our imagery would have left the Greeks as cold. Clarity and simplicity of statement, the watchwords of the thinker, were the Greek poets' watchwords too. Never to them would the humblest flower that blows have brought thoughts that do often lie too deep for tears. A primrose by the river's brim was always a simple primrose and nothing more. That a skylark was like a glow-worm golden in a dell of dew or like a poet hidden in a light of thought, would have been straight nonsense to them. A skylark was just a skylark. Birds were birds and nothing else, but how beautiful a thing was a bird, "that flies over the foam of the wave with careless heart, sea-purple bird of spring"!

The Greeks were realists, but not as we use the word. They saw the beauty of common things and were content with it:

> *Bring white milk good to drink, from a cow without blemish;*
> *bright honey, too, the drops the bee in her flowery work distils,*
> *with water that purifies, drawn from a virgin spring—*

> *The strange glory of the narcissus...a wonder to all, immortal gods and mortal men. A hundred blossoms grew from the roots of it and very sweet was the fragrance, and all the wide sky above and all the land laughed and the salt wave of the sea.*

> *As flakes of snow fall thick of a winter's day, and the crests of the high hills are covered, and the farthest headlands and the meadow grass and the rich tillage of men. Over the inlets and the shore of the gray sea fast it falls and only the on-sweeping wave can ward it off.*

These three instances, from Æschylus, the *Hymn to Demeter*, and the *Iliad* are selected almost at random. There is hardly a Greek poem from which such examples could not be taken. The Greeks liked facts. They had no real taste for embroidery, and they detested exaggeration.

Sometimes, if rarely, the Greek idea of beauty is found in English poetry. Curiously, Keats, than whom no poet delights more in rich detail, has in the *Ode to Autumn* written a poem more like the Greek than any other in English; the concluding lines are pure Greek:

Then in a wailful choir the small gnats mourn
Among the river sallows, borne aloft
Or sinking as the light wind lives or dies;
And full-grown lambs loud bleat from hilly bourn;
Hedge-crickets sing; and now with treble soft
The red-breast whistles from a garden croft,
And gathering swallows twitter in the skies.

The things men live with, noted as men of reason note them, not slurred over or evaded, not idealized away from actuality, and then perceived as beautiful—that is the way Greek poets saw the world.

It follows that the fancy which must ever roam very far from home, played a humble role in Greek poetry. They never wanted to "splash at a ten-league canvas with brushes of comet's hair." What have not our lover-poets said of their beloved! Earth in her springtime, the starry heavens, sun and moon and dawn and sunset, have not sufficed for them:

Oh, thou art fairer than the evening air
Clad in the beauty of a thousand stars.

She seemed a splendid angel, newly dressed,
Save wings, for heaven—

Everyone can supply quotations for himself.

The Greek lover-poet kept his Greek sense for fact. Occasionally he would allow himself a brief flight of fancy: "Flower among the flowers, Zenophile is blooming. My girl is better than garlands sweet to smell." But as a rule hc was chary of imagery and of adjectives as well. One epithet or two, at most, contented him: "Golden Telesila," "Heliodora, delicate darling," "Demo with the lovely hair," "Wide-eyed Anticleia," "A forehead white as ivory above dark-lashed eyes." Such modest tributes were all that the girls whose beauty inspired the Greek sculptors could win from lovers who had been trained in the Greek way.

Everywhere fancy travels with a tight rein in the poetry of Greece, as everywhere in English poetry it is given free course. Byron uses no curb when he wants to describe a high mountain:

—the monarch of mountains.
They crowned him long ago
On a throne of rocks, in a robe of clouds,
With a diadem of snow.

When Æschylus has the same thing in mind, he will allow himself a single touch, but no more:

the mighty summit, neighbor to the stars.

Coleridge is not using his eyes when he perceives Mont Blanc

like some sweet beguiling melody,
So sweet, we know not we are listening to it—

Pindar is observing Ætna with accurate care:

Frost-white Ætna, nurse all year long of the sharp-biting snow.

Coleridge was letting his fancy wander where it pleased. He was occupied with what he happened to feel when he stood before the mountain. Obviously he might have felt almost anything else; there is no logical connection between the spectacle and his reaction. The Greek poet was a precise observer giving a truthful account of a great snow mountain. His attitude was that the mountain is the important thing, not this or that fanciful idea it might suggest to him. He felt limited by the facts; the English poet was completely independent of them.

Meleager prays for night to come as a Greek lover would do: "Morning star, herald of dawn, swiftly come as the evening star and bring again in secret her whom thou takest from me." Juliet's prayer is after the model of English poetry:

Come, gentle night; come, loving black-brow'd night.
Give me my Romeo: and when he shall die,
Take him and cut him out in little stars,
And he will make the face of heaven so fine,
That all the world will be in love with night—

"Gray dawn," says the Greek lover, "hater of those who love, why risest thou so swift around my bed where but now I nestled close to Demo? Would thou wouldst turn thy fleet steeds backward and be evening, O bearer of the sweet light that is so bitter to me." Not in that direct and literal fashion does the English lover cry out upon the dawn:

What envious streaks
Do lace the severing clouds in yonder east.
Night's candles are burnt out, and jocund day
Stands tiptoe on the misty morning tops—

The influence of the English Bible has had its share in making the Greek way hard for us. The language and the style of it have become to us those appropriate to religious expression, and Greek religious poetry which makes up much of the lyrical part of the tragedies, perhaps the greatest of all Greek poetry, is completely un-Hebraic. Hebrew and Greek are poles apart. Hebrew poetry is directed to the emotions; it is designed to make the hearer feel, not think. Therefore it is a poetry based on reiteration. Everyone knows the emotional effect that repetition produces, from the tom-tom in the African forest to the rolling sound of "Dearly beloved brethren, the Scripture moveth us—to acknowledge and confess our manifold sins and wickedness; and that we should not dissemble nor cloak them—when we assemble and meet together—to ask those things which are requisite and necessary—"

Nothing is gained for the idea by these repetitions; the words are synonyms; but the beat upon the ear dulls the critical reason and opens the way to gathering emotion. The method is basic in Hebrew poetry:

To cause it to rain on the earth where no man is, on the wilderness wherein there is no man.
Sing, O barren, thou that didst not bear; break forth into singing, thou that didst not travail with child—

The complete contrast this way of writing offers to the Greek can be seen most clearly in passages where the idea expressed is the same. In the Sermon on the Mount—the style of the New Testament is, of course, formed on that of the Old—occurs the passage:

Ask and it shall be given you; seek and ye shall find; knock and it shall be opened unto you: For every one that asketh receiveth; and he that seeketh findeth; and to him that knocketh it shall be opened.

This thought is expressed in the Greek way by Æschylus:

Men search out God and searching find him.

Not a word more is added. The poet felt the statement as it stood adequate for the idea and he had no desire to elaborate or ornament it.

The chorus in the *Agamemnon,* to which this sentence belongs, is a good instance of Greek brevity and straightforwardness:

He wills and it is done. One spoke, saying, God cares not when men tread underfoot holy things inviolate. But who spoke thus knew not God. We have seen with our eyes the price they pay whose breath is pride, who dare beyond man's daring, whose dwellings overflow with riches. The greatest good is not there,

> *wealth enough to keep misery away and a heart wise to use it. Gold is no bulwark to the arrogant, to him who spurns out of sight the great altar of God's justice. Temptation that persuades to evil, offspring intolerable of far-seeing destruction—when these constrain, there is no remedy. No hiding place can cover sin. It ever blazes forth, a light of death.*

All these ideas are found repeatedly in the Bible and are familiar through many a well-known verse from psalm or prophet, but written as the Hebrew writes they are so long that quotation here is impossible.

One parallel, however, must be given in full. A familiar and completely characteristic example of the Hebrew way is the description of wisdom in Job:

> *But where shall wisdom be found? and where is the place of understanding? The depth saith, It is not in me: and the sea saith, It is not with me. It cannot be gotten for gold, neither shall silver be weighed for the price thereof. It cannot be valued with the gold of Ophir, with the precious onyx, or the sapphire. The gold and the crystal cannot equal it: and the exchange of it shall not be for jewels of fine gold. No mention shall be made of coral, or of pearls: for the price of wisdom is above rubies. The topaz of Ethiopia shall not equal it, neither shall it be valued with pure gold. Whence then cometh wisdom? and where is the place of understanding?—Behold, the fear of the Lord, that is wisdom; and to depart from evil is understanding.*

The thought behind these sonorous sentences is simple: wisdom cannot be bought; it is the reward of righteousness. The effectiveness of the statement consists entirely in the repetition. The idea is repeated again and again with only slight variations in the imagery, and the cumulative effect is in the end great and impressive. It happens that a direct comparison with the Greek way is possible, for Æschylus too had his conception of the price of wisdom:

> *God, whose law it is that he who learns must suffer. And even in our sleep pain that cannot forget, falls drop by drop upon the heart, and in our own despite, against our will, comes wisdom to us by the awful grace of God.*

This passage is as characteristically Greek as the quotation from Job is Hebrew. There is little repetition, little enhancement, in the statement. The thought that wisdom's price is suffering and that it is always paid unwillingly although sent in truth as a gift from God, is stated almost as briefly and almost as plainly as is possible to language. The poet is preoccupied with his thought. He is concerned to get his idea across, not to emotionalize it. His sense for beauty is as unerring as the Hebrew poet's, but it is a different sense for beauty.

The same difference between the two methods is marked in another parallel where the wicked man is shown praying to deaf ears. In the Bible it runs:

> *When distress and anguish cometh then shall they call upon me but I will not answer; then they shall seek me but they shall not find me.*

The Greek expresses the bare idea, not a word more:

> *And does he pray, no one hears.*

Socrates and Phædrus once were discussing a certain piece of writing for which the younger man had a great admiration. He insisted that Socrates should feel the same. "Well," said the latter, "as to the sentiments, I submit to your judgment but as to the style, I doubt whether the author himself would be able to defend it. I speak under correction, but I thought he repeated himself two or three times, either from want of words or want of pains. And he seemed to me ambitious to show that he could say the same thing over in two or three ways—"

We are lovers of beauty *with economy*, said Pericles. Words were to be used sparingly like everything else.

Thucydides gives in a single sentence the fate of those brilliant youths who, pledging the sea in wine from golden goblets, sailed away to conquer Sicily and slowly died in the quarries of Syracuse: "Having done what men could, they suffered what men must." One sentence only for their glory and their anguish. When Clytemnestra is told that her son is searching for her to kill her, all she says of all she feels, is: "I stand here on the height of misery."

Macbeth at the crisis of his fate strikes the authentic note of English poetry. He is neither brief nor simple:

> *—all our yesterdays have lighted fools*
> *The way to dusty death. Out, out, brief candle!*
> *Life's but a walking shadow; a poor player*
> *That struts and frets his hour upon the stage—*

The English poet puts before his audience the full tragedy as they would never see it but for him. He does it all for them in words so splendid, in images so poignant, they are lifted to a vision that completely transcends themselves. The Greek poet lifts one corner of the curtain only. A glimpse is given, no more, but by it the mind is fired to see for itself what lies behind. The writer will do no more than suggest the way to go, but he does it in such a fashion that the imagination is quickened to create for itself. Pindar takes two lovers to the door of their chamber and dismisses them: "Secret are wise persuasion's keys unto love's sanctities." This is not Shakespeare's way with Romeo and Juliet. The English method is to fill the mind with beauty; the Greek method was to set the mind to work.

PINDAR
The Last Greek Aristocrat

"Pindar astounds," says Dr. Middleton in *The Egoist*, "but Homer brings the more sustaining cup. One is a fountain of prodigious ascent; the other, the unsounded purple sea of marching billows."

The problem anyone faces who would write about Pindar is how to put a fountain of prodigious ascent into words. Homer's unsounded purple sea is in comparison easy to describe. Homer tells a great story simply and splendidly. Something of his greatness and simplicity and splendor is bound to come through in any truthful account of him; the difficult thing would be to obscure it completely. The same is true of the tragedians. The loftiness and majesty of their thoughts break through our stumbling attempts at description no matter how little is left of the beauty of their expression. Even translation does not necessarily destroy thoughts and stories. Shelley's poet

hidden
In the light of thought,
Singing hymns unbidden
Till the world is wrought
To sympathy with hopes and fears it heeded not—

could be turned into another tongue without a total loss.

But this kind of poetry is at the opposite pole to Pindar's. Hopes and fears unheeded by the world he lived in were never his. The light of thought shed no glory of new illumination upon his mind. Such thinking as he did went along conventional, ready-made channels and could have moved no one to sympathy except the most stationary minds of his day. Nevertheless he was a very great poet. He is securely seated among the immortals. And yet only a few people know him. The band of his veritable admirers is and always has been small. Of all the Greek poets he is the most difficult to read, and of all the poets there ever were he is the most impossible to translate. George Meredith with his fountain of prodigious ascent gives half of the reason why. So, too, does Horace, who paints essentially the same picture of him:

Like to a mountain stream rushing down in fury,
Overflowing the banks with its rain-fed current,
Pindar's torrent of song sweeps on resistless,
Deep-voiced, tremendous.
Or by a mighty wind he is borne skyward,
Where great clouds gather.

Pindar is all that. One feels "life abundantly" within him, inexhaustible spontaneity, an effortless mastery over treasures of rich and incomparably vivid expression, the fountain shooting upward, irresistible, unforced—and beyond description. But in spite of this sense he gives of ease and freedom and power, he is in an equal degree a consummate craftsman, an artist in fullest command of the technique of his art, and that fact is the other half of the reason why he is untranslatable. His poetry is of all poetry the most like music, not the music that wells up from the bird's throat, but the music that is based on structure, on fundamental laws of balance and symmetry, on carefully calculated effects, a Bach fugue, a Beethoven sonata or symphony. One might almost as well try to put a symphony into words as try to give any impression of Pindar's odes by an English transcription.

We ourselves know little about that kind of writing. It is impossible to illustrate Pindar's poetry from English poetry. Metre was far more important to the Greeks than it is to us. That may seem a strange assertion. The rhythmic beauty and lovely sound of the verse of countless English poets is one of the characteristics we think most of in them. Even so, it is true that the Greeks thought more of metrical perfections. They would have in their poetry balanced measure answering measure, cunningly sought correspondence of meaning and rhythm; they loved a great sweep of varied movement, swift and powerful, yet at the same time absolutely controlled. The sound is beautiful in

Bare ruined choirs where late the sweet birds sang

and in

Under the glassy, cool, translucent wave

Nevertheless Shakespeare and Milton are painters with words more than they are master craftsmen in metrical effects. "A poem is the very image of life," Shelley said. No Greek poet would have thought about his art like that, hardly more than Bach would about his. The English-speaking race is not eminently musical. The Greek was, and the sound of words meant to them something beyond anything we perceive. Pindar's consummate craftsmanship, which produces the effect upon the ear of a great sweep of song, cannot be matched in English literature.

Pindar

But Kipling has something akin to him. The swift movement and the strong beat of the measure in some of his poems come nearer than anything else we have—if not to Pindar himself, at any rate to what an English reader unversed in the intricacies of musical composition can get from him. Compare

That night we stormed Valhalla, a million years ago—

with the two lines just quoted from Shakespeare and Milton, and Kipling's characteristic speed of movement and strength of stress become evident. Pindar could be as stately as Shakespeare and Milton on occasion; he could do anything he chose with words, but the measures he preferred have the sweep and lift Kipling shows so often:

Follow the Romany patteran
Sheer to the Austral Light,
Where the besom of God is the wild South wind,
Sweeping the sea-floors white.
The Lord knows what we may find, dear lass,
And the Deuce knows what we may do—
But we're back once more on the old trail, our own trail, the out trail,
We're down, hull-down, on the long trail, the trail that is always new.

In such lines the rhythm is of first importance. What they say is not of any especial consequence; the great movement holds the attention. The lines stay in the mind as music, not thoughts, and that is even truer of Pindar's poetry. His resources of vivid and beautiful metrical expression are immensely greater than Kipling's, and the compass of his music, too. The mirror Kipling holds up to him is a tiny thing; nevertheless we shall not find a better. It is worthy of note that Kipling himself declared that he was one of the little band of Pindar's lovers:

Me, in whose breast no flame hath burned
Life-long, save that by Pindar lit.

If Pindar's poetry is, when all is said and done, indescribable and his thoughts merely conventional, it would seem superfluous to write about him. It is anything but that to one who wants to understand Greece. Pindar is the last spokesman for the Greek aristocracy and the greatest after Homer. The aristocratic ideal, so powerful in shaping the Greek genius, is shown best of all in his poetry.

He was an aristocrat by race and by conviction, born in the late sixth century when aristocracy in Greece was nearing its end. The first democracy in the world was coming to birth in Athens. Pindar was the figure upon which much romantic pity and sympathy have been expended—the champion of a dying cause. The man who fights for a new cause does not receive that tribute. He is up against the immense force of stubborn resistance the new always arouses. He must give battle without trumpets and drums and with the probability that he will not live to see the victory. Indeed he cannot be sure that there will ever be a victory. Nevertheless he is far more to be envied than the man who tries to turn the tide back; and that is what Pindar did.

To judge him fairly one must consider what the ideal was that produced the aristocratic creed. It was founded upon a conception altogether different from the one behind tyranny, of all power in the hands of a single man. The tyrants departed from Greece unlamented, and never to be revived again even in wishful thinking, except for Plato's rulers who were to be given absolute power only upon the condition that they did not want it, a curious parallel to the attitude prescribed by the early Church. A man appointed to the episcopacy was required to say—perhaps still must say, forms live so long after the spirit once in them is dead—"I do not want to be a bishop. *Nolo episcopari.*" To the Fathers of the Church as to Plato, no one who desired power was fit to wield it.

But the case for the aristocracy was different. In the aristocratic creed, power was to be held by men who alone were immune to the temptations that beset, on the one hand, those struggling to be powerful and, on the other, those struggling to survive. The proper leaders of the world, the only ones who could be trusted to guide it disinterestedly, were a class from generation to generation raised above the common level, not by self-seeking ambition, but by birth; a class which a great tradition and a careful training made superior to the selfish greed and the servile meanness other men were subject to. As a class they were men of property, but position was not dependent upon wealth. The blood ran as blue in the veins of the poor noble as in the rich, and precedence was never a mere matter of money. Thus, absolutely sure and secure, free from the anxious personal preoccupations which distract men at large, they could see clearly on the lofty eminence they were born to, what those lower down could not catch a glimpse of, and they could direct mankind along the way it should go.

Nor was their own way, the aristocratic way, by any means a path of ease. They had standards not accessible to ordinary men, standards well-nigh impossible to men obliged to fight for their daily bread. An aristocrat must not tell a lie (except in love and war); he must keep his word, never take advantage of another, be cheated in a bargain rather than cheat by so much as a hair's breadth. He must show perfect courage, perfect courtesy, even to an enemy; a certain magnificence in the conduct of his life, a generous liberality as far as his means could be stretched, and he must take pride in living up to this severe code. Aristocrats subjected themselves as proudly and willingly to the exacting discipline of the gentleman as they did to the rigid discipline of the warrior. High privilege was theirs, but it was weighted by great responsibility. The burden of leadership lay upon them; they must direct and protect the unprivileged. Nobility of birth must be matched by nobility of conduct.

This was the creed of the aristocracy. Theoretically it is impeccable. Men placed by birth in a position where disinterestedness was easy were trained from childhood to rule other men for their greater welfare. Purely as a theory there is not another that can compete with it, except the one that all men are to be enabled to be disinterested, trained to be rulers, not of others, but each of his own self, and all interdependent, equally bound to give help and to accept it. This utopia, the merest dream so far, is the only conception that surpasses or even matches the conception of authority in the hands of the disciplined best. But most unfortunately for the world it did not work. There was no fault with the idea, only with its supporters. It was never allowed to work by those who upheld it. That is beyond dispute to us today. From the first moment that we catch sight of it in history it is a failure. Class privilege has become class prejudice, if it had ever been anything else; inherited power creates a thirst for acquiring more power; nobility of birth has no connection with spiritual nobility. The aristocrats always failed every time they had their chance. Their latest embodiment, the English House of Lords, endowed by birth with all the best the world could give—power, riches, reverential respect—fought throughout the nineteenth century with almost religious resolution every attempt to raise the condition, the wages or education, of the agricultural laborer.

We all know that by now; but Pindar did not. He believed that the great had and would use their power for the benefit of others. His poems express to perfection and for the last time in Greek literature the class consciousness of the old Greek aristocracy, their conviction of their own lofty moral and religious value. It has often been pointed out that the perfect expression of anything means that that thing has reached its culmination and is on the point of declining. *La clarté parfaite, n'est elle pas le signe de la lassitude des idées?* The statue of the man throwing the discus, the charioteer at Delphi, the stern young horsemen of the Parthenon frieze, and the poetry of Pindar—all show the culmination of the great ideal Greek aristocracy inspired just before it came to an end: physical perfection which evokes mysteriously the sense of spiritual perfection. Every poem Pindar wrote is a tribute to that union.

The games, the great games, had belonged time out of mind to the aristocrats. Only they had money enough and leisure enough to undergo the strenuous discipline of the athlete for the reward of a crown of wild olives. When Pindar lived, the bourgeois were beginning to take part in them, but professionalism had not yet come into being. Almost all his poems that we have are songs in honor of a noble victor at one of the four chief games—the Pythian near Delphi, the Isthmian at Corinth, the Nemean in Argolis, and, most glorious of all, the Olympic at Olympia. These triumphal odes are written in a way peculiar to Pindar. No other poems that praise physical achievement, poems of battle and adventure and the like, bear the least resemblance to them, and it is Pindar's creed as an aristocrat that marks them out. Anyone who has not read him would expect his songs to centre in the encounter he celebrates, to describe the thrilling scene when the chariots went whirling down the race course, or the light flashing feet of the runners carried them past the breathless crowd, or two splendid young bodies locked together in the tension of the wrestling match. Nothing light was at stake. A victory meant the glory of a lifetime. The soul-stirring excitement together with the extreme beauty of the spectacle would seem to give a theme fitted to the heart's desire of a poet. But Pindar dismisses all of it. He hardly alludes to the contest. He describes nothing that happened. A good case could be made out for his never having been present at a game. He sings praises to a victor and he disdains to mention a detail of the victory. His attention is fixed upon the young hero, not upon his achievement. He sees him as the noble representative of the noble, showing in himself the true ideal for humanity. He sees him as a religious figure, bringing to the god in whose honor the game was held the homage of a victory won by the utmost effort of body and spirit. What did this or that outside event matter—the way a horse ran or a man, or the way they looked, or the way they struggled? Pindar was glorifying one who had upheld the traditions of the great past upon which all the hope of the world depended.

In all his odes there is a story of some hero of old told with solemnity. The hero of the present, the victor, is pointed back to what men in other ages did and so shown what men in future ages could do. Pindar gives him a model upon which to form himself and make himself fit to join the august company of the noble dead. Pindar in his own eyes had a mission to the world lofty enough to employ worthily the great endowments of genius and noble blood he had been born to. He was the preacher and the teacher divinely appointed to proclaim the glory of the golden past and to summon all the nobly born and the highly placed to live their own lives in the light of that glory. This was his great charge, and no man on earth, however powerful, could make him think himself inferior. He felt not the slightest degree of subserviency. He spoke to his patron invariably as one equal to another. So they were in his eyes. In point of birth, they were both aristocrats; in point of achievement, the glory of an Olympic victory did not surpass the glory of his poetry. When summoned to Sicily to make an ode in honor of one or another of the mighty tyrants there who often competed in the games, he would admonish him and exhort him exactly as he would any lesser noble. Indeed, in the many poems he wrote to Hieron the Magnificent, the tyrant of Syracuse, he speaks more plainly even than elsewhere. "Become what you really are," he bids the great ruler. Pindar will show him his true self and spur him not to sink below it. "Be straight-tongued"—in the old aristocratic tradition, which is ever "in harmony with God, and shoulder the yoke which God has laid upon you."

There is nothing quite so unique in literature as these solemn admonitory poems dedicated to the praise of a powerful ruler and a popular hero crowned in an athletic victory, and written in a way that is the very reverse of the popular, never condescending to one word of flattery. "Wherefore seeing we are compassed about with so great a cloud of witnesses, let us run with patience the race that is set before us." Something like that Pindar said to his victorious athletes, and no other poems written to praise an exploit, athletic or military or of any sort, ever said anything in the least like that—as witness all the poets laureate.

He is different from them all. His subjects were chosen for him just as theirs were, and no doubt he too was paid for his poems; but these were matters of no importance to him. The thing that mattered was that he always would and could write exactly as he pleased. His odes were written at command, but how they were written was his affair alone. He was loftily sure of his own position. There never was a writer more proudly conscious of superiority. He is "an eagle soaring sunward," he declares, while below him the other poets "vainly croak like ravens," or "feed low like chattering crows." His odes are "radiant blossoms of song" "an arrow of praise that will not miss the mark" they are "a torch, a flame, a fiery dart" "a golden goblet full of foaming wine."

"I will set ablaze the beloved city with my burning song. To every quarter of the earth my word shall go, swifter than noble horse or winged ship." "Within Apollo's golden vale I build a treasure-house of song. No rain of winter sweeping to the uttermost parts of the sea upon the wings of the wind, no storm-lashed hurricane, shall lay it low, but in pure light the glorious portal shall proclaim the victory."

Such poetry proves its sublime descent. The power to write it, Pindar says in many an ode, comes from God alone. It is no more to be acquired than noble blood by the baseborn. Can excellence be learned? Socrates was to ask the Athenians that question again and again in a later day, but Pindar first propounded it and his answer was, No. "Through inborn glory a man is mighty indeed, but he who learns from teaching is a twilight man, wavering in spirit." That is the *ne plus ultra* of the aristocratic creed, and so stated it cannot be refuted. To us today the theory of the aristocracy has almost ceased to be. The fact that there are aristocrats remains. Power, of poetry or anything else, comes to a man by birth; it cannot be taught in the public schools.

The Greeks put Pindar with Æschylus and Thucydides, in the "austere" school of writing, the severe and unadorned. It seems a curious judgment in view of his power of rich and vivid expression, which is one of his most marked characteristics, but there is much truth in it. Pindar is austere. Splendor can be cold, and Pindar glitters but never warms. He is hard, severe, passionless, remote, with a kind of haughty magnificence. He never steps down from his frigid eminence. Aristocrats did not stoop to lies, and his pen would never deviate from the strict truth in praising any triumph. He would glorify a victor so far as he was really glorious, but no further. As he himself puts it, he would not tell "a tale decked out with dazzling lies against the word of truth." Only what was in actual fact nobly praiseworthy would be praised by him. "Now do I believe," he says, "that the sweet words of Homer make great beyond the fact the story of Odysseus, and upon these falsities through Homer's winged skill there broods a mysterious spell. His art deceives us... But as for me, whoever has examined can declare if I speak crooked words." Again, "In ways of single-heartedness may I walk through life, not holding up a glory fair-seeming but false." And in another ode:

Forge thy tongue on an anvil of truth
And what flies up, though it be but a spark,
Shall have weight.

Nevertheless, also strictly in the aristocratic tradition, he would leave the truth unsaid if it was ugly or unpleasant, offensive to delicate feeling. "Believe me," he writes, "not every truth is the better for showing its face unveiled." He adds:

That which has not the grace of God is better far in silence.

The reserve which has always been held to characterize gentlefolk is stamped on everything he wrote. "It is fitting," he writes, "for a man to utter what is seemly and good," and in one way and another the idea is repeated throughout the odes. Essentially the same feeling makes him unwilling to touch with his pen the torments of the damned in hell which so many great writers have loved to linger on. The joys of the saved, yes:

Their boon is life forever freed from toil.
No more to trouble earth or the sea waters
With their strong hands,
Laboring for the food that does not satisfy.
But with the favored of the gods they live
A life where there are no more tears.
Around those blessed isles soft sea winds breathe,
And golden flowers blaze upon the trees,
Upon the waters, too.

But as for the others, "those bear anguish too great for eye to look upon." A gentleman will not join the staring crowd. Neither Virgil nor Dante would have tempted Pindar to journey in their company.

If Pindar had lived where he belonged by all his convictions and ideas—in the sixth century, or the seventh, instead of the fifth, he would be that not uncommon figure among men of exceptional gifts, a man of genius moving with the tide and not great enough to perceive that the flow is feeble and the ebb is near. But Pindar's life was lived when the tide of Greek achievement was at fullest flow, and he withstood it. Marathon, Thermopylæ, Salamis—he had no part in them nor in the exultant and solemn triumph the land felt when the Persian power was broken. Not an echo of these heroic events is in his poetry. His city, Thebes, did not join in the glorious struggle. She refused to help, and her poet took his stand with her. He acted as the aristocrats always act in the face of whatever threatens to disturb things as they are. He did concede praise to the chief defender of Greece, Athens, in two famous lines,

O shining white and famed in song and violet-wreathed,
Fortress of Hellas, glorious Athens, city of God,

but that was the utmost he could do for the new cause. What was dawning in Greece would give light to the world for all ages to come, but Pindar would not look at it. He kept his eyes fixed on the past. He used his genius, his grave and lofty spirit, his moral fervor, to defend a cause that was dying through the unworthiness of its own supporters. And that, not the difficulty of understanding his poetry, is at bottom the reason why he has not meant more and has become to the world a name without a content. What has the man who is bent wholly on the past to say to those who come after him? Æschylus, also an aristocrat, was able to discard the idea of being set apart by noble birth and become the spokesman for the new freedom which after Salamis leveled old barriers. His poetry is permeated with aspiration toward a good never known before, and with insight into loftier possibilities for humanity than had ever yet been discerned. He saw Athens no longer divided into ruler and ruled, but the common possession of a united people. To compare this spirit with Pindar's is to see why with all his great gifts Pindar essentially failed. Æschylus is greatly daring as the leader to new heights must be; Pindar is cautious and careful, as the defensive always must be. Stray within safe limits, he constantly urges. The aristocrats must attempt nothing further if they are to keep what they have. He warns them solemnly not only against ambition, but against aspiration as well. It is dangerous; it tempts a man to stray from the old roads to the unknown. Be content, he tells the victor in the games. Seek nothing further. Man's powers are bounded by his mortality; it is sheer folly to think that that can ever be transcended. "Strive not thou to become a god. The things of mortals best befit mortality." And again, "Desire not the lift of the immortals, but drink thy fill of what thou hast and what thou canst." "May God give me," he prays, "to aim at that which is within my power." An Olympic victory is the height of human achievement, as is also in a different sense the splendor and dignity and remoteness from all things vulgar of a great prince's court, as Hieron's in Syracuse. That height once gained, all that remains is to defend it and keep it inviolate for nobles and tyrants forever.

As a result, Pindar is often sad. The brilliant odes of victory have an undercurrent of dejection. It is a discouraging task to defend in perpetuity. Hieron's festal board is spread; the wine sparkles in the golden cups; the highborn gather to celebrate; they chant the praise of driver and steeds that won the glorious race—and the mournfulness of all things human weighs down the poet's heart. That terrifying page has been reached in the book of man's destiny which Flaubert says is entitled "Accomplished Desires." There is nothing to look forward to. The best has been achieved, with the result that hope and endeavor are ended. Then turn your eyes away from the future. It can bring nothing that is better; it may bring much that is worse. The past alone is safe, and the brief moment of the present. This point of view has no especial distinction; it is not profound, neither deeply melancholy nor poignantly pathetic. It is hardly more than dissatisfaction, a verdict of "Vanity of vanities; all is vanity." "Brief is the growing time of joy for mortals and brief the flower's bloom that falls to earth shaken by grim fate. Things of a day! What are we and what are we not. Man is a shadow's dream." That is Pindar's highest contribution toward solving the enigma of human life.

Only in a very minor capacity does he still speak to the world as the greatest interpreter of the Greek aristocracy at its greatest moment. In his true and sovereign capacity as a mighty poet he has almost ceased to speak. It is our irreparable loss that his peculiar beauties of language and rhythm cannot ever be transferred in any degree into English. It is our still more irreparable loss that this man of genius used his great gifts to shed light only upon the past and turned away from the present which was so full of promise for the future of all the world to come.

THE ATHENIANS AS PLATO SAW THEM

Once upon a time—the exact date cannot be given but it was not far from 450 B.C.—an Athenian fleet cast anchor near an island in the Ægean as the sun was setting. Athens was making herself mistress of the sea and the attack on the island was to be begun the next morning. That evening the commander-in-chief, no less a one, the story goes, than Pericles himself, sent an invitation to his second in command to sup with him on the flag-ship. So there you may see them sitting on the ship's high poop, a canopy over their heads to keep off the dew. One of the attendants is a beautiful boy and as he fills the cups Pericles bethinks him of the poets and quotes a line about the "purple light" upon a fair young cheek. The younger general is critical: it had never seemed to him that the color-adjective was well chosen. He preferred another poet's use of rosy to describe the bloom of youth. Pericles on his side objects: that very poet had elsewhere used purple in the same way when speaking of the radiance of young loveliness. So the conversation went on, each man capping the other's quotation with one as apt. The entire talk at the supper table turned on delicate and fanciful points of literary criticism. But, nonetheless, when the battle began the next morning, these same men, fighting fiercely and directing wisely, carried the attack on the island.

The literal truth of the charming anecdote I cannot vouch for, but it is to be noted that no such story has come down to us about the generals of any other country except Greece. No flight of fancy has ever conceived of a discussion on color-adjectives between Cæsar and the trusty Labienus on the eve of crossing the Rhine, nor, we may feel reasonably assured, will any soaring imagination in the future depict General Grant thus diverting himself with General Sherman. That higher truth which Aristotle claimed for poetry over history is here perfectly exemplified. The little story, however apocryphal, gives a picture true to life of what the Athenians of the great age of Athens were like. Two cultivated gentlemen are shown to us, of a great fastidiousness, the poets their familiar companions, able the evening before a battle to absorb themselves in the lesser niceties of literary criticism, but, with all this, mighty men of action, soldiers, sailors, generals, statesmen, any age would be hard put to it to excel. The combination is rarely found in the annals of history. It is to be completely civilized without having lost in the process anything of value.

Civilization, a much abused word, stands for a high matter quite apart from telephones and electric lights. It is a matter of imponderables, of delight in the things of the mind, of love of beauty, of honor, grace, courtesy, delicate feeling. Where imponderables are the things of first importance, there is the height of civilization, and if, at the same time, the power to act exists unimpaired, human life has reached a level seldom attained and very seldom surpassed. Few individuals are capable of the achievement; periods of history which have produced such men in sufficient numbers to stamp their age are rare indeed.

Pericles, according to Thucydides, held the Athens of his day to be one of them. The most famous of his sayings gives, in brief but to perfection, the height of civilization attained with undiminished power to act. The Athenians, he says, are "lovers of beauty without having lost the taste for simplicity, and lovers of wisdom without loss of manly vigor."

We need no proof that the Greeks of the fifth century B.C. had not lost their manly vigor. Marathon, Thermopylæ, Salamis, are names that will forever be immortal for valor matched against overwhelming numbers, and the grandsons of those same great warriors whom Pericles was addressing were themselves engaged in a stern and bitter war. But it is difficult for us today to realize how important the imponderables were in Greece. The poet Sophocles, so the story is told, in his extreme old age was brought into court by his son who charged him with being incompetent to manage his own affairs. The aged tragedian's sole defense was to recite to the jurors passages from a play he had recently written. Those great words did not fall on deaf ears. Judge a man who could write such poetry not competent in any way? Who that called himself Greek could do that? Nay: dismiss the case; fine the complainant; let the defendant depart honored and triumphant. Again, when Athens had fallen and her Spartan conquerors held high festival on the eve of destroying the city altogether, razing to the ground the buildings, not a pillar to be left standing on the Acropolis, one of the men charged with the poetical part of the entertainment—even Spartans must have poetry to their banquet—gave a recitation from Euripides, and the banqueters, stern soldiers in the great moment of their hard-won triumph, listening to the beautiful, poignant words, forgot victory and vengeance, and declared as one man that the city such a poet had sprung from should never be destroyed. So important were imponderables to the Greeks. Poetry, all the arts, were matters of high seriousness, which it appeared perfectly reasonable that the freedom of a man and a city's life might hang upon.

It is clear that in Greece the values were different from our own today. Indeed we are not able really to bring into one consistent whole their outlook upon life; from our point of view it seems to involve a self-contradiction. People so devoted to poetry as to make it a matter of practical importance must have been, we feel, deficient in the sense for what is practically important, dreamers, not alive to life's hard facts. Nothing could be further from the truth. The Greeks were pre-eminently realists. The temper of mind that made them carve their statues and paint their pictures from the living human beings around them, that kept their poetry within the sober limits of the possible, made them hard-headed men in the world of everyday affairs. They were not tempted to evade facts. It is we ourselves who are the sentimentalists. We, to whom poetry, all art, is only a superficial decoration of life, make a refuge from a world that is too hard for us to face by sentimentalizing it. The Greeks looked straight at it. They were completely unsentimental. It was a Roman who said it was sweet to die for one's country. The Greeks never said it was sweet to die for anything. They had no vital lies.

The great funeral oration of Pericles, delivered over those fallen in the war, stands out as unlike all other commemoration speeches ever spoken. There is not a trace of exaltation in it, not a word of heroic declamation. It is a piece of clear thinking and straight talking. The orator tells his audience to pray that they may never have to die in battle as these did. He does not suggest or imply to the mourning parents before him that they are to be accounted happy because their sons died for Athens. He knows they are not and it does not occur to him to say anything but the truth. His words to them are:

> *Some of you are of an age at which they may hope to have other children, and they ought to bear their sorrow better. To those of you who have passed their prime, I say: Congratulate*

yourselves that you have been happy during the greater part of your days; remember that your life of sorrow will not last long, and take comfort in the glory of those who are gone.

Cold comfort, we say. Yes, but people so stricken cannot be comforted, and Pericles knew his audience. They had faced the facts as well as he had. To read the quiet, grave, matter-of-fact words is to be reminded by the force of opposites of all the speeches everywhere over the tombs of the Unknown Soldier.

Completely in line with this spirit is the often quoted epitaph on the Lacedemonians who fell at Thermopylæ. Every one of them fell, as they knew beforehand they would. They fought their battle to the death with no hope to help them and by so dying they saved Greece, but all the great poet who wrote their epitaph found it fitting to say for them was:

O passer-by, tell the Lacedemonians that we lie here in obedience to their laws.

We rebel; something more than that, we feel, is due such heroism. But the Greeks did not. Facts were facts and deeds spoke for themselves. They did not need ornament.

Often we are repelled by words that seem to us wanting in common human sympathy. When Œdipus appears for the last time before his exile and speaks his misery, all that his friends say is:

These things were even as thou sayest.

And to his wish that he had died in infancy they answer:

I also would have had it thus.

The attitude seems hard but it is always to be borne in mind that the Greeks did not only face facts, they had not even a desire to escape from them. When Iphigenia says that Orestes must die but Pylades may go free, he refuses to take his life on such terms, but he refuses like a Greek and not a modern. It is not love of his friend alone that constrains him but also fear of what people would say, and he knows it and speaks it straight: "Men will whisper how I left my friend to die. Nay—I love you and I dread men's scorn." That is honest but we cannot any more be honest like that. It shocks us. The combination that resulted in the Athenian is baffling to us, lovers of beauty who held poetry and music and art to be of first importance—in their schools the two principal subjects the boys learned were music and mathematics—and at the same time, lovers of fact, who held fast to reality. Pindar prays: "With God's help may I still love what is beautiful and strive for what is attainable." "What I aspire to be and am not, comforts me," would never have appealed to a Greek.

The society these men made up whose sense of values is so strange to us, can be in some sort reconstructed, an idea of what their ways and their manner of life was like is to be had, even though the historical records, as usual, say nothing about the things we most want to know. Stories like those given above were not told of the Greeks because one man or two, a Pericles, a Socrates, had such notions. The golden deeds of a nation, however mythical, throw a clear light upon its standards and ideals. They are the revelation that cannot be mistaken of the people's conscience, of what they think men should be like. Their stories and their plays tell more about them than all their histories. To understand the mid-Victorians one must go not to the history writers but to Dickens and Anthony Trollope. For the Athenians of the great age we turn not to Thucydides, the historian, interested in Athens rather than her citizens, but to two writers unlike in every respect but one, their power to understand and depict the men they lived with: to Aristophanes, who made fun of them and scolded them and abused them and held them up for themselves to see in every play he wrote, and to Plato, who, for all that his business lay with lofty speculations on the nature of the ideal, was a student and lover of human nature too, and has left us in the personages of his dialogues characters so admirably drawn, they still live in his pages.

Many of the men met there are known to us from other writers. Some of the most famous persons of the day take part in the discussions. Whether all of them were real people or not there is no means of knowing, but there can be no doubt that they all are true to life, and that they seemed to Plato's hearers perfectly natural men, such as any upper-class Athenian was used to. Nothing else is credible. To suppose that Plato's idealism extended to his dramatis personæ, and that he put his doctrines in the mouths of personages who would appear unreal and absurd to his pupils, is to insult their intelligence and his. It is true that he does not give a cross-section of Athens, any more than Trollope does of England. A few people "not in society" make their appearance—a man who earns his living by giving recitations from Homer; a soothsayer, to Plato on the same social level as a clergyman to Sir Roger de Coverley—but the people he really knows are the gentlemen of Athens and he knows them as Trollope knows his parsons and his M.P.'s.

This society he introduces us to is eminently civilized, of men delighting to use their minds, loving beauty and elegance, as Pericles says in the funeral oration, keenly alive to all the amenities of life, and, above all, ever ready for a talk on no matter how abstract and abstruse a subject: "When we entered the house"—the speaker is Socrates—"we found Protagoras walking in the cloister; a train of listeners accompanied him; he, like Orpheus, attracting them by his voice and they following. Then, as Homer says, 'I lifted up my eyes and saw' Hippias the Elean sitting in the opposite cloister and many seated on benches around him. They were putting to him questions on physics and astronomy and he was discoursing of them. Also Prodicus the Cean was there,

Plato

still in bed—the day, be it noted, was just dawning—and beside him on the couches near, a number of young men. His fine deep voice re-echoed through the room." Socrates begs Protagoras to talk to them of his teaching and when the great man agrees, "As I suspected that he would like a little display and glorification in the presence of Prodicus and Hippias, I said, 'But why should we not summon the rest to hear?' 'Suppose,' said Callias, the host, 'we hold a council in which you may sit and discuss?' This was agreed upon and great delight was felt at the prospect of hearing wise men talk." And so they all settle down happily to argue about the identity of virtue and knowledge and whether virtue can be taught.

It is, one perceives, a leisured society. Socrates speaks to the young Theætetus of "the ease which free men can always command. They can have their talk out in peace, wandering at will from one subject to another, their only aim to attain the truth." But the direct witness is hardly needed; an atmosphere of perfect leisure is the setting of all the dialogues and to immerse oneself in them is to be carried into a world where no one is ever hurried and where there is always time and to spare. "I went down yesterday to the Piræus with Glaucon," so the *Republic* begins, "to offer up my prayers to the goddess and also to see how they would celebrate the festival. When we had finished and were turned toward the city, Polemarchus appeared and several others who had been at the procession. 'You are on your way to the city?' he said. 'But do you see how many we are? And are you stronger than all these? If not, you will have to stay.' 'But,' said I, 'may there not be an alternative? May we not persuade you to let us go?' 'Can you, if we refuse to listen? And you may be sure we shall. Stay and see the torch race on horseback this evening. And there will be a gathering of young men and we will have a good talk.'"

After some such fashion nearly every dialogue begins. The most charmingly leisured of them is, perhaps, the *Phœdrus*. "Where are you bound?" Socrates asks Phædrus, to which the young man answers that he is going for a walk outside the wall to refresh himself after a morning spent in talk with a great rhetorician: "You shall hear about it if you can spare time to accompany me." Well, Socrates says, he so longs to hear it that he would go all the way to Megara and back rather than miss it. With this, Phædrus begins to be doubtful if he can do justice to the great man: "Believe me, Socrates, I did not learn his very words—oh, no. Still, I have a general notion of what he said and can give you a summary." "Yes, dear lad," replies Socrates, "but you must first of all show what you have under your cloak—for that roll I suspect is the actual discourse, and much as I love you, I am not going to have you exercise your memory at my expense." Phædrus gives in—he will read the whole essay; but where shall they sit? Oh, yes, under "that tallest plane-tree, where there is shade and gentle breezes and grass on which to sit or lie." "Yes," Socrates answers, "a fair resting place, full of summer sounds and scents, the stream deliciously cool to the feet, and the grass like a pillow gently sloping to the head. I shall lie down and do you choose the position you can best read in. Begin." A number of hours are spent under that plane-tree, discussing "the nature of the soul—though her true form be ever a theme of large and more than mortal discourse" and "beauty shining in company with celestial forms" and "the soul of the lover that follows the beloved in modesty and holy fear" and "the heavenly blessings of friendship" and "all the great arts, which require high speculation about the truths of nature" and men who "are worthy of a proud name befitting their serious pursuit of life. Wise, I may not call them, for that is a great name which belongs to God alone—lovers of wisdom is their fitting title." That is the way two gentlemen would while away a summer morning in the Athens of Plato.

It is a society marked also by an exquisite urbanity, of men gently bred, easy, suave, polished. The most famous dinner-party that was ever given was held at the house of Agathon the Elegant, who declared to his guests as they took their places that he never gave orders to his servants on such occasions: "I say to them: Imagine that you are our hosts and I and the company your guests; treat us well and we shall commend you." Into this atmosphere of ease and the informality past masters in the social art permit themselves, an acquaintance is introduced by mistake who had not been invited, a mishap with awkward possibilities for people less skilled in the amenities than our banqueters. Instantly he is made to feel at home, greeted in the most charming fashion: "'Oh, welcome, Arisdodemus,' and Agathon, 'you are just in time to sup with us. If you come on any other matter put it off and make one of us. I was looking for you yesterday to invite you if I could have found you.'"

Socrates is late. It appears that he has fallen into a meditation under a portico on the way. When he enters, "Agathon begged that he would take the place next to him 'that I may touch you and have the benefit of that wise thought which came into your mind in the portico.' 'How I wish,' said Socrates, taking his place as he was desired, 'that wisdom could be infused by touch. If that were so how greatly should I value the privilege of reclining at your side, for you would fill me with a stream of wisdom plenteous and fair, whereas my own is of a very questionable sort.'" An argument is started and Agathon gives way: "I cannot refute you, Socrates." "Ah no," is the answer. "Say rather, dear Agathon, that you cannot refute the truth, for Socrates is easily refuted." It is social intercourse at its perfection, to be accounted for only by a process of long training. Good breeding of that stamp was never evolved in one generation nor two, and yet these men were the grandsons of those that fought at Marathon and Salamis. Heroic daring and the imponderables of high civilization were the inheritance they were born to.

Through the dialogues moves the figure of Socrates, a unique philosopher, unlike all philosophers that ever were outside of Greece. They are, these others, very generally strange and taciturn beings, or so we conceive them, aloof, remote, absorbed in abstruse speculations, only partly human. The completest embodiment of our idea of a philosopher is Kant, the little stoop-shouldered, absent-minded man, who moved only between his house and the university, and by whom all the housewives in Königsberg set their clocks when they saw him pass on his way to the lecture-room of a morning. Such was not Socrates. He could not be, being a Greek. A great many different things were expected of him and he had to be able to meet a great many different situations. We ourselves belong to an age of specialists, the result, really, of our belonging to an age that loves comfort. It is obvious that one man doing only one thing can work faster, and the reasonable conclusion in a world that wants a great many things, is to arrange to have him do it. Twenty men making each a minute bit of a shoe, turn out far more than twenty times the number of shoes that the cobbler working alone did, and in consequence no one must go barefoot. We have our reward in an ever-increasing multiplication of the things everyone needs but we pay our price in the limit set to the possibilities of development for each individual worker.

In Greece it was just the other way about. The things they needed were by comparison few, but every man had to act in a number of different capacities. An Athenian citizen in his time played many parts. Æschylus was not only a writer of plays; he was an entire theatrical staff, actor, scenic artist, costumer, designer, mechanician, producer. He was also a soldier who fought in the ranks, and had probably held a civic office; most Athenians did. No doubt if we knew more about his life we should find that he had still other avocations. His brother-dramatist, Sophocles, was a general and a diplomat and a priest as well; a practical man of the theatre too, who made at least one important innovation. There was no artist class in Greece, withdrawn from active life, no literary class, no learned class. Their soldiers and their sailors and their politicians and their men of affairs wrote their poetry and carved their statues and thought out their philosophy. "To sum up"—the speaker is Pericles—"I say that Athens is the school of Greece and that the individual Athenian in his own person seems to have the power of adapting himself to the most varied forms of action with the utmost versatility and grace"—that last word a touch so peculiarly Greek.

So Socrates was everything rather than what we expect a learned man and a philosopher to be. To begin with, he was extremely social; he delighted above all in company. "I am a lover of knowledge," he says of himself, "and men are my teachers." He would have them gentlemen, however. He liked a man who had been brought up to do things properly. "A narrow, keen, little legal mind—one who knows not how to wear his cloak like a gentleman" is his dismissal of an objectionable person.

He takes us sometimes into very illustrious company indeed. Just before a great public funeral he meets an acquaintance on his way from the Agora who tells him the Council are about to choose the orator for the occasion, and asks: "Do you think you could speak yourself if they were to choose you?" "It would be no great wonder if I could," Socrates answers, "considering the admirable mistress I have in the art of speaking—she who has made so many good speakers, one of whom was the best among all the Greeks—Pericles." "I suppose you mean Aspasia," says the other. "Yes, I do," replies Socrates. "Only yesterday I heard her composing an oration about these very dead. She had been told, as you were saying, that the Athenians were going to choose a speaker and she repeated to me the sort of speech he should deliver, partly improvising and partly putting together fragments of the funeral oration which Pericles spoke, but which, as I believe, she composed." "Can you remember what Aspasia said?" the friend asks, and is told, "I ought to be able, for she taught me and she was ready to strike me because I kept forgetting." The oration is then rehearsed and at its close Socrates, who has declared that he is afraid Aspasia will be angry with him for giving publicity to her speech, warns his hearer, "Take care not to tell on me to her and I will repeat to you many other excellent political speeches of hers."

At that famous supper table in Agathon's house where a company of young men was gathered not easily matched for brilliancy by any other age; Agathon himself, who had just been awarded the first prize for a play, Aristophanes, greatest of comedians, that gilded youth, Alcibiades, among the brilliant always the most brilliant—by these and their like, Socrates, when he enters, is treated as a boon companion, beloved, admired, and the best of company. They joke with him and make fun of him with an undertone of loving delight in him, all of which Socrates receives with amused tolerance and the complete assurance of the man of the world. "Don't answer him, dear Agathon," calls out Phædrus, the young man who took that walk to the tall plane-tree, "for if he can only get a companion to whom he can talk, especially a good-looking one, he will be of no use for anything else."

In the conversation that follows, it appears that he can do all the things young men admire most, the world over. "He can drink any quantity of wine," says Alcibiades, "and not get drunk." This declaration is made in humorous despair, after he has insisted on Socrates' draining a two-quart wine jar, which Socrates does with entire composure. Alcibiades himself, when he first appeared at the door, "crowned with a garland of ivy and violets," had asked, "Will you have a very drunken man as companion?" And all the rest of the company had already echoed Aristophanes' suggestion that they avoid deep drinking because they had all drunk too much the day before—"except Socrates, who can always drink or not, and will not care which we do."

So, too, he is the typical young man's hero in his power to endure hardship. Alcibiades and he had messed together in one campaign and the young man says, "I had an opportunity of seeing his extraordinary power of sustaining fatigue. And his endurance was simply marvelous when we were cut off from supplies—there was no one to be compared with him." It was winter and very cold, and everybody else "had on an amazing quantity of clothes and their feet done up in felt and fleeces," but Socrates, "in ordinary dress and with bare feet, marched on the ice better than the others." Yet with all this, "if we had a feast he was the only person who had real powers of enjoyment."

The Symposium ends with the narrator's confesssion that they all did finally drink too much, and he himself fell asleep until the dawn, when, on waking up, he found everybody else asleep except Socrates, Aristophanes and Agathon. The two latter were still drinking while Socrates discoursed to them. He was arguing "that the true artist in tragedy would be an artist in comedy also. To which the others had to assent, being drowsy and not quite up to the argument. And first Aristophanes dropped off, then Agathon. Socrates having laid both to sleep, departed. At the Lyceum he took a bath and passed the day as usual."

He could make schoolboys feel equally at home with him: "His friend, Menexenus, came and sat down by us and Lysis followed. I asked, 'Which of you two boys is the older?' He answered that it was a matter of dispute between them. 'Which is the better looking?' The two lads laughed. 'I shan't ask you which is the richer,' I said, 'for you two are friends, are you not?' 'Certainly,' they replied. 'And friends have all things in common,' I said, 'so that one of you cannot be richer than the other.' 'No, indeed,' they agreed."

Follows a talk on friendship, broken off by the boys' tutors who bid them go home as it is getting late. "I said, however, a few words to the lads at parting: 'O Menexenus and Lysis, here is a joke: you two boys and I, an old boy who would fain be one of you, think we are friends and yet we have not been able to discover what is a friend!'"

Such a conclusion or rather absence of conclusion, illustrates the attitude peculiar to Socrates among all the great teachers of the world. He will not do their thinking for the men who come to him, neither in matters small nor great. In the *Cratylus* where that young man and his friend approach him with a question about language and how names are formed, all the satisfaction they get is: "If I had not been a poor man I might have heard the fifty-drachma course of the great Prodicus, which is a complete education in grammar and language—these are his own words—and then I should have been able at once to answer your question. But, indeed, I have only heard the single-drachma course, and therefore I do not know the truth about such matters. Still, I will gladly assist you in the investigation of them." The investigation, however, ends with: "This may be true, Cratylus, but is also very likely to be untrue; and therefore I would not have you be too easily persuaded of it. Reflect well, for you are young and of an age to learn. And when you have found the truth, come and tell me." To which the young man answers—he must have been very young—"I will do as you say, Socrates."

This ironic inconclusiveness is his most distinctive characteristic. Always when he is convicting his world of that dark crime in Greece, ignorance, as always when he is—so unobtrusively—leading them on to great thoughts and the conception of their high calling, he assumes that he is in the same case with his hearers, or worse. His habitual manner is a charming diffidence. "I know it may all be quite wrong," he seems to say. He suggests merely—with a question mark. It is the way of the most sophisticated people in the *ne plus ultra* of civilized society.

One other illustration must be given to show the deep seriousness which underlay that attitude so whimsical and deprecatory. It is taken from the talk during the summer stroll with Phædrus—"Is not the road to Athens made for conversation?" The younger man asks if they are not near the place where Boreas is said to have carried off Orithya: "The little stream is delightfully clear and bright. I can fancy there might be maidens playing near. Tell me, Socrates, do you believe the tale?" "The wise are doubtful,"

Socrates answers, "and I should not be singular if, like them, I too, doubted. I might have a rational explanation that Orithya was playing when a northerly gust carried her over the rocks, and therefore she was said to have been carried off by Boreas. Now I quite acknowledge that these allegorical explanations are very nice, but he is not to be envied who has to make them up: much labor and ingenuity will be required of him; he will have to go on and rehabilitate Hippo-centaurs and chimæras dire. Gorgons and winged steeds flow in apace, and numberless inconceivable and portentous natures. And if he would fain reduce them to the rules of probability it will take up a deal of time. Now I have no leisure for such enquiries; shall I tell you why? I must first know myself, as the Delphic inscription says; to be curious about things not my concern while I am still in ignorance of my own self, would be absurd. And therefore I bid farewell to all that sort of thing. I want to know about myself: am I a monster more complicated and swollen with passion than the serpent Typho, or a creature of a gentler and simpler sort, to whom Nature has given a lowlier and a diviner destiny?"

The complete lack of dogmatism in an avowed teacher is startling, not to say repellent, to most of us today, accustomed as we are and devoted as we are to ex cathedra utterances and ipse dixits. But in Athens, in Platonic Athens, at least, the idea that each man must himself be a research worker in the truth if he were ever to attain to any share in it, seemed rather to attract than to repel. Plato, it may be fairly admitted, knew something about the Greek way in such respects. For years and years after Socrates' death he taught the men of Athens in the world's first Academy, and there is no suggestion anywhere that he paid for his kind of teaching by unpopularity. If the Platonic dialogues point to any one conclusion beyond another, it is that the Athenian did not want someone else to do his thinking for him.

In a sense, therefore, extraordinary man though he was, Socrates yet holds up the mirror to his own age. A civilized age, where the really important matters were not those touched, tasted, or handled, an age whose leaders were marked by a devotion to learning and finding out the truth, and an age able to do and dare and endure, still capable of an approach to the heroic deeds of a past only a few years distant. Mind and spirit in equal balance was the peculiar characteristic of Greek art. Intellectuality and exquisite taste balanced by an immense vitality was the distinctive mark of the people—as Plato saw them.

ARISTOPHANES AND THE OLD COMEDY

"True comedy," said Voltaire, "is the speaking picture of the Follies and Foibles of a Nation." He had Aristophanes in mind, and no better description could be given of the Old Comedy of Athens. To read Aristophanes is in some sort like reading an Athenian comic paper. All the life of Athens is there: the politics of the day and the politicians; the war party and the anti-war party; pacifism, votes for women, free trade, fiscal reform, complaining taxpayers, educational theories, the current religious and literary talk—everything, in short, that interested the average citizen. All was food for his mockery. He was the speaking picture of the follies and foibles of his day.

The mirror he holds up to the age is a different one from that held up by Socrates. To turn to the Old Comedy from Plato is a singular experience. What has become of that company of courteous gentlemen with their pleasant ways and sensitive feelings and fastidious tastes? Not a trace of them is to be found in these boisterous plays, each coarser and more riotous than the last. To place them in the audience is much more difficult than to imagine Spenser or Sir Philip Sidney listening to Pistol and Doll Tearsheet, just to the degree that Elizabeth's court was on a lower level of civilization than the circle around Pericles, and Aristophanes capable of more kinds of vulgarity and indecency than Shakespeare ever dreamed of.

None the less there is a close relationship between the comedy of Athens and the comedy of sixteenth-century England. The *Zeitgeist* of those periods of splendor and magnificent vigor was in many points, the most important points, alike. The resemblance between Aristophanes and certain of the comedy parts of Shakespeare jumps to the eye. The spirit of their times is in them. There is the same tremendous energy and verve and vitality; the same swinging, swashbuckling spirit; the same exuberant, effervescing flow of language; the same rollicking, uproarious fun. Falstaff is a character out of Aristophanes raised to the *n*th power; Poins, Ancient Pistol, Mistress Quickly, might have come straight out of any of his plays.

The resemblance is not on the surface only. The two men were alike in the essential genius of their comedy. In those supreme ages of the drama, Elizabethan England and the Athens of Pericles, the step from the sublime to the ridiculous was easily taken. Uproarious comedy flourished side by side with gorgeous tragedy, and when one passed away the other passed away too. There is a connection between the sublime and the ridiculous. Aristophanes' comedy and, pre-eminently, Shakespeare's comedy, and theirs alone, has a kinship with tragedy. "The drama's laws the drama's patrons give." The audiences to whose capacity for heightened emotion *Lear* and the Œdipus Rex were addressed, were the same that delighted in Falstaff and in Aristophanes' maddest nonsense, and when an age succeeded in no wise less keen intellectually, but of thinner emotions, great comedy as well as great tragedy departed.

Greek drama had reached its summit and was nearing its decline when Aristophanes began to write. Of the Old Comedy, as it is called, we have little; none of the plays of Aristophanes' often successful rivals, and only eleven of the many he himself wrote; but the genre is clearly to be seen in those eleven. There were but three actors. A chorus divided the action by song and dance (there was no curtain) and often took part in the dialogue. About half-way through, the plot, a very loose matter at best, came practically to an end, and the chorus made a long address to the audience, which aired the author's opinions and often had nothing to do with the play. After that would follow scenes more or less connected. A dull picture, this, of a brilliantly entertaining reality. Nobody and nothing escaped the ridicule of the Old Comedy. The gods came in for their share; so did the institutions dearest to the Athenians; so did the most popular and powerful individuals, often by name. The freedom of speech is staggering to our ideas.

In the passages that follow the metres of the originals have been reproduced, as they are an essential part of the comic effect. When the *Acharnians* opens a man is explaining how the war started:

For men of ours—I do not say the City,
Remember that—I do not say the City,
But worthless fellows, just bad money, coins
No mint has ever seen, kept on denouncing
The men of Megara. Trifles, I grant,
—Our way here—but some tipsy youngsters then
Go steal from Megara a hussy there.
Then men of Megara come here and steal
Two of Aspasia's minxes. And those three,
No better than they should be, caused the war.
For then in wrath Olympian Pericles
Thundered and lightened and confounded Greece.
Enacting laws against the Megarians
That sounded just like drinking songs—

But it was not only the great who had cause to feel uneasy. Any man might suddenly find himself mocked at by name. The *Wasps* opens with two servants discussing their master's father:

FIRST SLAVE: He's got a strange disease
Nobody knows—Or will you try a guess?

(*Looking at audience.*)

Amynias down there, Pronapes' son,
Says it's a dice-disease, but he's quite off.

SECOND SLAVE: Ah—diagnosing from his own disease.

FIRST SLAVE: But Sosias here, in front declares he knows That it's a drink disease.

SECOND SLAVE: No—no—confound it!
That's the disease of honest gentlemen.

The names, of course, were changed as the audience changed. In a town that was small enough for everyone to know everyone else, the possibilities the method offered were endless.

The best known of Aristophanes' plays are the *Birds*, where Athens is shown up in contrast to the utopian city the birds build in the clouds; *The Frogs*, a parody of popular writers; the *Clouds*, which makes fun of the intelligentsia and Socrates who "walks on air and contemplates the sun" and three plays about women, the *Thesmophoriazusæ*, the *Lysistrata*, and the *Ecclesiazusœ*, in which the women take hold of literature, the war, and the state, to the great betterment of all.

The characters have little in common with Plato's. The delightful host of the *Symposium*, the courteous, witty Agathon, is a different person as seen by Aristophanes. In the *Thesmophoriazusæ* Euripides and an elderly man, Mnesilochus, are walking along a street:

EURIPIDES: That house is where great Agathon is living,
The tragic poet.

MNESILOCHUS: Agathon? Don't know him.

EURIPIDES: Why, he's the Agathon—

MNESILOCHUS: (*interrupting*) A big dark fellow, eh?

EURIPIDES: Oh, no, by no means. Haven't you ever seen him?
But let us step aside. His servant's coming.
He's got some myrtle and a pan of charcoal.
He's going to pray for help in composition.

SERVANT: Let sacred silence rule us here.
Ye people all, lock up your lips,
For the Muses are reveling there within,
The Queens of poetry-making.
Let the air be still and forget to blow,
And the gray sea wave make never a sound—

MNESILOCHUS: Stuff and nonsense—

EURIPIDES: *Will* you be quiet!

SERVANT: (*scandalized*) What's this that I hear?

MNESILOCHUS: Oh, just as you said.
It's the air that's forgetting to blow.

SERVANT: He's making a play.
First the keel he will lay
With neatly joined words all new,
Then the bottom he'll round,
And chisel the sound,
And fasten the verses with glue.
A maxim he'll take,
And an epithet make;
And call by new names what is old.
He'll form it like wax

And fill in the cracks,
And cast it at last in a mold.

(*Enter Agathon. He has on a silk dress and his hair is in a net.*)

MNESILOCHUS: Who are you? Were you born a man?
No, you're a woman surely.

AGATHON: Know, sir, I choose my dress to suit my writing.
A poet molds himself upon his poems,
And when he writes of women he assumes
A woman's dress and takes on woman's habits.
But when he sings of men a manly bearing
Is his therewith. What we are not by nature
We take unto ourselves through imitation.

Socrates fares no better. Aristophanes had noted well the homely imagery Socrates loved to illustrate high discourse with. In the *Clouds* a father goes to "The thinking-school" to enter his son, and there as he is being shown around, he sees a curious spectacle:

FATHER: Well now. Who's that—that man up in the basket?

STUDENT: Himself!

FATHER: Who *is* Himself?

STUDENT: Why, Socrates.

FATHER: Dear me. That Socrates? Oh, call him for me.

STUDENT: Really, I haven't time. Call him yourself.

FATHER: O Socrates! O—dear—sweet—Socrates!

SOCRATES: Mortal! Why call you on me?

FATHER: Tell me, please,
What are you doing up there in a basket?

SOCRATES: I walk on air and con-template the sun.
I could not search into celestial matters
Unless I mingled with the kindred air
My subtle spirit here on high. The ground
Is not the place for lofty speculations.
The earth would draw their essence to herself.
The same too is the case with watercress.

FATHER: Well, well. Thought draws the essence into watercress.

The two passages illustrate a further point: they presuppose an educated audience, perfectly at home in the best thought and literature of the day. It is the presupposition of all the plays. The intellectual side of the society Plato knew is constantly suggested. Much of the fun in *The Frogs* turns on parodies of Æschylus and Euripides which imply an exhaustive acquaintance with them on the part of the spectators, and as Æschylus is said to have written ninety plays and Euripides seventy-five, it meant something substantial in the way of culture to be well-read in them. Occasionally too we catch a faraway glimpse of people by whom the arts are taken seriously. In the *Clouds*, the father who entered his son in Socrates' thinking-school, finds him much the worse therefor. He pours out his complaints:

I told him to go and fetch his harp and help the supper along
By singing us good Simonides' Ram or another fine old song.
But he replied that to sing at meals was coarse and quite out of style,
And Simonides now was obsolete—had been for a good long while.
I really could hardly restrain myself at his finicking, poppycock ways,
But I did and I asked him to give us then a selection from Æschylus' plays.
But he answered, "Æschylus is to me an unmitigated bore,

A turgid, swollen-up, wind-bag thing that does nothing but ramp and roar."
When he talked like that my bosom began to heave extremely fast,
But I kept myself in and politely said, "Then give us one of the last,
Of the very newest you young men like." And he started a shameful thing
Euripides wrote, the sort of stuff no gentleman ever would sing,
Then, then, I could bear no more. I confess, I stormed and struck him too,
And he turned on me, his own father, he did, and beat me black and blue.

SON: And rightly too when you dared to blame that wisest of poets—he
Who is high over all, Euripides.

FATHER: The boy's just a fool, I see.

But these are only shadowy glimpses, and few and far between, at that. Aristophanes' Athens is for the most part inhabited by a most disreputable lot of people, as unplatonic as possible. The *Plutus* begins with a scene where a blind man is groping his way along a street, followed by an elderly, respectable-appearing man and his slave. The slave asks his master why they are following a blind man:

CHREMYLUS: I'll tell you why, straight out. Of all my slaves
I know you are the best, most constant—thief.
Well—I have been a good, religious man,
But always poor—no luck.

SLAVE: And so you have.
CHREMYLUS: While a church robber, and those thieves who live
On politics, get rich.

SLAVE: And so they do.

CHREMYLUS: So then I went to ask—not for myself,
I've pretty well shot all my arrows now—
But for my son, my only son. I prayed
That he might change his ways and turn into
A scoundrel, wicked, rotten through and through,
And so live happily forever after.
The god replied, the first man I fell in with
To follow.

SLAVE: Yes—Quite good. Of course, a blind man
Can see it's better nowadays to be
A rotten scoundrel.

The man in front proves to be Wealth himself, not aware of his power because he is blind. The two others proceed to enlighten him.

CHREMYLUS: Why, everything there is, is just Wealth's slave.
The girls, now, if a poor man comes along,
Will they look at him? But just let a rich one,
And he can get a deal more than he wants.
SLAVE: Oh, not the sweet, good, modest girls. They never
Would ask a man for money.

CHREMYLUS: No? What then?

SLAVE: Presents—the kind that cost a lot—that's all.

CHREMYLUS: Well, all the voting's done for Wealth of course.
You man our battleships. You own our army.
When you're an ally, that side's sure to win.
Nobody ever has enough of you.
While all things else a man can have too much of—
Of love.

SLAVE: Of loaves.

Aristophanes

CHREMYLUS: Of literature.

SLAVE: Of candy.

CHREMYLUS: Of fame.

SLAVE: Of figs.

CHREMYLUS: Of manliness.

SLAVE: Of mutton.

This kind of invective has a certain familiar ring in our ears. Writers who hold their own country and their own times to be the worst possible ever, can, it appears, trace their descent back through a great many centuries.

The playwright most like Aristophanes, the man whose sense of humor was most akin to his, lived in an age as unlike his as Shakespeare's was like it. The turbulent democracy that gave birth to the Old Comedy, and the England over whose manners and customs Queen Victoria ruled supreme, had little in common, and yet the mid-Victorian Gilbert of *Pinafore* fame saw eye to eye with Aristophanes as no other writer has done. The differences between Aristophanes and Gilbert are superficial; they are due to the differences of their time. In their essential genius they are alike.

The unknown is always magnificent. Aristophanes wears the halo of Greece, and is at the same time softly dimmed by the dust of centuries of scholarly elucidation. A comparison, therefore, with an author familiar and beloved and never really thought about wears a look of irreverence—also of ignorance. Dear nonsensical Gilbert, and the magnificent Aristophanes, poet, political reformer, social uplifter, philosophical thinker, with a dozen titles to immortality—how is it possible to compare them? The only basis for true comparison, Plato says, is the excellence that is peculiar to each thing. Was Aristophanes really a great lyric poet? Was he really bent on reforming politics or ending democracy? Such considerations are beside the point. Shakespeare's glory would not be enhanced if Hamlet's soliloquy was understood as a warning against suicide, or if it could be proved that in *Pericles* he was attacking the social evil. The peculiar excellence of comedy is its excellent fooling, and Aristophanes' claim to immortality is based upon one title only: he was a master maker of comedy, he could fool excellently. Here Gilbert stands side by side with him. He, too, could write the most admirable nonsense. There has never been better fooling than his, and a comparison with him carries nothing derogatory to the great Athenian.

Striking resemblances, both general and particular, emerge from such a comparison. The two men fooled in the same way; they looked at life with the same eyes. In Gilbert's pages Victorian England lives in miniature just as Athens lives in Aristophanes' pages. Those sweet pretty girls, those smart young dragoons, those match-making mammas; those genial exponents of the value of a title, a safe income, a political pull; that curious union of sentimental thinking and stoutly practical acting; that intimate savor of England in the eighteen eighties—who has ever given it so perfectly as he? He was one of the cleverest of caricaturists, but the freedom Aristophanes enjoyed was not his, and his deft, clear-cut pictures of dishonesty and sham and ignorance in high places are very discreet and always nameless. Essentially, however, he strikes with the same weapon as his Greek predecessor. He, too, ridicules the things dearest to his countrymen: the aristocracy in *Lolanthe*; army training in the *Pirates*; the navy in *Pinafore*; English society in *Utopia Limited*; and so on, through all his thirteen librettos. It is never cruel, this ridicule, as Aristophanes' sometimes is, but this difference is the inevitable result of the enormous difference between the two men's environment. The Athenian was watching cold and hunger and bitter defeat draw ever nearer to Athens. The Englishman wrote in the safest and most comfortable world mankind has ever known. But underneath that difference their fundamental point of view was the same.

They were topical writers, both of them, given over to the matters of the moment, and yet Aristophanes has been laughed with for two thousand years, and Gilbert has survived a half century of such shattering change, his England seems almost as far away from us. They saw beneath the surface of the passing show. They wrote of the purely ephemeral and in their hands it became a picture not of the "Follies and Foibles" of a day and a nation, but of those that exist in all nations and all ages and belong to the permanent stuff of human nature.

Of the two, Aristophanes has the bigger canvas, leagues to Gilbert's inches, but the yardstick is not a measure of art and the passages that follow will show how closely they resemble each other in the quality of their humor. It is true that Aristophanes wrote for an audience on a higher level intellectually than Gilbert's, made up of the keenest minds, the most discriminating critics, the theatre has ever known. It would be impossible to imagine the Victorians listening delightedly to hundreds of lines on end that were nothing except exquisitely skillful parodies of Browning and Tennyson. In the vital matter of an audience the Athenian was greatly more fortunate than the Englishman, and his plays have inevitably a far wider scope. None the less, it remains true that while the difference in their intellectual appeal may quite well have been due to the difference between the people each wrote for, their resemblances are far more striking and are certainly due to a close kinship of spirit.

Even in matters of technique, which is wont to vary so greatly from age to age, there are many similarities. To both men the fooling is the point, not the plot. In that subtle, individual thing, the use of metre, they are strikingly alike. The metre of a comic song is as important as its matter. No one understood that more clearly than Gilbert:

All children who are up in dates and floor you with 'em flat,
All persons who in shaking hands, shake hands with you like that.

Aristophanes understood it too as none better:

Come listen now to the good old days when the children, strange to tell,
Were seen not heard, led a simple life, in short were brought up well.

This jolly line is a favorite with him but he uses an endless variety. Examples will be found in the passages translated, in all of which, as I have already said, except the one indicated, I have reproduced the original metres. The effect of them is essentially that of Gilbert's.

A device of pure nonsense in Gilbert, which seems peculiarly his own, and which he uses, for example, in the second act of *Patience*, is the appeal to something utterly irrelevant that proves irresistible:

GROSVENOR (*wildly*): But you would not do it—I am sure you would not. (*Throwing himself at* BUNTHORNE'S *knees, and clinging to him.*) Oh, reflect, reflect! You had a mother once.

BUNTHORNE: Never!

GROSVENOR: Then you had an aunt! (BUNTHORNE *deeply affected.*) Ah!
I see you had! By the memory of that aunt, I implore you.

Precisely the same nonsensical device is used by Aristophanes. In the *Acharnians* the magic appeal before which all opposition melts is, not to an aunt, but to a scuttle of coal, as it might have been a few years back in England. Fuel was scarce in Athens just then; war was raging.

The scene is a street in Athens. A man, Dikæopolis by name, has said something in favor of Sparta, Athens' enemy. The crowd is furious:

DIKÆOPOLIS: This I know, the men of Sparta, whom we're cursing all day long,
Aren't the only ones to blame for everything that's going wrong.

CROWD: Spartans not to blame, you traitor? Do you dare tell such a lie?
At him! At him, all good people. Stone him, burn him. He shall die.

DIKÆOPOLIS: Won't you hear me, my dear fellows?

CROWD: Never, never. Not a word.

DIKÆOPOLIS: Then I'll turn on you, you villains. Would you kill a man unheard?
I've a hostage for my safety, one that's very dear to you.
I will slaughter him before you. (*Goes into house at back of stage.*)

CROWD: What is it he's gone to do?
How he threatens. You don't think he's got a child of ours in there?

DIKÆOPOLIS: (*From behind stage*) I've got something. Now, you scoundrels, tremble, for I will not spare.
Look well at my hostage. This will test your mettle, every soul. (*He comes out lugging something behind him.*)
Which among you has true feeling for—a scuttle full of coal?

CROWD: Heaven save us! Oh, don't touch it. We'll give in. Say what you please.

In the *Lysistrata* occurs the following:

FIRST SPEAKER: For through man's heart there runs in flood
A natural and a noble taste for blood.

SECOND SPEAKER: To form a ring and fight—

THIRD SPEAKER: To cut off heads at sight—

ALL: It is our right.

Matter and manner are perfectly Gilbert's. Any one not knowing the author would inevitably assign it to him, to the *Princess Ida,* perhaps, along with:

We are warriors three,
Sons of Gama Rex,
Like most sons are we,
Masculine in sex.
Bold and fierce and strong, ha! ha!
For a war we burn,
With its right or wrong, ha! ha!
We have no concern.

Aristophanes was amused by grand talk that covered empty content. In the first scene of the *Thesmophoriazusæ* two elderly men enter, one with the lofty air that befits a Poet and Philosopher, the other an ordinary, cheerful old fellow. He speaks first:

MNESILOCHUS: Might I, before I've lost my wind entirely, Be told, where you are taking me, Euripides?

EURIPIDES: (*solemnly*) You may not hear the things which presently
You are to see.

MNESILOCHUS: What's that? Say it again.
I'm not to hear—?

EURIPIDES: What you shall surely see.

MNESILOCHUS: And not to see—?

EURIPIDES: The things you must needs hear.

MNESILOCHUS: Oh, how you talk. Of course you're very clever.
You must mean I must not either hear or see?

EURIPIDES: They two are twain and by their nature diverse,
Each one from other.

MNESILOCHUS: What's that—diverse?

EURIPIDES: Their elemental parts are separate.

MNESILOCHUS: Oh, what it is to talk to learned people!

Gilbert was amused by the same thing. In the second act of the *Princess Ida* the first scene is the hall of the Women's University. The principal has been addressing the faculty and students, and as she finishes asks:

Who lectures in the Hall of Arts today?

LADY BLANCHE: I, madam, on Abstract Philosophy.
There I propose considering at length
Three points—the Is, the Might Be, and the Must.
Whether the Is, from being actual fact,
Is more important than the vague Might Be,
Or the Might Be, from taking wider scope,
Is for that reason greater than the Is:
And lastly, how the Is and Might Be stand
Compared with the inevitable Must!

PRINCESS: The subject's deep.

Every kind of sham is dear to Aristophanes but especially the literary sham. He is forever making fun of him. In the *Birds* Peisthetærus, an Athenian, is helping the birds found their new city in the clouds, which is called Cloud-cuckoo-town. To it flock the quacks and the cranks. A priest has just been chased off the stage when enter a poet, singing:*

O Cloud-cuckoo-town!
Muse, do thou crown
With song her fair name,
Hymning her fame.

PEISTHETÆUS: What sort of thing is this? I say,
Who in the world are you, now, pray?

POET: A warbler of a song,
Very sweet and very strong.
Slave of the Muse am I,
Eager and nimble and spry,
—As Homer says.

PEISTHETÆUS: Does the Muse let her servants wear
That sort of long, untidy hair?

POET: Oh, we who teach the art
Of the drama, whole or part,
Servants of the Muse must try
To be eager and nimble and spry,
—As Homer says.

PEISTHETÆUS: That nimbleness, no doubt is why
You're all in rags. You are too spry.

POET: Oh, I've been making lovely, lovely lays,
Old and new-fashioned too, in sweetest praise
Of your Cloud-cuckoo-town.
...And won't you see
If you have something you can give to ME?

Gilbert enjoyed the sham artist quite as much. In *Patience* the officers of the Dragoons are on the stage:

COLONEL: Yes, and here are the ladies.

DUKE: But who is the gentleman with the long hair?

(BUNTHORNE *enters, followed by the ladies, two by two.*)

BUNTHORNE: (*Aside*) Though my book I seem to scan
In a rapt ecstatic way,
Like a literary man
Who despises female clay,
I hear plainly all they say.
Twenty love-sick maidens they!

(*Exit ladies.*)

BUNTHORNE: (*Alone*) Am I alone
And unobserved? I am!
Then let me own
I'm an æsthetic sham!
This air severe
Is but a mere
Veneer!
This costume chaste
Is but good taste
Misplaced!

Both writers make the same kind of jokes about military matters and the like. In the *Knights* the two generals introduced were among the most famous of their time:

DEMOSTHENES: How goes it, poor old chap?

NICIAS: Badly. Like you.

DEMOSTHENES: Let's sing a doleful ditty and then weep. (*Both sing, break down and sob.*)

DEMOSTHENES: No use in whimpering. We'd do better far
To dry our tears and find some good way out.

NICIAS: What way? You tell me.

DEMOSTHENES: No. Do you tell me.
If you won't speak I'll fight you.

NICIAS: No, not I.
You say it first and then I'll say it after.

DEMOSTHENES: Oh, speak for me and say what's in my heart.

NICIAS: My courage fails. If only I could say it
Neatly and sweetly, like Euripides.
Well, then, say SERT, like that, and say it smartly.

DEMOSTHENES: All right. Here goes: SERT.

NICIAS: Good! Have courage now.
Say first SERT and then DE, repeating fast
The two words, very fast.

DEMOSTHENES: Ah, yes. I get you.
Sert de, sert de sert, DESERT!

NICIAS: You have it.
Well, doesn't it sound nice?

DEMOSTHENES: It's HEAVENLY.
But—but—

NICIAS: What's that?

DEMOSTHENES: They FLOG deserters.

Gilbert's jokes, of course, were in a lighter vein. War seemed remote to the mid-Victorian. The passage most like the one quoted from Aristophanes is the marching song of the Police in the *Pirates*:

MABEL: Go, ye heroes, go to glory,
Though ye die in combat gory,
Ye shall live in song and story,
Go to immortality!

POLICE: Though to us it's evident,
Tarantara! tarantara!
These intentions are well meant,
Tarantara!
Such expressions don't appear,
Tarantara, tarantara,
Calculated men to cheer,
Tarantara!
Who are going to meet their fate
In a highly nervous state,
Tarantara!

Politicians in Athens and in London seem very much the same. In the *Plutus* a slave, Carion, meets one. He asks:

You're a good man, a patriot?

POLITICIAN: Oh, yes,
If ever there was one.

CARION: And, as I guess,
A farmer?

POLITICIAN: I? Lord save us. I'm not mad.

CARION: A merchant then?

POLITICIAN: Ah, sometimes I have had
To take that trade up—as an alibi.

CARION: You've some profession surely.

POLITICIAN: No, not I.

CARION: How do you make a living?

POLITICIAN: Well, there're several
Answers to that. I'm Supervisor General
Of all things here, public and private too.

CARION: A great profession that. What did you do to qualify for it?

POLITICIAN: I WANTED it.

So Gilbert in the song of the duke and duchess in the *Gondoliers*:

To help unhappy commoners, and add to their enjoyment,
Affords a man of noble rank congenial employment;
Of our attempts we offer you examples illustrative:
The work is light, and, I may add, it's most remunerative.
Small titles and orders
For Mayors and Recorders
I get—and they're highly delighted.
M. P.'s baronetted,
Sham Colonels gazetted,
And second-rate Aldermen knighted.

In the *Knights* an oracle has just foretold that Athens will be ruled some day by a sausage-seller. At that moment one enters and is greeted with enthusiasm.

DEMOSTHENES: Dear Sausage-seller, rise, our Saviour and the State's.

SAUSAGE-SELLER: What's that you say?

DEMOSTHENES: O happy man and rich!
Nothing today, tomorrow everything.
O Lord of Athens, blest through you!

SAUSAGE-SELLER: I see, sir,
That you must have your joke. But as for me,
I've got to wash the guts and sell my sausage.

DEMOSTHENES: But you are going to be our greatest man.

SAUSAGE-SELLER: Oh, I'm not fit for that.

DEMOSTHENES: What's that?
Not fit?
Is some good action weighing on your conscience?
Don't tell me that you come of honest folk?

SAUSAGE-SELLER: Oh, dear me, no sir. Bad 'uns, out and out.

DEMOSTHENES: You lucky man. Oh, what a start you've got
For public life.

SAUSAGE-SELLER: But I don't know a thing except my letters.

DEMOSTHENES: Ah, the pity is that you know anything.
A parallel passage is Sir Joseph's song in *Pinafore*:
I grew so rich that I was sent
By a pocket borough into Parliament.
I always voted at my party's call,
And I never thought of thinking for myself at all.
I thought so little they rewarded me
By making me the Ruler of the Queen's Navee!

The woman joke, of course, is well to the fore with both men. It is ever with us. *Plus ça change, plus c'est la même chose*. Any number of passages might be selected.

The song of the duchess in the *Gondoliers* is completely in the customary style:

On the day when I was wedded
To your admirable sire,
I acknowledge that I dreaded
An explosion of his ire.

I was always very wary,
For his fury was ecstatic—
His refined vocabulary
Most unpleasantly emphatic.

Giving him the very best, and getting back the very worst—
That is how I tried to tame your great progenitor—at first!

But I found that a reliance on my threatening appearance,
And a resolute defiance of marital interference,
Was the only thing required for to make his temper supple,
And you couldn't have desired
A more reciprocating couple.
So with double-shotted guns and colours nailed unto the mast,
I tamed your insignificant progenitor—at last!

Aristophanes' ladies are of quite the same kind. They form the chorus of the *Thesmophoriazusæ*, and they begin their address to the audience as follows:

We now come forward and appeal to you to hear how the men all flout us,
And the foolish abuse and the scandals let loose the silly things tell about us.
They say all evil proceeds from us, war, battles, and murder even;
We're a tiresome, troublesome, quarrelsome lot, disturbers of earth and of heaven.
Now, we ask you to put your minds on this: if we're really the plague of your lives,
Then tell us, please, why you're all so keen to get us to be your wives?
Pray, why do you like us to be at home, all ready to smile and greet you,
And storm and sulk if your poor little wife isn't always there to meet you?
If we're such a nuisance and pest, then why—we venture to put the question—
Don't you rather rejoice when we're out of the way—a reasonable suggestion.
If we stay the night at the house of a friend—I mean, the house of a lady,

You hunt for us everywhere like mad and hint at
something shady.
Do you like to look at a plague and a pest? It seems you do,
for you stare
And ogle and give us killing looks if you see us anywhere.
And if we think proper to blush and withdraw, as a lady, no
doubt, should be doing,
You will try to follow us all the more, and never give
over pursuing.
But we can show you up as well.

The ways of a man we all can tell.
Your heart's in your stomach, every one,
And you'll do any one if you're not first done.
We know what the jokes are you love to make,
And how you each fancy yourself a rake.

Parallels such as these could be given indefinitely. The world moves slowly. Aristophanes in Athens, fifth century B.C., Gilbert in nineteenth-century England, saw the same things and saw the same humor in them. Some things, however, were seen by the Athenian which the Englishman was constrained not to see and this fact constitutes the chief point of difference between them. What a gulf divides the Old Comedy, so riotous and so Rabelaisian, and the decorous operettas that would never raise a blush on the cheek of Anthony Trollope's most ladylike heroine. A gulf indeed, but it is the gulf between the two periods. England's awful arbiter of morals, the formidable Queen in her prime, was the audience that counted in Gilbert's day, and it may be stated with certainty that Aristophanes himself would have abjured indecency and obscenity in that presence. Equally certainly, if he had lived in the age, *par excellence*, of gentility, he would have tempered his vigor, checked his swiftness, moderated his exuberance. Gilbert is an Aristophanes plentifully watered down, a steady and stolid-y, jolly Bank-holiday, everyday Aristophanes, a mid-Victorian Aristophanes.

The question is irresistibly suggested, if Gilbert had lived in those free-thinking, free-acting, free-speaking days of Athens, "so different from the home life of our own dear Queen," would he too have needed a Lord High Chamberlain

To purge his native stage beyond a question
Of "risky" situation and indelicate suggestion.

There are indications that point to the possibility, had he not been held down by the laws the Victorian patrons of the drama gave. He could not but submit to these limitations, and only rarely, by a slip as it were, is a hint given of what he might have done if there had not always been before him the fear of that terrible pronunciamento: We are NOT amused!

But Aristophanes' audiences set no limits at all. Were Plato's characters found among them, the meditative Phædrus, the gentle-mannered Agathon, Socrates, the philosophic, himself? Beyond all question. They sat in the theatre for hours on end, applauding a kind of Billingsgate Falstaff at his worst never approached; listening to violent invectives against the men—and the women—of Athens as a drunken, greedy, venal, vicious lot; laughing at jokes that would have put Rabelais to the blush.

Such a theatre to our notions is not a place gentlemen of the Platonic stamp would frequent. A polite Molière comedy would be the kind of thing best suited to them, or if they must have improprieties to divert them, they should be suggested, not shouted. But our Athenians were not French seventeenth-century nobles, nor yet of Schnitzler's twentieth-century Vienna; they were vigorous, hardy, hearty men; lovers of good talk but talk with a body to it, and lovers quite as much of physical prowess; hard-headed men, too, who could drink all night and discuss matters for clear heads only; realists as well, who were not given to drawing a veil before any of life's facts. The body was of tremendous importance, acknowledged to be so, quite as much as the mind and the spirit.

Such were Plato's gentlemen and such were Aristophanes' audiences. The comic theatre was a means of working off the exuberant energy of abounding vitality. There were no limitations to the subjects it could treat or the way of treating them. The result is that the distinctive quality of the Old Comedy cannot be illustrated by quotation. The most characteristic passages are unprintable. Something completely indecent is caricatured, wildly exaggerated, repeated in a dozen different ways, all fantastically absurd and all incredibly vulgar. The truth is that the jokes are often very funny. To read Aristophanes through at a sitting is to have Victorian guide posts laid low. He is so frank, so fearless, so completely without shame, one ends by feeling that indecency is just a part of life and a part with specially humorous possibilities. There is nothing of Peeping Tom anywhere, no sly whispering from behind a hand. The plainest and clearest words speak everything out unabashed. Life looks a coarse and vulgar thing, lived at the level of nature's primitive needs, but it never looks a foul and rotten thing. Degeneracy plays no part. It is the way of a virile world, of robust men who can roar with laughter at any kind of slapstick, decent or indecent, but chiefly the last.

Look upon this picture and on this. It is impossible for us today to make a coherent whole out of Aristophanes' Athens and Plato's. But if ever a day comes when our intelligentsia is made up of our star football players we shall be on the way to understanding the Athenians—as Aristophanes saw them.

* Except the first four lines this quotation is not in the original metre, which varies from line to line as English metre does not.

HERODOTUS
The First Sight-seer

THE SLAVE IN GREECE

Herodotus is the historian of the glorious fight for liberty in which the Greeks conquered the overwhelming power of Persia. They won the victory because they were free men defending their freedom against a tyrant and his army of slaves. So Herodotus saw the contest. The watchword was freedom; the stake was the independence or the enslavement of Greece; the issue made it sure that Greeks never would be slaves.

The modern reader cannot accept the proud words without a wondering question. What of the slaves these free Greeks owned? The Persian defeat did not set them free. What real idea of freedom could the conquerors at Marathon and Salamis have had, slave-owners, all of them? The question shows up, as no other question could, the difference between the mind of today and the mind of antiquity. To all the ancient world the freeing of slaves would have been sheer nonsense. There always had been slaves. In every community the way of life depended on them; they were a first necessity, accepted as such without a thought—literally; nobody ever paid any attention to them. Life in Greece as everywhere else was founded on slaves, but in all Greek literature up to the age of Pericles they never come into sight except as individuals here and there; the old nurse in the *Odyssey*, or the good swineherd, whose condition is accepted as naturally as any fact in nature. That is true from Homer to Æschylus, who makes Clytemnestra say to Cassandra, the Trojan princess, now her slave:

If one is a slave
It is well to serve in an old family
Long used to riches. Every man who reaps
A sudden harvest, wealth past all his hopes,
Is savage to his slaves beyond the common.
From us expect such use as custom grants.

From the time immemorial that was the attitude in all the world. There was never anywhere a dreamer so rash or so romantic as to imagine a life without slaves. The loftiest thinkers, idealists, and moralists never had an idea that slavery was evil. In the Old Testament it is accepted without comment exactly as in the records of Egypt and Mesopotamia. Even the prophets of Israel did not utter a word against it, nor, for that matter, did St. Paul. What is strange is not that the Greeks took slavery for granted through hundreds of years, but that finally they began to think about it and question it.

To Euripides the glory belongs of being the first to condemn it. "Slavery," he wrote:

That thing of evil, by its nature evil,
Forcing submission from a man to what
No man should yield to.

He was, as usual, far in advance of his age. Even Plato, a generation later, could not keep pace with him. He never spoke against slavery; in his old age he actually advocated it. Still, there are signs that he was troubled by it. He says, "A slave is an embarrassing possession." He had reached a point when he could not feel at ease with slaves, and he does not admit them to his ideal Republic.

Except for this mild and indirect opposition and for Euripides' open attack, we have no idea how or why the opposition to slavery spread, but by Aristotle's time, a generation after Plato, it had come out into the open. Aristotle himself, for all his extraordinary powers of mind, looked at the matter purely from the point of view of common sense and social convenience. Slaves were necessary to carry on society as constituted, and he did not want any other kind of society. With no expressed or implied disapproval he defines a slave as "a machine which breathes, a piece of animated property," an instance of the cold, clear statement of fact which so often opens people's eyes and shocks them into opposition. Opponents to slavery increased. "There are people," Aristotle writes—he does not include himself—"who consider owning slaves as violating natural law because the distinction between a slave and a free person is wholly conventional and has no place in nature, so that it rests on mere force and is devoid of justice."

That is the point Greek thought had reached more than two thousand four hundred years ago. Less than a hundred years ago America had to fight a great war before slavery was abolished. The matter for wondering is not that Herodotus saw nothing odd in slave-owners being the champions of freedom, but that in Greece alone, through all ancient and almost all modern times, were there men great enough and courageous enough to see through the conventional coverings that disguised slavery, and to proclaim it for what it was. A few years after Aristotle the Stoics denounced it as the most intolerable of all the wrongs man ever committed against man.

Socrates, when the young Theætetus was introduced to him as a lad of brilliant promise, said to him that he felt sure he had thought a great deal. The boy answered, Oh, no—not that, but at least he had wondered a great deal. "Ah, that shows the lover of wisdom," Socrates said, "for wisdom begins in wonder."

There have been few men ever who wondered more than Herodotus did. The word is perpetually on his pen: "A wonder was told me" "In that land there are ten thousand wonders" "Wonderful deeds, those" "It is a thing to be wondered at." In this disposition he was the true child of his age—the great age of Greece. During his life his countrymen were using their freedom, newly secured to them by the Persian defeat, to wonder in all directions. They were no longer obliged to spend their best powers on war. Fighting occurred, but only sporadically. The Athenians on the whole were peaceful and prosperous; they had leisure to sit at home and think about the universe and dispute with Socrates, or to travel abroad and explore the world. In any case, to be active. Leisure meant activity in those days. Nobody wanted anything else. Energy and high spirits and vitality marked the fifth century in Athens.

Herodotus, spiritually an Athenian although a native of Halicarnassus, summed up in himself the vigor of his times. He set out to travel over the earth as far as a man could go. What strength of will and also of body that called for under the travelling conditions of the day, it is impossible for us to realize. The first part of St. Paul's journey to Rome gives a picture of the hazards that had to be faced at sea four hundred years after Herodotus, and a companion picture for the land is Xenophon's description of the endless miles on foot or horseback through the burning wastes of Asia Minor to Babylon. It required a hungering and thirsting for knowledge and all the explorer's zest to send a man on the travels Herodotus undertook; undertook, too, with keen enjoyment. He was the first sight-seer in the world, and there has never been a happier one. If he could see something new, discomforts and difficulties and dangers were nothing to him. He seems never to have noticed them. He never wrote about them. He filled his book with the marvels to rejoice a man's heart—marvels of which the great earth was full. Oh, wonder that there were such goodly creatures in it!

Just how far he travelled is hard to say. What he heard he gives with as great interest as what he saw, and he is so objective, so absorbed in whatever he is describing, he generally leaves himself out. But he certainly went as far east as Persia and as far west as Italy. He knew the coast of the Black Sea and had been in Arabia. In Egypt he went up the Nile to Assouan. It seems probable that he went to Cyrene; his descriptions often read like those of an eye witness. That is less true of Libya and Sicily, but it is quite possible that he had been in both countries. In fact, his journeys practically reached to the boundaries of the known world, and the information he gathered reached far beyond. He knew a good deal about India. For instance, there were wild trees there that bore wool, superior in whiteness and quality to sheep's wool. The Indians made beautiful fine clothing from it. With India his information about the East stopped. He had heard a report of great deserts on the further side, but that was all. Of the West he writes:

> *I am unable to speak with certainty. I can learn nothing about the islands from which our tin comes, and though I have asked everywhere I have met no one who has seen a sea on the west side of Europe. The truth is no one has discovered if Europe is surrounded by water or not.*
>
> *I smile at those who with no sure knowledge to guide them describe the ocean flowing around a perfectly circular earth.*

This is an example of the way the Greek mind worked. The great river Ocean encircling the earth had been described by Homer, the revered, even sacred, authority, and by Hesiod, second only to Homer, and yet Herodotus with never a qualm at possible impiety permits himself a smile. Quite as characteristic is his matter-of-fact statement that the priestess at Delphi had been more than once bribed to give an oracle favorable to one side in a dispute. This was attacking the Greek holy of holies—like accusing the pope of taking bribes. Herodotus had a great respect for the Delphic oracle, but to his mind that was no reason to suppress a charge which he had investigated and believed to be true—and most assuredly no reason to abstain from investigation. When an authority, no matter how traditionally sacrosanct, came into conflict with a fact, the Greeks preferred the fact. They had no inclination to protect "sound doctrine taught of old." A new force had come into the world with Greece, the idea of Truth to which personal bias and prejudice must yield.

Herodotus is a shining instance of the strong Greek bent to examine and prove or disprove. He had a passion for finding out. The task he set himself was nothing less than to find out all about everything in the world. He is always called the "father of history," but he was quite as much the father of geography, of archæology, of anthropology, of sociology, of whatever has to do with human beings and the places in which they live. He was as free from prejudice as it is possible to be. The Greek contempt for foreigners—in Greek, "barbarians"—never touched him. He was passionately on Athens' side in her struggle against Persia, yet he admired and praised the Persians. He found them brave and chivalrous and truthful. Much that he saw in Phœnicia and Egypt seemed admirable to him, and even in uncivilized Scythia and Libya he saw something to commend. He did not go abroad to find Greek superiority. An occasional inferiority quite pleased him. He quotes with amusement Cyrus' description of a Greek market as "a place set apart for people to go and cheat each other on oath."

"All men," he writes, "if asked to choose the best ways of ordering life would choose their own." Darius once asked some Greeks what would induce them to devour the dead bodies of their

Herodotus

parents, and when they answered in horror that nothing could make them do an act so atrocious, he had some men from India brought in whose custom it was to do this very thing. He asked them how they could be persuaded to burn their dead instead of eating them. They cried out in abhorrence and begged him not to utter such abominable words. "As Pindar says," concludes Herodotus, "custom is king." The story is characteristic of his indulgent attitude toward all men's ways, however queer. He was that rare person, a lover of mankind. He liked people, all of them. But he liked them more than he admired them, and he never idealized them. Plutarch even accuses him, so markedly kind and fairminded as he was, of actual malignity because heroes in his book are not consistently heroical. It is true that he lived in an age of heroism and never really believed in heroes. But his gentle scepticism worked both ways. He never judged or condemned. The weakness and fallibility of the human kind aroused only his sympathy. If his heroes are imperfectly great, his villains are never perfectly villainous. He looked at them all with dispassionate and equal interest.

Everything everywhere in the world of men was of interest to him. He tells us how the homely girls in Illyria get husbands, how the lake dwellers keep their children from falling into the water, what Egyptian mosquito nets are like, that the King of Persia when travelling drinks only boiled water, what the Adrymachidæ do to fleas, how the Arabians cut their hair, that the Danube islanders get drunk on smells, how the Scythians milk their mares, that in Libya the woman with the most lovers is honored, how the streets of Babylon are laid out, that physicians in Egypt specialize in diseases, and so on, and so on. Bits of information that have nothing to do with what he is writing about keep straying in; but he is so intensely interested in them himself, the reader's interest is caught too. Is not that really extraordinary? he says to us—or extremely diverting—or remarkably sensible? And we follow him; we are surprised and diverted and approving. Of course this is only to say that he has the *sine qua non* of a writer—he is never dull; but to avoid dullness in what is often a guidebook is an achievement. Some part of it is due to his perfect, his unsurpassed, ease in writing. He has no mannerisms, not a particle of self-consciousness; he is always simple, direct, and lucid, always easy to read. His countryman, Dionysius of Halicarnassus, said he was the first to give Greece the idea that an expression in prose could have the worth of a verse of poetry.

He is often accused of being credulous even to the point of silliness. It is said that he accepted with the naïve simplicity of a child everything he was told, no matter how preposterous. There is no truth whatsoever in the charge. Precisely the contrary is true: his turn of mind was sceptical; he was a born investigator. The word history, which was first used in our sense by him, means investigation in Greek. His book begins, "This is an account of the investigations [historia] made by Herodotus of Halicarnassus." He started on them prepared to scrutinize everything he heard. When different and equally probable accounts of an event were given him he wrote them all down and left the final judgment to his reader. "I cannot positively state whether this was done or that," he will say. "For myself," he remarks in a notable passage, "my duty is to report all that is said, but I am not obliged to believe it all—a remark which applies to my whole History."

Even these few quotations show the temper of his mind, his sense of responsibility as a reporter, and his care in weighing evidence. But of course in his day the unknown was so great, what was actually known was so limited, no borderline had yet been drawn between the credible and the incredible. It is often impossible to make out why Herodotus accepts one thing and rejects another purely on the ground of what can and cannot happen. Doves, he says firmly, do not ever speak even though the holy women at Dodona declare that they do, but he does not question the story that a mare gave birth to a rabbit. He is sure that no matter what the Egyptian priests assert, it is not true that the phoenix wraps up the dead body of his parent in a mass of myrrh and carries it from Arabia to the Temple of the Sun in Heliopolis where he buries it. On the other hand it seems to him quite reasonable that there are headless creatures in Libya with eyes in their breasts, and that cats in Egypt have the singular habit of jumping into the fire. He had a standard of what was possible and what was not, but it was so different from ours it escapes us. After all, wherever he went he saw so many strange things, it was easy to believe there were even stranger ones in the vast beyond.

But when he was on ground he knew he was a shrewd judge of the improbable. He writes:

> *In the highest tower in Babylon, in the topmost chamber, there is a great couch on which the god himself is reported to sleep. So the priests told me, but I do not believe it.*
>
> *I cannot say with confidence how the man escaped, for the account given me made me wonder. They say he jumped into the sea and swam eighty stadia under water, never rising to the top. If I may give my own opinion, it is that he got off in a boat.*

But he is always mildly tolerant of other people's explanations and never dogmatic about his own. Of the storm that wrecked Xerxes' fleet he writes:

> *It lasted three days. At length the Magi charming the wind and sacrificing to the Nereids succeeded in laying the tempest—or perhaps it ceased of itself.*

When he was sight-seeing in Thessaly he was told that a famous gorge he visited was caused by Neptune, and he remarks:

> *It seemed plain to me that it was the result of an earthquake. Many people think earthquakes are the work of Neptune.*

What he himself thought about the gods is not easy to make out. The heavenly powers play a leading part in his history, and omens, oracles, prayers, and prophets are very important to him. Yet it would be hard to find a more coldly rationalistic statement than the one he makes early in his book:

> *Where the gods come from, whether they always existed, what they looked like, was, so to speak, unknown till yesterday. Homer and Hesiod lived not more than four hundred years ago and it was they who made the gods for the Greeks and gave them their names and shapes.*

His book is really a bridge from one era to another. He was born in an age of deep religious feeling, just after the Persian Wars; he lived on into the scepticism of the age of Pericles; and by virtue of his kindly tolerance and keen intellectual interest he was equally at home in both.

Historians often forget that the proper study of history is men. Marshalled facts and reasoned analyses tend to cover up human nature. That was not Herodotus' way. People are always to the fore in his book. It is fortunate for us that he is the reporter of Marathon, Thermopylæ, Salamis, names which shine like stars through the endless, senseless wars that make up most of the world's history. In his hands they are the scenes of a great drama written in plain human terms. The disposing causes are men's arrogance and greed for conquest and their power to defend what is dear to them against overwhelming odds.

Only the last part of the *History* has to do with the Persian Wars. Two thirds of the book are taken up with Herodotus' journeys and what he learned on them. These earlier chapters have the effect, more and more as one reads on, of a slowly unrolling stage setting. The whole of the known world is presented as the fitting background to the tremendous conflict that is to decide whether freedom or tyranny is the stronger, whether the West is to be enslaved by the East. Darius, the Great King, makes his appearance. He is ruler of most of the world. Myriads of men serve him; his wealth is limitless; his magnificence fabulous; his cruelty fantastic. He is the Orient in person, its barbaric pearl and gold, its helpless millions, its disregard for human life and suffering. Over against him stands Greece, "a rocky land and poor," a speaker in Herodotus tells Darius, where, as Pericles put it, the people "love beauty with economy" economy, the very opposite to the lavishness and exaggeration of the grandiose East.

Herodotus describes the amused astonishment of the Persian Army at learning that the prize for an Olympic victory was a crown of wild olives. He tells about a pillar he saw, one of the many the Great King set up to mark his approbation when he passed a place that pleased him. It was inscribed: "These springs are the best and most beautiful of waters. They were visited by Darius, the best and most beautiful of men." By sheer force of contrast the words recall the epitaph on the dead at Thermopylæ: "Stranger, tell the Spartans that we lie here in obedience to their words."

The contrast is never stressed by Herodotus, but in one story after another it comes out so clearly that it needs no emphasis. "The immortals are near to men to watch over deeds of justice and kindliness," wrote Hesiod, and so all Greeks believed. Whatever the strange deities of the East required, it was not justice nor kindliness. "It is a Persian custom to bury people alive," says Herodotus. "One of Darius' daughters-in-law had fourteen young children of the best Persian families buried alive." Imperial Rome, always inclined to Oriental ways, took over this custom of killing the young with the old. Little boys and girls were, if not buried alive, at any rate put to death with a guilty father. But Greece was different. When the young sons of a man who had betrayed his city to the Persians were brought to the general commanding the Spartan forces after Leonidas fell at Thermopylæ, he dismissed them. "They are boys," Herodotus reports him as saying. "What part could boys have in the guilt of siding with the Persians?"

What underlay the Spartan general's action was not only the belief that the innocent must not suffer with the guilty; even more basic was the conviction of the value of each individual, no matter how defenseless. This idea never touched even the surface of Oriental life. No law or custom there lent it support. In Greece it was based on something deeper than law or custom. Once, Herodotus says, ten of the ruling party in Corinth went to a house with the purpose of killing a little boy there who an oracle had declared would grow up to destroy the city.

> *The mother, thinking it a friendly visit, brought her son when they asked to see him, and put him in the arms of one of them. Now they had agreed on the way there that whoever first received the child should dash it to the ground. But it happened that the baby smiled at the man who took it and so he was unable to kill it and handed it to another. Thus it passed through the hands of all the ten and no one of them would kill it. Then they gave it back to the mother and went away and began to blame each other, but especially him who had first held the child.*

"A tyrant disturbs ancient laws," Herodotus writes, "violates women, kills men without trial. But a people ruling—first, the very name of it is so beautiful; and secondly, a people does none of these things." Only the tyrant was known throughout the East. When the Great King was on his march to Greece a very rich noble of Lydia entertained not only him and his courtiers, but his multitudinous host of soldiers as well. He set sumptuous feasts before all, Herodotus says, and in return begged humbly that one of his five sons, all in the army, might remain with him. "You make such a request?" said the king. "You who are my slave and bound to give me all that is yours, even to your wife?" He ordered the body of the eldest youth to be cut in two and placed on either side of the road where the army was to pass. The Persians were slaves, so called and so treated; the richest and most powerful claimed nothing as their right; they were completely at the disposal of the king. Herodotus tells another story. A noble, who had for years enjoyed the royal favor and then had lost it, was invited to dine with the king. After he had feasted on the meat placed before him, he was presented with a covered basket. Lifting the lid he saw the head and hands and feet of his only son. "Do you know now," the king asked pleasantly, "the kind of animal you have been eating?" The father had learned the lesson slaves must master, self-control. He answered with perfect composure, "I do know, indeed—and whatever the king is pleased to do pleases me." That was the spirit of the East from time immemorial, first clearly recorded for the world in Herodotus' book. Little, poor, barren Greece was free. "You know perfectly what it is to be a slave," Herodotus reports some Greeks as saying to a Persian official who was urging them to submit to Xerxes. "Freedom you have never tried, to know how sweet it is. If you had you would urge us to fight for it not with our spears only, but even with hatchets." As the war with the Persians draws nearer in Herodotus, it is seen more and more clearly as a contest not of flesh and blood only, but of spiritual forces which are incompatible.

A brief prologue introduces the action. A revolt broke out in the Greek cities on the coast of Asia Minor which were subject to Darius. Athens sent help. The Athenians marched to Sardis, the capital of Lydia, and they burned the splendid town. To Darius it was incredible that any people on earth should so defy him. "Who are the Athenians?" he demanded; and he ordered that every time he dined, an attendant should say to him three times: "Sire, remember the Athenians." There is no doubt that Herodotus understood dramatic requirements. The stage has been set for Marathon.

When the curtain rises for the drama proper the nephew of Darius, who has been entrusted with the charge of carrying out the vengeance of the king, is leading the Persian Army into

Greece, vast forces by sea and by land. Before him heralds come demanding from the Greek cities "earth and water," the tokens of submission; and all as far south as Thebes give them. One, Eritræa, separated from Athens only by a narrow strait, refuses, but she is quickly captured and burned to the ground. Athens is next, seemingly a most trifling obstacle to that great host. She has no one in all Greece to help her except a little band of soldiers sent by Platæa, a town grateful for favors in the past. Away to the south the chief military power of Greece, Sparta, is no more ready to submit to Persia than Athens, and would be a strong ally. But, as democracies always do, Athens has waited too long to make her plans. The Persians are almost upon her when Pheidippides starts his race to enlist help for her. In Sparta the next day he urges: "Lacedæmonians, the Athenians entreat you. Do not suffer them to fall into bondage to barbarians." But there are some days yet to the full moon, and until the moon was full the Spartans would not march. "We will come as soon after that as we can," the herald is told. Events, however, do not wait on the moon. The Persian fleet is already at anchor in the curving bay of Marathon.

Herodotus was born about that time. The fight must often have been described to him by men who had taken part in it. He explains the strategy very clearly. The Athenian formation was the exact reverse of the enemy's who trusted to their centre, leaving their wings to inferior troops. Miltiades threw his chief strength into the wings. The centre was weak so that the Persians easily broke through it and rushed on in pursuit. Then the Athenian wings closed in behind, shutting the foe off from their ships and cutting them down. The defeat was complete. The fleet after sailing down the coast to within sight of Athens put out to sea. The Persians had gone. It was an incredible contest and an incredible victory. How could it happen like that—the little band of defenders victors over the mighty armament? We do not understand. But Herodotus understood, and so did all Greeks. A free democracy resisted a slave-supported tyranny. The Athenians at Marathon had advanced at a run; the enemy's officers drove them into battle by scourging them. Mere numbers were powerless against the spirit of free men fighting to defend their freedom. Liberty proved her power. A wave of exultant courage and faith swept through the city, and Athens started on her career.

Ten years passed before the curtain rose for the last act. Darius was kept from the terrible vengeance he vowed he would take by a war which occupied him until he died. He had to leave it to his son to revenge the Persian defeat. He too was to remember the Athenians. Xerxes was not eager for the enterprise, but in actual fact he was helpless. It was written in the decrees of Fate that he should undertake it. The power of the Persians had grown too great, their self-confidence too assured. The gods who hated beyond all else the arrogance of power had passed judgment upon them. The time had come when the great empire should be broken and humbled. Insolent assurance will surely, soon or late, be brought low, Herodotus says, just as Æschylus wrote:

All arrogance will reap a harvest rich in tears.
God calls men to a heavy reckoning
For overweening pride.

False dreams sent by heaven to Xerxes aroused his ambition and he determined to conquer Greece. Herodotus marshals with solemnity the preparations for the invasion: the slow assembling of the vast army; a canal dug across a great isthmus and the Hellespont bridged for an easy passage by sea and land; food commandeered and water supplies sought out; enormous stores of provisions amassed along the route. Then the pomp and splendor of the start which was signalled by the very heavens. As the army began its march "the sun quit his seat in the sky and disappeared. And yet there were no clouds and the air was serene." Science today says that that eclipse happened two years later, but the ten-year-old boy Herodotus was then could not be expected to mark the date accurately, and a sense for dramatic appropriateness is so general, the older men he depended on for his facts would never have failed to bring together the darkening of the sun and the fall of the Persian power.

At the Hellespont a halt was made for the king to review his forces. On a lofty throne of white marble he watched the army filling shores and plain, and the ships crowding so close, they hid the water. Thus gazing he shed tears. "There came upon me," he told one standing by, "a sudden pity when I thought of the shortness of man's life and considered all this host, so numerous, fated so soon to die." "Nay, King," the other answered. "Weep rather for this, that brief as life is there never yet was or will be a man who does not wish more than once to die rather than to live."

The great army swept on to Greece, drinking the rivers dry as they advanced. Town after town at their approach sent the earth and water which showed that they were no longer free, but already under the Persian yoke. Athens did not send them. There was terror and despair there, too. The oracle at Delphi had spoken to Athenian envoys and had told them to fly to the ends of the earth and make their minds familiar with horrors. Still, the Athenians did not submit. Their cause seemed hopeless. Sparta was as determined as Athens to resist, but her policy was shortsighted. Her heart was in defending only the Peloponnesus; she refused at first to consider anything else. And still the Athenians stood firm. Xerxes' general sent an ambassador to Athens to offer most generous terms, everything good, in short—except freedom. "Tell the general," was the answer, "that the Athenians say, as long as the sun moves in his present course we will never come to terms with Xerxes." When that spirit takes possession of men miracles may be looked for.

Sparta was finally aroused. She sent a little band of soldiers north to defend Thermopylæ, the pass over which the Persians must advance. There was a long and heroic defense which in the end failed. Leonidas, the Spartan commander, sent away the other Greeks who had been fighting with him, "being anxious," Herodotus says, "that they should not perish, but he and the Spartans would not desert their post, for they held that to be dishonorable." As they waited for the attack which they knew would be the last, one of them said he had heard the Persians were so numerous that when they shot their arrows they hid the sky. "Good," said another. "Then we will fight in the shade." Men like that would make the enemy suffer before they fell. Herodotus describes them "advancing from the fortification which had hitherto protected them, as for certain death, while on the other side the Persian officers flogged their men forward. Thus they fought at Thermopylæ." And Xerxes, coming to the battlefield when all was over, looked at the many dead and sent for a Greek exile he had in his train. "In what way can we conquer these men?" he asked. "Come, tell me." But no one could tell him that.

Athens had been abandoned. The priestess at Delphi had spoken again. "Zeus gives a wooden wall to Pallas Athena," she said, "which shall preserve you and your children." When the messengers brought this answer back there was great dispute as to what it meant, but, Herodotus says, "a certain man lately risen to eminence whose name was Themistocles, prevailed." He said the wooden wall was the ships, and the entire populace left the city. The women and children were taken to places of safety; the fleet sailed to the island of Salamis, where the other Greeks assembled. Athens had the largest force and was entitled to the leadership, but she did not press her claim when she saw it would be bitterly contested. "She thought," Herodotus explains, "the great thing was that Greece should be saved," not that she should get the honor which was clearly her due. She withdrew and saw, without a protest, Sparta, always her rival, chosen in her stead. That was the greatest moment in her history. If she could have kept that vision of what was really important and what was not, there would have been no Peloponnesian War.

The victory, even so, belonged to the Athenian Themistocles. He made the plan which forced the Persians to fight in the narrow waters around Salamis where their numbers helped to defeat them. Xerxes watched the battle from the shore.

A king sat on the rocky brow
That looks on sea-born Salamis,
And ships by thousands lay below,
And men by nations—all were his.
He counted them at break of day,
And when the sun set where were they?

The victorious Greeks distrusted the evidence of their own eyes. They had gone into battle almost despairing. "The night before," Herodotus says, "fear and dismay had taken possession of them." Now they could not believe the awful menace was ended. They held themselves ready for another attack. But the Persian ships put out to sea; they were gone never to return. Liberty had again proved her power. Just before the attack the Greek leaders told their men, "When we join battle with the Persians, before all else remember freedom." Æschylus, who was there, says they advanced upon the foe with a shout of:

For freedom, sons of Greece,
Freedom for country, children, wives,
Freedom for worship, for our fathers' graves.

Awe fell upon the victors as they watched the mighty armament depart. "It is not we who have done this," Themistocles said.

THUCYDIDES

The Thing That Hath Been Is That Which Shall Be

THE SPINNING BALL

The greatest sea power in Europe and the greatest land power faced each other in war. The stake was the leadership of Europe. Each was fighting to strengthen her own position at the expense of the other: in the case of the sea power to hold her widely separated empire; in the case of the land power to challenge that empire and win one for herself. Both, as the war began, were uneasily conscious that an important and even decisive factor might be an Asiatic nation, enormous in extent of territory, which had a foothold in Europe and was believed by many to be interested in watching the two chief Western powers weaken and perhaps destroy each other until in the end she herself could easily dominate Europe.

The year was 431 B.C., when Athens was mistress of the sea, when Sparta had the best army in the world—and Persia saw a prospect of being rid of both at no more cost than encouraging first one and then the other.

Historians today generally reject the idea that history repeats itself and may therefore be studied as a warning and a guide. The modern scientific historian looks at his subject very much as the geologist does. History is a chronicle of fact considered for itself alone. There is no pattern in the web unrolled from the loom of time and no profit in studying it except to gain information. That was not the point of view of the Greek historian of the war between Athens and Sparta, whose book is still a masterpiece among histories. Thucydides would never have written his history if he had thought like that. Knowledge for the sake of knowledge had little attraction for the Athenians. They were realists. Knowledge was to be desired because it had value for living; it led men away from error to right action. Thucydides wrote his book because he believed that men would profit from a knowledge of what brought about that ruinous struggle precisely as they profit from a statement of what causes a deadly disease. He reasoned that since the nature of the human mind does not change any more than the nature of the human body, circumstances swayed by human nature are bound to repeat themselves, and in the same situation men are bound to act in the same way unless it is shown to them that such a course in other days ended disastrously. When the reason why a disaster came about is perceived people will be able to guard against that particular danger. "It will perhaps be found," he writes, "that the absence of storytelling in my work makes it less attractive to listen to, but I shall be satisfied if it is considered useful by all who wish to know the plain truth of the events which happened and will according to human nature happen again in the same way. It was written not for the moment, but for all time."

The man who looked thus at the historian's task was a contemporary of the events he related. Thucydides was one of the Athenian generals during the first years of the war. Then fate intervened and turned a soldier into an investigator, for he was exiled when the war was in its tenth year. He tells the reason:

> *The general sent to the other commander of the district, Thucydides son of Olorus, the author of this history, who was about half a day's sail from Amphipolis, and urged him to come to their aid. He sailed in haste with seven ships which happened to be at hand, wishing above all to reach Amphipolis before it surrendered. But the citizens capitulated. On the evening of the same day Thucydides and his ships arrived.*

He reached the town just too late. Athens punished unsuccessful officers, and from then on Thucydides occupied the post of an observer. "Because of my exile," he writes, "I was enabled to watch quietly the course of events."

Extraordinary as the statement is, it is proved true by the book he wrote. From being one of the men his country trusted most he had become a man without a country, a fate in those days little better than death, and, as far as we can judge, he had done nothing to deserve it. Yet he was able "to watch quietly the course of events," free from bitterness and bias, and to produce a history as coldly impartial as if it had dealt with a far-distant past. He looked at Athens exactly as he did at Sparta, with no concern to give a bit of praise here or blame there. What occupied his mind was something above and beyond the deadly and destructive contest he was recounting. He saw his subject in its eternal aspect—*sub specie œternitatis*. Underneath the shifting surface of the struggle between two little Greek states he had caught sight of a universal truth. Throughout his book, through the endless petty engagements on sea and land which he relates with such scrupulous care, he is pointing out what war is, why it comes to pass, what it does, and, unless men learn better ways, must continue to do. His *History of the Peloponnesian War* is really a treatise on war, its causes and its effects.

The war broke out in 431. A succession of petty quarrels had led up to it, insufficient, all put together, to give any adequate reason for a fight to the death between the two chief states of Greece. Aristophanes held them up to ridicule, declaring that the whole business started because some tipsy youngsters from Athens went off to a neighboring town and

stole from Megara a hussy there.
Then men of Megara came here and stole
Two of Aspasia's minxes. And those three,
No better than they should be, caused the war.
For then in wrath Olympian Pericles
Thundered and lightened and confounded Greece.

What Aristophanes parodied Thucydides dismissed. The real cause of the war was not this or that trivial disturbance, the revolt of a distant colony, the breaking of an unimportant treaty, or the like. It was something far beneath the surface, deep down in human nature, and the cause of all the wars ever fought. The motive power was greed, that strange passion for power and possession which no power and no possession satisfy. Power, Thucydides wrote, or its equivalent wealth, created the desire for more power, more wealth. The Athenians and the Spartans fought for one reason only—because they were powerful, and therefore were compelled (the words are Thucydides' own) to seek more power. They fought not because they were different—democratic Athens and oligarchical Sparta—but because they were alike. The war had nothing to do with differences in ideas or with considerations of right and wrong. Is democracy right and the rule of the few over the many wrong? To Thucydides the question would have seemed an evasion of the issue. There was no right power. Power, whoever wielded it, was evil, the corruptor of men.

A historian who lived some two hundred years later, Polybius, also a Greek, gives an admirably clear and condensed account

Thucydides

of Thucydides' basic thesis. Human history, he says, is a cycle which excess of power keeps revolving. Primitive despots start the wheel rolling. The more power they get the more they want, and they go on abusing their authority until inevitably opposition is aroused and a few men, strong enough when they unite, seize the rule for themselves. These, too, can never be satisfied. They encroach upon the rights of others until they are opposed in their turn. The people are aroused against them, and democracy succeeds to oligarchy. But there again the evil in all power is no less operative. It brings corruption and contempt for law, until the state can no longer function and falls easily before a strong man who promises to restore order. The rule of the one, of the few, of the many, each is destroyed in turn because there is in them all an unvarying evil—the greed for power—and no moral quality is necessarily bound up with any of them.

The revolution of the cycle Thucydides watched brought results so terrible that he believed an account of them would be a warning which men could not disregard. The fact of first importance for them to realize, which the Peloponnesian War threw into clear relief, was that great power brought about its own destruction. Athens' triumphant career of empire building ended in ruin. Her immensely rich sea empire had seemed for a long time the exemplar of successful power politics. In reality she had grown too powerful. She acted in the invariable way with the invariable result; she abused her power and she was overwhelmingly defeated. So far Thucydides saw.

We can see farther. The cause of humanity was defeated. Greece's contribution to the world was checked and soon ceased. Hundreds of years had to pass before men reached again the point where Greek thought left off.

At the beginning of the sixth century, a hundred and fifty years before Thucydides' war, the Athens we know was born. She had been a little state ruled by a landed aristocracy that slowly as commerce increased turned into an aristocracy of wealth. Wars were infrequent. The main fighting up to the fifth century had been within the state itself, where the idea of the rights of man was gaining ground and the old order was weakening. Fortunately for the city, the early sixth century was marked by the coming forward of a great and good man, Solon, too great and too good to want power for himself. He saw as keenly as Thucydides that power worked out in evil and that greed was its source and its strength. "Men are driven on by greed to win wealth in unrighteous ways," he wrote, "and he who has most wealth always covets twice as much." Of power he said, "Powerful men pull the city down," than which there could be no greater condemnation from a Greek, utterly dependent as every man in those days was upon his city. Solon made over the government in accordance with the new spirit of the times. He gave the common people a share in it, and he laid the foundation for the first democracy in the world. It is true that an interlude followed after his retirement when a strong man profited by violent quarrels between the classes to take control himself, but on the whole he respected Solon's constitution. Democracy even under a tyranny continued to advance, and the city kept peace with her neighbors. The important island of Salamis, it is true, was taken away from Megara, a near neighbor, at the instigation of no less a person than Solon himself; but it was the only case of its kind.

That was well for Athens. A few years after the tyrant had been put down, in the great and memorable year 490 when the little city had to decide between fighting Persia or being enslaved, she did not have to guard also against enemies in Greece. There has never been a war fought for purer motives than the war against Persia. Marathon and Salamis are still words that "send a ringing challenge down through the generations." Their victories still seem a miracle as they seemed to the men who won them. The mighty were put down from their seats and those of low degree exalted, and for fifty years and more Persia could do nothing to Greece.

What followed was one of the most triumphant rebirths of the human spirit in all history, when the bitter differences that divide men were far in the background and freedom was in the air—freedom in the great sense, not only equality before the law, but freedom of thought and speech. Surely, we think, then, at any rate, in this sad and suffering world

> *Joy was it at that season but to live.*

There is no joy in the pages of Thucydides. A great change came over Athens in a brief space of time. Two quotations are enough to show it.

As the curtain rises in the *Suppliants* (held by many, and in my opinion with truth, to be one of Euripides' early plays) an expedition sent by Argos against Thebes has been defeated, and the Thebans have done what was utterly abhorrent to every Greek: they have refused to allow the enemy to bury their dead. Their leader comes to Athens for help "because," he tells Theseus, the Athenian king, "Athens of all cities is compassionate." As Theseus hesitates to take on the quarrel, however righteous, of another state his mother tells him it is his duty. The city's honor is at stake as well as his own.

> *Look to the things of God.*
> *Know you are bound to help all who are wronged.*
> *Bound to constrain all who destroy the law.*
> *What else holds state to state save this alone,*
> *That each one honors the great laws of right.*

Theseus acknowledges that what she says is true. Athens is the defender of the defenseless, the enemy of the oppressor. Wherever she goes freedom follows.

Only a few years later, Thucydides has Pericles, his ideal statesman, give this warning to the Athenians:

> *Do not think you are fighting for the simple issue of letting this or that state become free or remain subject to you. You*

have an empire to lose. You must realize that Athens has a mighty name in the world because she has never yielded to misfortunes and has today the greatest power that exists. To be hated has always been the lot of those who have aspired to rule over others. In face of that hatred you cannot give up your power—even if some sluggards and cowards are all for being noble at this crisis. Your empire is a tyranny by now, perhaps, as many think, wrongfully acquired, but certainly dangerous to let go.

The difference between these two ideas of Athens is extraordinary. It cannot be explained by the difference between a poet and a historian. Euripides knew the world as well as Thucydides did. Few have ever known it better. It was Athens that was different. The two men were spokesmen each of his own time. In less than a generation the city that had been the champion of freedom had earned the name of the Tyrant City.

Back in 480, after the final defeat of the Persians, the Athenians had been chosen to lead the new confederacy of free Greek states. It was a lofty post and they were proud to hold it, but the role demanded a high degree of disinterestedness. Athens could be the leader of the free only if she considered the welfare of others on the same level with her own. During the war with Persia she had been able to do that. She had shown herself at a great crisis not meanly preoccupied with her own advantage, but honorable, generous, just as Euripides saw her. As head of the league, too, for a time she had not let her power corrupt her. But only for a short time. The temptation to acquire still more power proved as always irresistible. Very soon the free confederacy was being turned into the Athenian Empire. There are changes, even violent ones, in a state which do not affect the character of the people. But this change went deep down to the very roots of religion and morality.

To the men who fought against Persia, their astonishing victory was a proof of the belief that divine justice ruled the world. It worked, indeed, in a mysterious way; nevertheless, those who trampled on the rights of others would be punished no matter how strong they were, a nation as surely as an individual. The arrogance that springs from a consciousness of power was the sin Greeks had always hated most. In their earliest literature, throughout the stories of their mythology, it was sure to draw down the wrath of the gods upon the individual, and what it did to a nation they had seen for themselves when the proud power of Persia was crushed at Salamis. Their greatest leader Solon had declared that earthly justice mirrored the justice of heaven. Their greatest poet Æschylus wrote:

Gold is never a bulwark,
No defense to those who spurn
God's great altar of justice.

But these convictions were swept away by the rising tide of money and power as Athens turned on her associates in the league and forced them to become her subjects. To the young men of the empire the old belief was proved false by the facts. Gold, as far as they could see, was actually an impregnable defense. Certainly they could see their city prospering by doing wrong to other cities. Where, then, was the divine power of justice? What was there to frighten a man if he injured those who could not injure him? Why should Thucydides and his contemporaries go on believing that the wicked would certainly be painfully punished and the good substantially rewarded? The younger generation of the Periclean age had only to use their eyes to be emancipated from the union between refraining from evil and being safe. A man who took every means to gain his own advantage at the expense of others most obviously did not have to live in terror of being struck dead by lightning. Suddenly, in imperial, invincible Athens the profit motive for doing right was taken away, along with the restraining fear of an odious penalty accurately meted out for each misdeed. The debit and credit system ceased to work, and the brilliant young men of the day, full of ambition and pride of possession, had nothing to take its place. To be sure, they continued to flock to the plays of Æschylus and Sophocles, but with all their intellect they did not understand them. They watched the *Oresteia* without a notion that the dramatist was showing them the supreme power of goodness, and they applauded the *Antigone*, never dreaming that they were looking at the lofty beauty of disinterested action.

This drastic change was understood by one person in that brilliant and corrupted city. Thucydides saw that the foundation stone of all morality, the regard for the rights of others, had crumbled and fallen away. It had been the acknowledged foundation when Euripides wrote the *Suppliants*, not only of dealings between man and man, but also between state and state. The state embodied the idea of honorable men. But when Thucydides wrote, Athens had won an empire by dismissing that idea. In the big business of power politics it was not only necessary, it was right, for the state to seize every opportunity for self-advantage. Thucydides was the first probably to see, certainly to put into words, this new doctrine which was to become the avowed doctrine of the world. He makes Pericles explicitly deny that fair dealing and compassion are proper to the state as they are to the individual. A country pursuing her own way with no thought of imposing that way on others might, he points out, keep to such ideas, but not one bent upon dominion. "A city that rules an empire," he writes, "holds nothing which is to its own interest as contrary to right and reason."

That was the spirit in Athens when the Peloponnesian War broke out. The growing power of the Athenian Empire aroused her most powerful competitor. Sparta took the field against her.

All readers approach Thucydides with a preconception in favor of Athens. The Spartans have left the world nothing in the way of art or literature or science. Nevertheless it must be said that the Spartan ideal has remained persistent from their day to our own, the manifestation of an instinct hardly weakened through the last two thousand years. It is not an adult point of view. Sparta looked at things the way schoolboys do, very much like Kipling's Stalky & Co. The ideal Spartan was plucky, indifferent to hardship and pain, a first-rate athlete. The less he talked or, for that matter, thought, the better. It was for him emphatically not to reason why, but always to do and die. He was a soldier and nothing else. The purpose of the Spartan state was war. The Athenians were realistic in their attitude toward war as toward everything else. They saw nothing attractive in dying on the battlefield. Pericles, in the oration Thucydides reports him as delivering over those who had fallen in battle, does not urge his hearers to go and do likewise, but bids them pray that if they fight it will be in less dangerous circumstances. War was a bad business in Athens. Nevertheless it was a necessity; the only way a state could take what belonged to others and, having taken, keep it. War could, of course, be very profitable.

The Spartans had the sentimental, not the business, view of war. It was by no means a necessary evil; it was the noblest form of human activity. They felt a great admiration for battlefields. Tyrtæus, the poet they adored, expressed to perfection their romantic emotions. In a poem which reaches a height of sentimentality rarely attained even by bards of martial lays, he says:

The youth's fair form is fairest when he dies.
Even in his death the boy is beautiful,
The hero boy who dies in his life's bloom.
He lives in men's regret and women's tears.
More sacred than in life, more beautiful by far,
Because he perished on the battlefield.

The idea that underlay the young Spartans' training was their obligation to maintain the power of the state and ignore everything that did not directly contribute to it. All the other possibilities of life—imagination, love of beauty, intellectual interests—were put aside. The goal of human aspiration and achievement was to uphold the fatherland. Only what helped the state was good; only what harmed it was bad. A Spartan was not an individual but a part of a well-functioning machine which assumed all responsibility for him, exacted absolute submission from him, molded his character and his mind, and imbued him with the deep conviction that the chief end of man was to kill and be killed. Plutarch writes:

> *In Sparta, the citizens' way of life was fixed. In general, they had neither the will nor the ability to lead a private life. They were like a community of bees, clinging together around the leader and in an ecstasy of enthusiasm and selfless ambition belonging wholly to their country.*

Athens was a democracy. The General Assembly to which every Athenian belonged was the final authority. The executive body was a Council of Five Hundred for which all citizens were eligible. Officials were chosen by lot or elected by the people.

The state did not take responsibility for the individual Athenian; the individual had to take responsibility for the state. The result was, of course, a totally different idea of what the state was from that in Sparta. In Athens there was never a notion that it was a kind of mystic entity, different from and superior to the people who made it up. Athenian realism blocked any idea like that. The idea of the Athenian state was a union of individuals free to develop their own powers and live in their own way, obedient only to the laws they passed themselves and could criticize and change at will. And yet underneath this apparently ephemeral view of law was the conviction peculiarly Athenian which dominated the thought and the art of the fifth century—that the unlimited, the unrestrained, the lawless, were barbarous, ugly, irrational. Freedom strictly limited by self-control—that was the idea of Athens at her greatest. Her artists embodied it; her democracy did not. Athenian art and Athenian thought survived the test of time. Athenian democracy became imperial and failed.

Imperial autocracy when it came to fighting proved the stronger. Year by year as the war went on the weakness of Athenian popular government became more and more evident in comparison with the stern discipline and undistracted policy of Sparta. Athens was moved this way or that as the man of the moment chose. One such person, the unprincipled but brilliant Alcibiades, from whom Socrates had expected great things, persuaded the people to send an expedition to conquer Sicily. He was a remarkable man, and in his hands the venture might have turned out well. Certainly the obvious reason why it failed is that it was carried out as badly as possible. Alcibiades was recalled almost as soon as the Athenian fleet reached Sicily. By that time popular feeling was hot against him because of a charge of sacrilege brought by his enemies. He had better sense than to face a populace seething with fervor to defend religion by making an example of the irreligious, and he transferred his allegiance to Sparta, where he proved very useful.

Sheer mismanagement wrecked the Sicilian expedition. The Athenian people were led by men too small for the part to which they aspired. They were misled. They underestimated the strength of the enemy until it was too late. They trusted implicitly to their sea power and it failed them. In the final sea fight around Syracuse the Athenians were outmaneuvered and the great fleet was defeated. The disaster was complete. The ships were abandoned and the army started to retreat by land with no food, no provisions of any sort. After days of marching, the desperate, starving men were divided; the van lost touch with the rear, and it was easy for the Syracusans to overwhelm first one and then the other. The last scene was on the bank of a river where the Athenians, mad with thirst, rushed down to the water not seeing or not caring that the enemy was upon them. The river was soon flowing red with blood, but they fought each other to get to it and they drank of it as they died.

All who were taken alive were made slaves. The greater part of them were put in the stone quarries near Syracuse where nature did the torturing without need of human assistance. The frightful heat by day and the bitter cold by night insured the survival of very few. Thucydides writes their epitaph: "Having done what men could they suffered what men must."

There has never been, there could not be, a more complete defeat. To inflict on the enemy what the Athenians suffered in Sicily is still the brightest hope that can animate a nation going to war. But it was not the worst disaster the war brought Athens. The climax of Thucydides' history is his picture of what happened within the city to the individual Athenians during the years of fighting. It is a picture of the disintegration of a great people. He shows how swift the process was by two stories he tells, one early in the war, the other late. The first is about the revolt of an important island tributary. Athens sent a fleet to subdue her and then in furious anger voted to kill the men and enslave the women and children. In the debate before the vote was taken the popular leader of the moment warned the Athenians not to be misled by the three deadly foes of empire: pity, enjoyment of discussion, and the spirit of fair dealing. He carried the meeting, and a ship was dispatched with the fatal order. Then, still true to the spirit of Euripides' Athens, the Athenians came to themselves. A second ship was sent to overtake the first, or at any rate to get to the island in time to prevent the massacre. The eagerness was such that the rowers were fed at their oars, taking no rest until they landed in time.

The second story concerns another offending island, seven years later. This was little Melos, of no importance in herself, who wanted only to be neutral. But those seven years had left their mark on Athens. This time she did not have to be warned against pity and fair dealing. The conversation Thucydides gives between the envoys of the Athenians and the men of Melos shows what war did to the people who once had stood, as Herodotus said, in the perpetual choice between the lower and the higher, always for the higher.

To a plea from the Melians that they have done no wrong and that to make war on them will be contrary to all justice, the envoys reply: "Justice is attained only when both sides are equal. The powerful exact what they can and the weak yield what they must."

"You ignore justice," the Melians answer, "and yet it is to your interest, too, to regard it, because if you ever are defeated you will not be able to appeal to it."

"You must allow us to take the risk of that," the Athenians say. "Our point is that we want to subjugate you without trouble to ourselves and that this will be better for you too."

"To become slaves?" ask the Melians. "Well—it will save you from a worse fate."

"You will not consent to our remaining at peace, your friends, but not your allies?"

"No," the Athenians answer. "We do not want your friendship. It would appear a proof of our weakness whereas your hatred is a proof of our power. Please remember that with you the question is one of self-preservation. We are the stronger."

"Fortune does not always side with the strong," the Melians say. "There is hope that if we do our utmost we can stand erect."

"Beware of hope," the Athenians reply. "Do not be like the common crowd who when visible grounds for hope fail betake themselves to the invisible, religion and the like. We advise you to turn away from such folly. And may we remind you that in all this discussion you have not advanced one argument that practical men would use."

The Melians were unpractical and they fought. They were conquered with little trouble to Athens. She put the men to death and made slaves of the women and children. She had reached a point where she did not care to use fine words about ugly facts, and the reason was that they had ceased to look ugly to her.

Vices by then, Thucydides says, were esteemed as virtues. The very meaning of words changed; deceit was praised as shrewdness, recklessness held to be courage, loyalty, moderation, generosity, scorned as proofs of weakness. "That good will which is the chief element in a noble nature was laughed out of court and vanished. Every man distrusted every other man." That was where the race for power brought the Athenians in the end.

Sparta was better off. Her ideal of the duty of death on a battlefield was guaranteed not to satisfy men for long, but it was better by far than the lack of any ideal shown in the Athenians' talk to the Melians. Athens was conquered in 404. Violent party strife divided the city, and the aristocratic coterie, always pro-Sparta, finally got the upper hand. There was another revolution of the power cycle.

The succeeding one came more quickly. Sparta could not rule other nations. Athens had taxed them heavily, but except for that she had not interfered with them. Sparta's methods are explained by the remark of an Athenian who admired her, to the effect that the will of any Spartan citizen was absolute law in the subject states. She was never able to understand any way but her own, and the other Greeks did not take kindly to that. They were not docile and they did not like obedience. She could not hold them long. The Spartan Empire lasted only a few years. Toward the end of the war she had made an alliance with her old arch-enemy, Persia, which helped her greatly in reducing Athens. But soon afterwards the two allies quarreled. Sparta was defeated and Persia took away the sea empire she had taken away from Athens.

That was the result of twenty-seven years of war. It seems at first sight a triumph of futility, but it was worse than that. Very many Athenians were killed during those years. Fortunately for us, some who were of an age to fight—Socrates, Plato, Thucydides himself, and others equally familiar—did not die on battlefields; but it cannot be doubted that among all who did, there were those who would have led the world up to new heights. The flame that burned so brightly in fifth-century Athens would have given more and still more light to the world if these dead had not died, and died truly in vain.

> *The cause of all these evils was the desire for power which greed and ambition inspire.*
>
> —*Thucydides* III, 83

XENOPHON

The Ordinary Athenian Gentleman

To turn from Thucydides to Xenophon is a pleasant, but surprising, experience. The lives of the two men overlapped, although Xenophon was much the younger. Both were Athenians and soldiers; both lived through the war and saw the defeat of Athens. Yet they inhabited different worlds; worlds so different, they seem to have no connection with each other. Thucydides' world was a place racked and ruined and disintegrated by war, where hope was gone and happiness was unimaginable. Xenophon's was a cheerful place with many nice people in it and many agreeable ways of passing the time. There was hunting, for instance. He writes a charming essay about it: of the delights of the early start, in winter over the snow, to track the hare with hounds as keen for the chase as their masters; in spring "when the fields are so full of wildflowers, the scent for the dogs is poor" or a deer may be the quarry, first-rate sport; or a wild boar, dangerous, but delightfully exciting. Such rewards, too, as the hunter has: he keeps strong and young far longer than other men; he is braver, and even more trustworthy—although why that should be our author does not trouble to explain. A hunting man just is better than one who does not hunt and that is all there is to it. Ask any fox-hunting squire in English literature. Hunting is a good, healthy, honest pleasure, and a young man is lucky if he takes to it. It will save him from city vices and incline him to love virtue.

At what period in Thucydides' history were the Athenians going a hunting, one wonders. Did that man of tragic vision ever watch a hunt? Did he ever listen to stories about the size of the boar that had been killed? Was he ever at a dinner-party where any stories were told over the wine? The imagination fails before the attempt to put him there, even if Socrates had been a guest as he was at a dinner Xenophon went to and reported. It followed more closely, we must suppose, the fashion of the day for such parties than did Plato's famous supper at Agathon's house, where conversation was the only entertainment. Agathon's guests were the élite of Athens and wanted lofty discourse for their diversion. The guests at Xenophon's dinner, except for himself and Socrates, were ordinary people who would quickly have been bored by the speeches in the *Symposium*. But no one could possibly have been bored at the party Xenophon describes. It was from first to last a most enjoyable occasion. There was some good talk at the table, of course—Socrates would see to that; and now and then the discourse turned to matters sober enough to have engaged even Thucydides' attention. But for the most part, it was lighthearted as befitted a good dinner. There was a great deal of laughter when, for instance, Socrates defended his flat nose as being preferable to a straight one, and when a man newly married refused the onions. There was music, too, and Socrates obliged with a song, to the delighted amusement of the others. A pleasant interlude was afforded by a happy boy, and

Xenophon's description reveals his power of keen observation and quick sympathy. The lad had been invited to come with his father, a great honor, but he had just won the chief contest for boys at the principal Athenian festival. He sat beside his father, regarded very kindly by the company. They tried to draw him out, but he was too shy to speak a word until someone asked him what he was most proud of, and someone else cried, "Oh, his victory, of course." At this he blushed and blurted out, "No—I'm not." All were delighted to have him finally say something and they encouraged him. "No? Of what are you proudest, then?" "Of my father," he said, and pressed closer to him. It is an attractive picture of Athenian boyhood in the brilliant, corrupt city where Thucydides could find nothing good.

As was usual, entertainment had been provided for the guests. A girl did some diverting and surprising feats. The best turn was when she danced and kept twelve hoops whirling in the air, catching and throwing them in perfect time with the music. Watching her with great attention Socrates declared that he was forced to conclude, "Not only from this girl, my friends, but from other things, too, that a woman's talent is not at all inferior to a man's." A pleasant thing to know, he added, if any of them wanted to teach something to his wife. A murmur passed around the table: "Xanthippe" and one of the company ventured, "Why do not you, then, teach good temper to yours?" "Because," Socrates retorted, "my great aim in life is to get on well with people, and I chose Xanthippe because I knew if I could get on with her I could with anyone." The explanation was unanimously voted satisfactory.

A little desultory talk followed that finally turned upon exercise, and Socrates said, to the intense delight of all, that he danced every morning in order to reduce. "It's true," one of the others broke in. "I found him doing it and I thought he'd gone mad. But he talked to me and I tell you he convinced me. When I went home—will you believe it? I did not dance: I don't know how;

but I waved my arms about." There was a general outcry, "Oh, Socrates, let us see you, too."

By this time the dancing girl was turning somersaults and leaping headfirst into a circle formed by swords. This displeased Socrates. "No doubt it is a wonderful performance," he conceded. "But pleasure? In watching a lovely young creature exposing herself to danger like that? I don't find it agreeable." The others agreed, and a pantomime between the girl and her partner, a graceful boy, was quickly substituted: "The Rescue of the Forsaken Ariadne by Bacchus." It was performed to admiration. Not a word was spoken by the two actors, but such was their skill that by gestures and dancing they expressed all the events and emotions of the story with perfect clarity to the spectators. "They seemed not actors who had learned their parts, but veritable lovers." With that the party broke up, Socrates walking home with the nice boy and his father. Of himself Xenophon says nothing throughout the essay except at the very beginning when he explains that he was one of the guests and decided to given an account of the dinner because he thought what honorable and virtuous men did in their hours of amusement had its importance. One can only regret that so few Greek writers agreed with him.

Another pleasant picture he gives of domestic Athens has an interest not only as a period piece but because it shows a glimpse of that person so elusive in all periods, the woman of ancient Greece. A man lately married talks about his wife. She was not yet fifteen, he says, and had been admirably brought up "to see as little, and hear as little, and ask as few questions as possible." The young husband had the delightful prospect of inscribing on this blank page whatever he chose. There was no doubt in his mind what he should start with. "Of course," Xenophon reports him as saying, "I had to give her time to grow used to me; but when we had reached a point where we could talk easily together, I told her she had great responsibilities. I took up with her what I expected of her as a housekeeper. She said wonderingly, 'But my mother told me I was of no consequence, only you. All I had to do, she said, was to be sensible and careful.'" Her husband was quick to seize the cue. Kindly but weightily he explained to the young thing that her life henceforth was to be a perpetual exercise in carefulness and good sense. She would have to keep stock of everything brought into the house; oversee all the work that went on; superintend the spinning, the weaving, the making of clothes; train the new servants and nurse the sick. At this point the girl's spirits seem to have risen a little for she murmured that she thought she would like to take care of sick people. But her husband kept steadily on. Of course she would stay indoors. He himself enjoyed starting the day with a long ride into the country—very healthful as well as very pleasant. But for a woman to be roaming abroad was most discreditable. However, she could get plenty of exercise, at the loom, or making beds, or supervising the maids. Kneading bread was said to be as good exercise as one could find. All that sort of thing would improve her health and help her complexion—very important in keeping herself attractive to her husband. Artificial substitutes were no good: husbands always knew when their wives painted, and they never liked it; white and red stuff on the face was disgusting when a man was aware of it, as a husband must be. The essay ends happily with the declaration, "Ever since, my wife has done in all respects just as I taught her."

It is as hard to fit the dutiful young wife and the happily important husband and their immaculate household into Thucydides' Athens as it is to put Thucydides himself at the table beside Socrates watching the girl with the hoops. There is no use trying to make a composite picture out of Xenophon and Thucydides. The only result would be to lose the truth on each side. Thucydides' truth was immeasurably more profound. In life's uneasy panorama he could discover unchanging verities. He could probe to the depths the evils of his time and perceive them all grounded in the never varying evils of human nature.

In Sparta's victory over Athens he saw what the decision of war was worth as a test of values, and that war would forever decide matters of highest importance to the world if men continued to be governed by greed and the passion for power. What he knew was truth indeed, with no shadow of turning and inexpressibly sad.

But Xenophon's truths were true, too. There were pleasant parties and well-ordered homes and nice lads and jolly hunters in war-wracked Greece. History never takes account of such pleasantries, but they have their importance. The Greek world would have gone insane if Thucydides' picture had been all-inclusive. Of course, Xenophon's mind was on an altogether lower level. Eternal truths were not in his line. The average man in Periclean Athens can be seen through Xenophon's eyes as he cannot be through Thucydides' or Plato's. In Xenophon there are no dark, greed-ridden schemers such as Thucydides saw in Athens; neither are there any Platonic idealists. The people in his books are ordinary, pleasant folk, not given to extremes in any direction and convincingly real, just as Xenophon himself is. Here is a picture he draws of one of them:

> *He said that he had long realized that "unless we know what we ought to do and try our best to do it God has decided that we have no right to be prosperous. If we are wise and do take pains he makes some of us prosperous, although not all. So to start with, I reverence him and then do all I can to be worthy when I pray to be given health and strength of body and the respect of the Athenians and the affection of my friends and an increase of wealth—with honor, and safety in war—with honor."*

These eminently sensible aspirations strike a true Greek note. The man who uttered them and the man who recorded them were typical Athenian gentlemen. What Xenophon was comes through clearly in his writings—a man of good will and good sense, kindly, honest, pious; intelligent, too, interested in ideas, not the purely speculative kind, rather those that could be made to work toward some rational, practical good. His friends were like him; they were representative Athenians of the better sort.

In another way, too, Xenophon represented his times. His life shows the widely separated interests and varied occupations which made the Periclean Athenians different from other men. As a young man he came to Athens from his father's estate in Attica, to be educated out of country ways; he joined the circle around Socrates, where young and old alike were, as Plato puts it, "possessed and maddened with the passion for knowledge," or, as he himself states, "wanting to become good and fine men and learn their duty to their family, their servants, their friends and their country." The Socrates he listened to did not, like Plato's Socrates, discourse upon "the glorious sights of justice and wisdom and truth the enraptured soul beholds, shining in pure light," or anything like that. This Socrates was a soberly thinking man, distinguished for common sense, and in Xenophon's record of him, the *Memorabilia,* what he chiefly does for his young friends is to give them practical advice on how to manage their affairs. A budding officer is told the way to make his men efficient soldiers; a conscientious lad, burdened with many female relatives, is shown how they can be taught to support themselves, and so on, while Xenophon listens entranced by such serviceable wisdom. How long Xenophon lived this delightful life of conversation is not known, but he was still young when he left it for the very opposite kind of life, that of a soldier. He was truly a man of his times, when poets and dramatists and historians were soldiers and generals and explorers.

In his campaigns he travelled far and saw the great world. He also got enough money to live on for the rest of his days by capturing and holding for ransom a rich Persian noble. Then he went back to Greece—but to Sparta, not Athens. Curiously, although he has left in his *Anabasis* an unsurpassed picture of what the democratic ideal can accomplish, he was himself no democrat. He came of a noble family and all his life kept the convictions of his class. He always loved Sparta and distrusted Athens. Even so, in the great crisis of his life, when he and his companions faced imminent destruction, he acted like a true Athenian, who knew what freedom was and what free men could achieve. When the Ten Thousand elected him general in order to get them out of their terrible predicament, he never tried out any Spartan ideas on them. He became as democratic a leader as there could possibly be of the freest democracy conceivable. The fact that the astonishing success which resulted had no permanent effect upon his point of view should not be surprising; a converted aristocrat is a rare figure in history. Xenophon never went back to Athens; indeed, a few years after his return to Greece he was fighting on the Spartan side against her and was declared an exile. The Spartans gave him an estate in the pleasant country near Olympia, where he lived for many years, riding and hunting and farming, a model country gentleman. Here he wrote a great many books on subjects as far apart as the dinner Socrates attended and the proper management of the Athenian revenues. With two or three exceptions the writings are quite pedestrian; sensible, straightforward, clearly written, but no more. There are a few sentences, however, scattered through them which show a surprising power of thought and far-reaching vision. Although, or perhaps because, he had fought much, he believed that peace should be the aim of all states. Diplomacy, he says, is the way to settle disputes, not war. He urges Athens to use her influence to maintain peace, and he suggests making Delphi a meeting place for the nations, where they can talk out their differences. "He who conquers by force," he says, "may fancy that he can continue to do so, but the only conquests that last are when men willingly submit to those who are better than themselves. The only way really to conquer a country is through generosity." The world has not yet caught up with Xenophon.

Xenophon

His best book, however, the book he really lives by, is on war. It is, of course, the *Anabasis,* the "Retreat of the Ten Thousand," a great story, and of great importance for our knowledge of the Greeks. No other piece of writing gives so clear a picture of Greek individualism, that instinct which was supremely characteristic of ancient Greece and decided the course of the Greek achievement. It was the cause, or the result, as one chooses to look at it, of the Greek love for freedom. A Greek had a passion for being left free to live his life in his own way. He wanted to act by himself and think for himself. It did not come natural to him to turn to others for direction; he depended upon his own sense of what was right and true. Indeed, there was no generally acknowledged source of direction anywhere in Greece except the oracles, difficult to reach and still more difficult to understand. Athens had no authoritarian church, or state either, to formulate what a man should believe and to regulate the details of how he should live. There was no agency or institution to oppose his thinking in any way he chose on anything whatsoever. As for the state, it never entered an Athenian's head that it could interfere with his private life: that it could see, for instance, that his children were taught to be patriotic, or limit the amount of liquor he could buy, or compel him to save for his old age. Everything like that a citizen of Athens had to decide himself and take full responsibility for.

The basis of the Athenian democracy was the conviction of all democracies—that the average man can be depended upon to do his duty and to use good sense in doing it. *Trust the individual* was the avowed doctrine in Athens, and expressed or unexpressed it was common to Greece. Sparta we know as the exception, and there must have been other backwaters; nevertheless, the most reactionary Greek might at any time revert to type. It is on record that Spartan soldiers abroad shouted down an unpopular officer; threw stones at a general whose orders they did not approve; in an emergency, put down incompetent leaders and acted for themselves. Even the iron discipline of Sparta could not completely eradicate the primary Greek passion for independence. "A people ruling," says Herodotus, "—the very name of it is so beautiful." In Æschylus' play about the defeat of the Persians at Salamis, the Persian queen asks, "Who is set over the Greeks as despot?" and the proud answer is, "They are the slaves and vassals of no man." Therefore, all Greeks believed, they conquered the slave-subjects of the Persian tyrant. Free men, independent men, were always worth inexpressibly more than men submissive and controlled.

Military authorities have never advocated this point of view, but how applicable it is to soldiers, too, is shown for all time by the *Anabasis*. The Ten Thousand got back safely after one of the most perilous marches ever undertaken just because they were not a model, disciplined army but a band of enterprising individuals.

The epic of the Retreat begins in a camp beside a little town in Asia not far from Babylon. There, more than ten thousand Greeks were gathered. They had come from different places: one of the leaders was from Thessaly; another from Bœotia; the commander-in-chief was a Spartan; on his staff was a young civilian from Athens named Xenophon. They were soldiers of fortune, a typical army of mercenaries who had gone abroad because there was no hope of employment at home. Greece was not at war for the moment. A Spartan peace was over the land. It was the summer of 401, three years after the fall of Athens.

Persia, however, was a hotbed of plots and counterplots that were bringing a revolution near. The late king's two sons were enemies, and the younger planned to take the throne from his brother. This young man was Cyrus, named for the great Cyrus, the conqueror of Babylon a hundred and fifty years earlier. His namesake is famous for one reason only: because when he marched into Persia Xenophon joined his army. If that had not happened he would be lost in the endless list of little Asiatic royalties forever fighting for no purpose of the slightest importance to the world. As it is, he lives in Xenophon's pages, gay and gallant and generous; careful for his soldiers' welfare; sharing their hardships; always first in the fighting; a great leader.

The Ten Thousand had enlisted under his banner with no clear idea of what they were to do beyond the matter of real importance, get regular pay and enough food. They earned their share of both in the next few months. They marched from the Mediterranean through sandy deserts far into Asia Minor living on the country, which generally meant a minimum of food and occasionally none at all. There was a large Asiatic contingent, a hundred thousand strong at the least, but they play very little part in the *Anabasis*. The Greeks are the real army Cyrus depends upon. As Xenophon tells the story they won the day for him when he met the king's forces. The battle of Cunaxa was a decisive victory for Cyrus. Only, he himself was dead, killed in the fighting as he struck at his brother and wounded him. With his death the reason for the expedition ceased to exist. The Asiatic forces melted away. The little Greek army was alone in the heart of Asia, in an unknown country swarming with hostile troops, with no food, no ammunition, and no notion how to get back. Soon there were no leaders either. The chief officers went to a conference with the Persians under a safe-conduct. Their return, eagerly awaited, was alarmingly delayed; and all eyes were watching for them when in the distance a man, one man all alone, was seen advancing very slowly, a Greek by his dress. They ran to meet him and caught him as he fell dying, terribly wounded. He could just gasp out that all the others were dead, assassinated by the Persians.

That was a terrible night. The Persian plan was clear. In their experience leaderless men were helpless. Kill the officers and the army would be a lot of sheep waiting to be slaughtered. The only thing wrong with the idea was that this was a Greek army.

Xenophon, all his friends dead, wandered away from the horrified camp, found a quiet spot and fell asleep. He dreamed a dream. He saw the thunderbolt of Zeus fall on his home and a great light shine forth, and he awoke with the absolute conviction that Zeus had chosen him to save the army. On fire with enthusiasm, he called a council of the under officers who had not gone to the conference. There, young and a civilian, he stood up and addressed them, hardened veterans all. He told them to throw off despair and "show some superiority to misfortune." He reminded them that they were Greeks, not to be cowed by mere Asiatics. Something of his own fire was communicated to them. He even got them laughing. One man who stubbornly objected to everything and would talk only of their desperate case, Xenophon advised reducing to the ranks and using to carry baggage; he would make an excellent mule, he told his appreciative audience. They elected him unanimously to lead the rear, and then had the general assembly sounded so that he could address the soldiers. He gave them a rousing talk. Things were black and might seem hopeless to others, but they were Greeks, free men, living in free states, born of free ancestors. The enemy they had to face were slaves, ruled by despots, ignorant of the very idea of freedom. "They think we are defeated because our officers are dead and our good old general Clearchus. But we will show them that they have turned us all into generals. Instead of one Clearchus they have ten thousand Clearchuses against them." He won them over and that very morning the ten thousand generals started the march back.

They had only enemies around them, not one man they could trust as a guide, and there were no maps in those days and no compasses. One thing only they were sure of: they could not go back by the way they had come. Wherever they had passed the food was exhausted. They were forced to turn northward and follow the course of the rivers up to the mountains where the Tigris and the Euphrates rise, through what is today the wilds of Kurdistan and the highlands of Georgia and Armenia, all inhabited by savage mountain tribes. These were their only source of provisions. If they could not conquer their strongholds and get at their stores they would starve. Mountain warfare of the most desperate character awaited them, waged by an enemy who knew every foot of the country, who watched for them on the heights above narrow valleys and rolled masses of rocks down on them, whose sharpshooters attacked them hidden in thickets on the opposite bank of some torrential icy river while the Greeks searched desperately for a ford. As they advanced ever higher into the hills, they found bitter cold and deep snow, and their equipment was designed for the Arabian desert.

Probably anyone today considering their plight would conclude that their only chance of safety would lie in maintaining strict discipline, abiding by their excellent military tradition, and obeying their leaders implicitly. The chief leaders, however, were dead; mountain fighting against savages was not a part of their military tradition; above all, being Greeks, they did not incline to blind obedience in desperate circumstances. In point of fact, the situation which confronted them could be met only by throwing away the rules and regulations that had been drilled into them. What they needed was to draw upon all the intelligence and power of initiative every man of them possessed.

They were merely a band of mercenaries, but they were Greek mercenaries and the average of intelligence was high. The question of discipline among ten thousand generals would otherwise certainly have been serious and might well have proved fatal, but, no less than our westward-faring pioneer ancestors who resembled them, they understood the necessity of acting together. Not a soldier but knew what it would mean to have disorder added to the perils they faced. Their discipline was a voluntary product, but it worked. When the covered wagons made their way across America any leader that arose did so by virtue of superior ability, which men in danger always follow willingly. The leaders of the Ten Thousand got their posts in the same way. The army was keen to perceive a man's quality and before long the young civilian Xenophon was practically in command.

Each man, however, had a share in the responsibility. Once when Xenophon sent out a reconnoitering force to find a pass through the mountains, he told them, "Every one of you is the leader." At any crisis an assembly was held, the situation explained and full discussion invited. "Whoever has a better plan, let him speak. Our aim is the safety of all and that is the concern of all." The case was argued back and forth, then put to the vote and the majority decided. Incompetent leaders were brought to trial. The whole army sat as judges and acquitted or punished. It reads like a caricature, but there has never been a better vindication of the average man when he is up against it. The ten thousand judges, which the ten thousand generals turned into on occasion, never, so far as Xenophon's record goes, passed an unjust sentence. On one occasion Xenophon was called to account for striking a soldier. "'I own that I did so,' he said. 'I told him to carry to camp a wounded man, but I found him burying him still alive. I have struck others, too, half-frozen men who were sinking down in the snow to die, worn-out men lagging behind where the enemy might catch them. A blow would often make them get up and hasten. Those I have given offense to now accuse me. But those I have helped, in battle, on the march, in cold, in sickness, none of them speak up. They do not remember. And yet surely it is better—and happier, too—to remember a man's good deeds than his evil deeds.' Upon this," the narrative goes on, "the assembly, calling the past to mind, rose up and Xenophon was acquitted."

This completely disarming speech for the defense shows how well Xenophon knew the way to manage men. There is wounded feeling in his words, but no anger, no resentment, above all, no self-righteousness. Those listening were convinced by his frankness of his honesty; reminded, without a suggestion of boasting, how great his services had been; and given to understand that far from claiming to be faultless, he appealed to them only to remember his deserts as well as his mistakes. He understood his audience and the qualities a leader must have, at least any leader who would lead Greeks. In a book he wrote on the education of the great Cyrus he draws a picture of the ideal general which, absurd as it is when applied to an Oriental monarch, shows to perfection the Greek idea of the one method that will make men who are worth anything independent, self-reliant men, willing to follow another man. "The leader," he writes, "must himself believe that willing obedience always beats forced obedience, and that he can get this only by really knowing what should be done. Thus he can secure obedience from his men because he can convince them that he knows best, precisely as a good doctor makes his patients obey him. Also he must be ready to suffer more hardships than he asks of his soldiers, more fatigue, greater extremes of heat and cold. 'No one,' Cyrus always said, 'can be a good officer who does not undergo more than those he commands.'" However that may be, it is certain that the inexperienced civilian Xenophon was could have won over the Ten Thousand in no other way. He was able to convince them that he knew best and they gave up their own ideas and followed him willingly.

He showed them too that even if they made him their leader, it was share and share alike between him and the army. On one occasion when he was riding up from his post in the rear to consult with the van, and the snow was deep and the marching hard, a soldier cried to him, "Oh, it's easy enough for you on horseback." Xenophon leaped from his horse, flung the man aside and marched in his place.

Always, no matter how desperate things seemed, the initiative which only free men can be counted on to develop got them through. They abandoned their baggage by common consent and threw away their loot. "We will make the enemy carry our baggage for us," they said. "When we have conquered them we can take what we want." Early in the march they were terribly harassed by the Persian cavalry because they had none of their own. The men of Rhodes could throw with their slings twice as far as the Persians. They set them on baggage mules, directed them to aim at the riders, but spare their mounts and bring them back, and from that time on the Persians kept them in horses. If they needed ammunition they sent bowmen who could shoot farther than the foe to draw down showers of arrows that fell short and could be easily collected. One way or another they forced the Persians into service. When they got to the hills they discarded the tactics they had been trained in. They gave up the solid line, the only formation they knew, and the army advanced by columns, sometimes far apart. It was merely common sense in the rough broken country, but that virtue belongs peculiarly to men acting for themselves. The disciplined military mind has never been distinguished for it.

So, always cold and sometimes freezing, always hungry and sometimes starving, and always, always fighting, they held their own. No one by now had any clear idea where in the world they were. One day, Xenophon, riding in the rear, putting his horse up a steep hill, heard a great noise in front. A tumult was carried back to him by the wind, loud cries and shouting. An ambush, he thought, and calling to the others to follow at full speed, he drove his horse forward. No enemy was on the hilltop; only the Greeks. They were standing, all faced the same way, with tears running down their faces, their arms stretched out to what they saw before them. The shouting swelled into a great roar, "The sea! The sea!"

They were home at last. The sea was home to a Greek. It was the middle of January. They had left Cunaxa on the seventh of September. In four months they had marched well on to two thousand miles in circumstances never surpassed before or since for hardship and danger.

The *Anabasis* is the story of the Greeks in miniature. Ten thousand men, fiercely independent by nature, in a situation where they were a law unto themselves, showed that they were preeminently able to work together and proved what miracles of achievement willing cooperation can bring to pass. The Greek state, at any rate the Athenian state, which we know best, showed the same. What brought the Greeks safely back from Asia was precisely what made Athens great. The Athenian was a law unto himself, but his dominant instinct to stand alone was counterbalanced by his sense of overwhelming obligation to serve the state. This was his own spontaneous reaction to the facts of his life, nothing imposed upon him from outside. The city was his defense in a hostile world, his security, his pride, too, the guarantee to all of his worth as an Athenian.

Plato said that men could find their true moral development only in service to the city. The Athenian was saved from looking at his life as a private affair. Our word "idiot" comes from the Greek name for the man who took no share in public matters. Pericles in the funeral oration reported by Thucydides says:

> *We are a free democracy, but we are obedient. We obey the laws, more especially those which protect the oppressed, and the unwritten laws whose transgression brings acknowledged shame. We do not allow absorption in our own affairs to interfere with participation in the city's. We differ from other states in regarding the man who holds aloof from public life as useless, yet we yield to none in independence of spirit and complete self-reliance.*

This happy balance was maintained for a very brief period. No doubt at its best it was as imperfect as the working out of every lofty idea in human terms is bound to be. Even so, it was the foundation of the Greek achievement. The creed of democracy, spiritual and political liberty for all, and each man a willing servant of the state, was the conception which underlay the highest reach of Greek genius. It was fatally weakened by the race for money and power in the Periclean age; the Peloponnesian War destroyed it and Greece lost it forever. Nevertheless, the ideal of free individuals unified by a spontaneous service to the common life was left as a possession to the world, never to be forgotten.

THE IDEA OF TRAGEDY

The great tragic artists of the world are four, and three of them are Greek. It is in tragedy that the pre-eminence of the Greeks can be seen most clearly. Except for Shakespeare, the great three, Æschylus, Sophocles, Euripides, stand alone. Tragedy is an achievement peculiarly Greek. They were the first to perceive it and they lifted it to its supreme height. Nor is it a matter that directly touches only the great artists who wrote tragedies; it concerns the entire people as well, who felt the appeal of the tragic to such a degree that they would gather thirty thousand strong to see a performance. In tragedy the Greek genius penetrated farthest and it is the revelation of what was most profound in them.

The special characteristic of the Greeks was their power to see the world clearly and at the same time as beautiful. Because they were able to do this, they produced art distinguished from all other art by an absence of struggle, marked by a calm and serenity which is theirs alone. There is, it seems to assure us, a region where beauty is truth, truth beauty. To it their artists would lead us, illumining life's dark confusions by gleams fitful indeed and wavering compared with the fixed light of religious faith, but by some magic of their own, satisfying, affording a vision of something inconclusive and yet of incalculable significance. Of all the great poets this is true, but truest of the tragic poets, for the reason that in them the power of poetry confronts the inexplicable.

Tragedy was a Greek creation because in Greece thought was free. Men were thinking more and more deeply about human life, and beginning to perceive more and more clearly that it was bound up with evil and that injustice was of the nature of things. And then, one day, this knowledge of something irremediably wrong in the world came to a poet with his poet's power to see beauty in the truth of human life, and the first tragedy was written. As the author of a most distinguished book on the subject says: "The spirit of inquiry meets the spirit of poetry and tragedy is born." Make it concrete: early Greece with her godlike heroes and hero-gods fighting far on the ringing plains of windy Troy; with her lyric world, where every common thing is touched with beauty—her twofold world of poetic creation. Then a new age dawns, not satisfied with beauty of song and story, an age that must try to know and to explain. And for the first time tragedy appears. A poet of surpassing magnitude, not content with the old sacred conventions, and of a soul great enough to bear new and intolerable truth—that is Æschylus, the first writer of tragedy.

Tragedy belongs to the poets. Only they have "trod the sunlit heights and from life's dissonance struck one clear chord." None but a poet can write a tragedy. For tragedy is nothing less than pain transmuted into exaltation by the alchemy of poetry, and if poetry is true knowledge and the great poets guides safe to follow, this transmutation has arresting implications.

Pain changed into, or, let us say, charged with, exaltation. It would seem that tragedy is a strange matter. There is indeed none stranger. A tragedy shows us pain and gives us pleasure thereby. The greater the suffering depicted, the more terrible the events, the more intense our pleasure. The most monstrous and appalling deeds life can show are those the tragedian chooses, and by the spectacle he thus offers us, we are moved to a very passion of enjoyment. There is food for wonder here, not to be passed over, as the superficial have done, by pointing out that the Romans made a holiday of a gladiator's slaughter, and that even today fierce instincts, savage survivals, stir in the most civilized. Grant all that, and we are not a step advanced on the way to explaining the mystery of tragic pleasure. It has no kinship with cruelty or the lust for blood.

On this point it is illuminating to consider our everyday use of the words tragedy and tragic. Pain, sorrow, disaster, are always spoken of as depressing, as dragging down—the dark abyss of pain, a crushing sorrow, an overwhelming disaster. But speak of tragedy and extraordinarily the metaphor changes. Lift us to tragic heights, we say, and never anything else. The depths of pathos but never of tragedy. Always the height of tragedy. A word is no light matter. Words have with truth been called fossil poetry, each, that is, a symbol of a creative thought. "The whole philosophy of human nature is implicit in human speech. It is a matter to pause over, that the instinct of mankind has perceived a difference, not of degree but of kind, between tragic pain and all other pain. There is something in tragedy which marks it off from other disaster so sharply that in our common speech we bear witness to the difference.

All those whose attention has been caught by the strange contradiction of pleasure through pain agree with this instinctive witness, and some of the most brilliant minds the world has known have concerned themselves with it. Tragic pleasure, they tell us, is in a class by itself. "Pity and awe," Aristotle called it, "and a sense of emotion purged and purified thereby." "Reconciliation," said Hegel, which we may understand in the sense of life's temporary dissonance resolved into eternal harmony. "Acceptance," said Schopenhauer, the temper of mind that says, "Thy will be done." "The reaffirmation of the will to live in the face of death," said Nietzsche, "and the joy of its inexhaustibility when so reaffirmed."

Pity, awe, reconciliation, exaltation—there are the elements that make up tragic pleasure. No play is a tragedy that does not call them forth. So the philosophers say, all in agreement with the common judgment of mankind, that tragedy is something above and beyond the dissonance of pain. But what it is that causes a play to call forth these feelings, what is the essential element in a tragedy, Hegel alone seeks to define. In a notable passage he says that the only tragic subject is a spiritual struggle in which each side has a claim upon our sympathy. But, as his critics have pointed out, he would thus exclude the tragedy of the suffering of the innocent, and a definition which does not include the death of Cordelia or of Deianira cannot be taken as final.

The suffering of the innocent, indeed, can itself be so differently treated as to necessitate completely different categories. In one of the greatest tragedies, the *Prometheus* of Æschylus, the main actor is an innocent sufferer, but, beyond this purely formal connection, that passionate rebel, defying God and all the powers of the universe, has no relationship whatever to the lovely, loving Cordelia. An inclusive definition of tragedy must cover cases as diverse in circumstance and in the character of the protagonist as the whole range of life and letters can afford it. It must include such opposites as Antigone, the high-souled maiden who goes with open eyes to her death rather than leave her brother's body unburied, and Macbeth, the ambition-mad, the murderer of his king and guest. These two plays, seemingly so totally unlike, call forth the same response. Tragic pleasure of the greatest intensity is caused by them both. They have something in common, but the philosophers do not tell us what it is. Their concern is with what a tragedy makes us feel, not with what makes a tragedy.

Only twice in literary history has there been a great period of tragedy, in the Athens of Pericles and in Elizabethan England. What these two periods had in common, two thousand years and more apart in time, that they expressed themselves in the same fashion, may give us some hint of the nature of tragedy, for far from being periods of darkness and defeat, each was a time when life was seen exalted, a time of thrilling and unfathomable possibilities. They held their heads high, those men who conquered at Marathon and Salamis, and those who fought Spain and saw the Great Armada sink. The world was a place of wonder; mankind was beauteous; life was lived on the crest of the wave. More than all, the poignant joy of heroism had stirred men's hearts. Not stuff for tragedy, would you say? But on the crest of the wave one must feel either tragically or joyously; one cannot feel tamely. The temper of mind that sees tragedy in life has not for its opposite the temper that sees joy. The opposite pole to the tragic view of life is the sordid view. When humanity is seen as devoid of dignity and significance, trivial, mean, and sunk in dreary hopelessness, then the spirit of tragedy departs. "Sometime let gorgeous tragedy in sceptred pall come sweeping by." At the opposite pole stands Gorki with *The Lower Depths.*

Other poets may, the tragedian must, seek for the significance of life. An error strangely common is that this significance for tragic purposes depends, in some sort, upon outward circumstance, on

> *pomp and feast and revelry,*
> *With mask, and antique pageantry—*

Nothing of all that touches tragedy. The surface of life is comedy's concern; tragedy is indifferent to it. We do not, to be sure, go to Main Street or to Zenith for tragedy, but the reason has nothing to do with their dull familiarity. There is no reason inherent in the house itself why Babbitt's home in Zenith should not be the scene of a tragedy quite as well as the Castle of Elsinore. The only reason it is not is Babbitt himself. "That singular swing toward elevation" which Schopenhauer discerned in tragedy, does not take any of its impetus from outside things.

The dignity and the significance of human life—of these, and of these alone, tragedy will never let go. Without them there is no tragedy. To answer the question, what makes a tragedy, is to answer the question wherein lies the essential significance of life, what the dignity of humanity depends upon in the last analysis. Here the tragedians speak to us with no uncertain voice. The great tragedies themselves offer the solution to the problem they propound. It is by our power to suffer, above all, that we are of more value than the sparrows. Endow them with a greater or as great a potentiality of pain and our foremost place in the world would no longer be undisputed. Deep down, when we search out the reason for our conviction of the transcendent worth of each human being, we know that it is because of the possibility that each can suffer so terribly. What do outside trappings matter, Zenith or Elsinore? Tragedy's preoccupation is with suffering.

But, it is to be well noted, not with all suffering. There are degrees in our high estate of pain. It is not given to all to suffer alike. We differ in nothing more than in our power to feel. There are souls of little and of great degree, and upon that degree the dignity and significance of each life depend. There is no dignity like the dignity of a soul in agony.

Here I and sorrows sit;
Here is my throne, bid kings come bow to it.

Tragedy is enthroned, and to her realm those alone are admitted who belong to the only true aristocracy, that of all passionate souls. Tragedy's one essential is a soul that can feel greatly. Given such a one and any catastrophe may be tragic. But the earth may be removed and the mountains be carried into the midst of the sea, and if only the small and shallow are confounded, tragedy is absent.

One dark page of Roman history tells of a little seven-year-old girl, daughter of a man judged guilty of death and so herself condemned to die, and how she passed through the staring crowds sobbing and asking, "What had she done wrong! If they would tell her, she would never do it again"—and so on to the black prison and the executioner. That breaks the heart, but is not tragedy, it is pathos. No heights are there for the soul to mount to, but only the dark depths where there are tears for things. Undeserved suffering is not in itself tragic. Death is not tragic in itself, not the death of the beautiful and the young, the lovely and beloved. Death felt and suffered as Macbeth feels and suffers is tragic. Death felt as Lear feels Cordelia's death is tragic. Ophelia's death is not a tragedy. She being what she is, it could be so only if Hamlet's and Laertes' grief were tragic grief. The conflicting claims of the law of God and the law of man are not what make the tragedy of the *Antigone.* It is Antigone herself, so great, so tortured. Hamlet's hesitation to kill his uncle is not tragic. The tragedy is his power to feel. Change all the circumstances of the drama and Hamlet in the grip of any calamity would be tragic, just as Polonius would never be, however awful the catastrophe. The suffering of a soul that can suffer greatly—that and only that, is tragedy.

It follows, then, that tragedy has nothing to do with the distinction between Realism and Romanticism. The contrary has always been maintained. The Greek went to the myths for their subjects, we are told, to insure remoteness from real life which does not admit of high tragedy. "Realism is the ruin of tragedy," says the latest writer on the subject. It is not true. If indeed Realism were conceived of as dealing only with the usual, tragedy would be ruled out, for the soul capable of a great passion is not usual. But if nothing human is alien to Realism, then tragedy is of her domain, for the unusual is as real as the usual. When the Moscow Art Players presented the *Brothers Karamazoff* there was seen on the stage an absurd little man in dirty clothes who waved his arms about and shuffled and sobbed, the farthest possible remove from the traditional figures of tragedy, and yet tragedy was there in his person, stripped of her gorgeous pall, but sceptred truly, speaking the authentic voice of human agony in a struggle past the power of the human heart to bear. A drearier setting, a more typically realistic setting, it would be hard to find, but to see the play was to feel pity and awe before a man dignified by one thing only, made great by what he could suffer. Ibsen's plays are not tragedies. Whether Ibsen is a realist or not—the Realism of one generation is apt to be the Romanticism of the next—small souls are his dramatis personæ and his plays are dramas with an unhappy ending. The end of *Ghosts* leaves us with a sense of shuddering horror and cold anger against a society where such things can be, and these are not tragic feelings.

The greatest realistic works of fiction have been written by the French and the Russians. To read one of the great Frenchmen's books is to feel mingled despair and loathing for mankind, so base, so trivial and so wretched. But to read a great Russian novel is to have an altogether different experience. The baseness, the beast in us, the misery of life, are there as plain to see as in the French book, but what we are left with is not despair and not loathing, but a sense of pity and wonder before mankind that can so suffer. The Russian sees life in that way because the Russian genius is primarily poetical; the French genius is not. *Anna Karenina* is a tragedy; *Madame Bovary* is not. Realism and Romanticism, or comparative degrees of Realism, have nothing to do with the matter. It is a case of the small soul against the great soul and the power of a writer whose special endowment is "*voir clair dans ce qui est*" against the intuition of a poet.

If the Greeks had left no tragedies behind for us, the highest reach of their power would be unknown. The three poets who were able to sound the depths of human agony were able also to recognize and reveal it as tragedy. The mystery of evil, they said, curtains that of which "every man whose soul is not a clod hath visions." Pain could exalt and in tragedy for a moment men could have sight of a meaning beyond their grasp. "Yet had God not turned us in his hand and cast to earth our greatness," Euripides makes the old Trojan queen say in her extremity, "we would have passed away giving nothing to men. They would have found no theme for song in us nor made great poems from our sorrows."

Why is the death of the ordinary man a wretched, chilling thing which we turn from, while the death of the hero, always tragic, warms us with a sense of quickened life? Answer this question and the enigma of tragic pleasure is solved. "Never let me hear that brave blood has been shed in vain," said Sir Walter Scott; "it sends an imperious challenge down through all the generations." So the end of a tragedy challenges us. The great soul in pain and in death transforms pain and death. Through it we catch a glimpse of the Stoic Emperor's Dear City of God, of a deeper and more ultimate reality than that in which our lives are lived.

ÆSCHYLUS
The First Dramatist

When Nietzsche made his famous definition of tragic pleasure he fixed his eyes, like all the other philosophers in like case, not on the Muse herself but on a single tragedian. His "reaffirmation of the will to live in the face of death, and the joy of its inexhaustibility when so reaffirmed" is not the tragedy of Sophocles nor the tragedy of Euripides, but it is the very essence of the tragedy of Æschylus. The strange power tragedy has to present suffering and death in such a way as to exalt and not depress is to be felt in Æschylus' plays as in those of no other tragic poet. He was the first tragedian; tragedy was his creation, and he set upon it the stamp of his own spirit.

It was a soldier-spirit. Æschylus was a Marathon-warrior, the title given to each of the little band who had beaten back the earlier tremendous Persian onslaught. As such, his epitaph would seem to show, he merited honor so lofty, no mention of his poetry could find place beside it:

> *Æschylus, the Athenian, Euphorion's son, is dead. This tomb in Gela's cornlands covers him. His glorious courage the hallowed field of Marathon could tell, and the longhaired Mede had knowledge of it.*

Did he fight elsewhere too? There is no answer to this or to any other question about him except in so far as it can be found in what he wrote. The epitaph, a statement that he was descended from an aristocratic family, and a few dates—of the production of this or that play, and of his death—make up all the facts that have come down. There was no Plato to draw his portrait with sure, intimate touches and make him a living human being forever. As with Shakespeare, we know him only as he permits us through his plays, a doubtful matter in the case of the greatest poets whose province is the whole of life and who can identify themselves with everything there is, delight in conceiving an Iago equally with an Imogen, as Keats once said. Even so, Æschylus' work, what we have of it, that is—seven plays only left from ninety—shows the main lines of his character and the temper of his mind as Shakespeare's, with its boundless range, does not. A conclusion, however, to be checked by the consideration that if we had all those ninety plays, and of Shakespeare's only seven tragedies, the exact reverse might appear to be the truth. And yet such is the overpowering impression each of Æschylus' plays makes of his grandeur of mind and spirit, of the heroic mold he was cast in, it is not possible to conceive of his writing anything that would not have been so stamped.

So much we can conclude about the man himself, but of his actual life there are almost no indications. He was used to the ways of a great house, we gather, and despised the *nouveau riche*—he takes him off in the Zeus of the *Prometheus*, "the upstart god" who "shows forth his power for his brief day, his little moment of lording it." If one is a slave, Clytemnestra tells the captive Trojan princess,

Portrait of Æschylus, in *The Tragic Drama of the Greeks*

It is very well to serve in an old family,
Long used to riches. For indeed the man
Who reaps a sudden harvest beyond hope,
Is savage to his slaves above the rule.

In this matter of his soldiering, too, there are passages that would appear to strike unmistakably the note of personal experience: "Our beds were close to the enemy's walls; our clothes were rotting with the wet; our hair full of vermin." That is not war as the novice sees it. Even more pointed are the words in Clytemnestra's announcement that Troy has fallen, when she pauses in the full flight of her tale of triumph to give a strange little realistic picture of a newly captured town:

The women have flung themselves on lifeless bodies, husbands, brothers—little children are clinging to the old dead that gave them life, sobbing from throats no longer free, above their dearest. And the victors—a night of roaming after battle has set them down hungry to breakfast on what the town affords, not billeted in order, but as chance directs.

That speech sounds oddly on a great queen's lips. It seems an old soldier's reminiscence, each clear detail part of a picture often seen. But these few passages are all there are that throw any light upon his way of life.

We are, the greatest of us, the product of our times. Æschylus lived in one of those brief periods of hope and endeavor which now and again light up the dark pages of history, when mankind makes a visible advance along its destined path without fear or faltering. A mere handful of men had driven back the hosts of the ruling world-power, so defeated that Persia was never again to repeat an invasion that had brought only disaster. The success of that great venture went thrillingly through the land. Life was lived at an intenser level. Peril, terror, and anguish had sharpened men's spirits and deepened their insight. A victory achieved past all hope at the very moment when utter defeat and the loss of all things seemed certain had lifted them to an exultant courage. Men knew that they could do heroic deeds, for they had seen heroic deeds done by men. This was the moment for the birth of tragedy, that mysterious combination of pain and exaltation, which discloses an invincible spirit precisely when disaster is irreparable. Up to that time the poets of Greece had looked with a direct and un-self-conscious gaze upon the world and found it good. The glory of brave deeds and the loveliness of natural things had contented them. Æschylus was the poet of a new era. He bridged the tremendous gulf between the poetry of the beauty of the outside world and the poetry of the beauty of the pain of the world.

He was the first poet to grasp the bewildering strangeness of life, "the antagonism at the heart of the world." He knew life as only the greatest poets can know it; he perceived the mystery of suffering. Mankind he saw fast bound to calamity by the working of unknown powers, committed to a strange venture, companioned by disaster. But to the heroic, desperate odds fling a challenge. The high spirit of his time was strong in Æschylus. He was, first and last, the born fighter, to whom the consciousness of being matched against a great adversary suffices and who can dispense with success. Life for him was an adventure, perilous indeed, but men are not made for safe havens. The fullness of life is in the hazards of life. And, at the worst, there is that in us which can turn defeat into victory.

In a man of this heroic temper, a piercing insight into the awful truth of human anguish met supreme poetic power, and tragedy was brought into being. And if tragedy's peculiar province is to show man's misery at its blackest and man's grandeur at its greatest, Æschylus is not only the creator of tragedy, he is the most truly tragic of all the tragedians. No one else has struck such ringing music from life's dissonance. In his plays there is nothing of resignation or passive acceptance. Great spirits meet calamity greatly. The maidens who form the chorus of the *Prometheus* demand full knowledge of all the evil before them: "For when one lies sick, to face with clear eyes all the pain to come is sweet." Antigone, about to do what means certain death to her, cries, "Courage! The power will be mine and the means to act." When Clytemnestra has struck her blow and her husband has fallen dead, she opens the palace doors and proclaims what she has done:

> *Here I stand where I struck. So did I. Nothing do I deny. Twice did I strike him and twice he cried out, and his limbs failed and he fell. The third stroke I gave him, an offering to the god of Hell who holds fast the dead. And there he lay gasping and his blood spouted and splashed me with black spray, a dew of death, sweet to me as heaven's sweet raindrops when the cornland buds.*

Prometheus, helpless and faced by irresistible force, is unconquered. There is no yielding in him, even to pronounce the one word of submission which will set him free; no repentance in dust and ashes before almighty power. To the herald of the gods who bids him yield to Zeus' commands, he answers:

> *There is no torture and no cunning trick,*
> *There is no force, which can compel my speech,*
> *Until Zeus wills to loose these deadly bonds.*
> *So let him hurl his blazing thunderbolt,*
> *And with the white wings of the snow,*
> *With lightning and with earthquake,*
> *Confound the reeling world.*
> *None of all this will bend my will.*

HERALD: Submit, you fool. Submit. In agony learn wisdom.

PROMETHEUS: Seek to persuade the sea wave not to break. You will persuade me no more easily.

With his last words as the universe crashes upon him, he asserts the justice of his cause: "Behold me, I am wronged"—greater than the universe which crushes him, said Pascal. In this way Æschylus sees mankind, meeting disaster grandly, forever undefeated. "Take heart. Suffering, when it climbs highest, lasts but a little time"—that line from a lost play gives in brief his spirit as it gives the spirit of his time.

He was a pioneer who hews his way through by the magnificence of sheer strength and does not stay to level and finish. There is no smooth perfection of form in him such as ever gives a hint that the summit has been reached and just beyond lies decadence. He could have heaved the mighty stones of the Mycenæan gate; he could not have polished the lovely beauty of the Praxiteles Hermes. Aristophanes, keenest of critics and true lover of Æschylus even when caricaturing him, describes his adjectives, those touchstones of a poet, as "new, torrent-swept timbers, blown loose by a giant at war," and the words recall that storm of "high-engendered battles," of "sulphurous and thought-executing fires, vaunt-couriers of oak-cleaving thunderbolts" that beat upon Lear's head. A kind of splendid carelessness goes with surpassing power. The labor of the file was not for Æschylus as it was not for Shakespeare. These are not to be pictured pacing the floor through nights of anguish, searching for *le mot unique*.

There is a kinship between the two. Shakespeare also had seen men achieve and suffer on a plane above the level of mere human life and had been moved by the high hope and courage of an age when heroes like those of Marathon and Salamis walked the earth. The sense of the wonder of human life, its beauty and terror and pain, and the power in men to do and to hear, is in Æschylus and in Shakespeare as in no other writer.

Thy friends are exultations, agonies,
And love and man's unconquerable mind.

These words from a nineteenth-century poet are as characteristic of both Shakespeare and Æschylus as anything either of them ever wrote.

One of Shakespeare's plays, indeed, *Macbeth*, is completely like Æschylus in conception, more so by far than any of Sophocles' or Euripides' plays. The atmosphere of Macbeth's castle and Agamemnon's palace is the same. It is always night there; a heavy murk is in the air; death drifts through the doorways. It is not a mere case of dark deeds done in both. Œdipus' palace is as deeply stained with blood; horror is there, and the slow footsteps of fate, clearly heard, ever inexorably drawing nearer to the doom that must be. But in the *Oresteia* and *Macbeth* the horror consists of the fact that those footsteps are not clearly heard; they are muffled; the ear listens and is not sure; what moves on is shrouded in blackness; the unknown is there and the mystery of evil.

It is impossible to show by quotations the similarity in the general impression the two tragedies make, but the way each is continually pointing to an undefined terror to come can be illustrated by many passages. Again and again in both plays the note of foreboding is struck. Some dreadful deed is impending—what, none may say, but any moment we may be face to face with it.

MACBETH

ACT I, SC. 3

MACBETH: If good, why do I yield to that suggestion
Whose horrid image doth unfix my hair,
And make my seated heart knock at my ribs,
Against the use of nature? Present fears
Are less than horrible imaginings.

ACT I, SC. 4

MACBETH: Stars, hide your fires!
Let not light see my black and deep desires;
The eye wink at the hand; yet let that be
Which the eye fears, when it is done, to see.

ACT I, SC. 5

LADY MACBETH: Come, thick night,
And pall thee in the dunnest smoke of hell,
That my keen knife sees not the wound it makes,
Nor heaven peep through the blanket of the dark,
To cry: "Hold, hold!"—

ACT III, SC. 4

MACBETH: (to the Ghost) Avaunt! and quit my sight! Let the
earth hide thee! Thy bones are marrowless, thy blood is cold!
Thou hast no speculation in those eyes
Which thou dost glare with...Hence, horrible shadow!
Unreal mockery, hence!

AGAMEMNON

CHORUS: But dark fear now
Shows me dim
Dreadful forms
Hid in night.
Men who shed the blood of men,
Their ways are not unseen of God.
Black the spirits that avenge...

Why for me so steadfastly
Hovers still this terror dark
At the portals of my heart prophetic...
Spirit of vengeance, your music is sung to no lyre.

Heart that throbs,
Breast that swells,
Tides of pain that shake the spirit,
Are you but fools?
Nay, you presage what shall be...

CASSANDRA: Where have you brought me—
and to what a house!

CHORUS: The house of Atreus' sons—

CASSANDRA: No—but a house God hates.
Murders and strangling deaths—
Kin...striking down kin. Oh, they kill men here.
House that knows evil and evil—the floor drips red.
O God, O God. What would they bring to pass?
Is there a woe that this house knows not?
Oh, dark deed, beyond cure, beyond hope.
—And help stands far away.

CASSANDRA: See them—those yonder by the wall—there, there!
So young—like forms that hover in a dream.
Children they seem, murdered by those they loved.
And in their hands is flesh—It is their own!
And inward parts—O load most horrible!
I see them...
Vengeance, I swear, from these is shaping still.

The similarity in the effect produced by these quotations is unmistakable, and it could be illustrated at far greater length. It is not a chance resemblance that through one drama come and go the weird sisters and through the other the three avenging furies of crime. Neither band could have found a place in Œdipus' palace.

Another notable resemblance: both poets can laugh. That can be said of no other tragedian. The poets, indeed, of whatsoever description, are not given to laughter; they are a serious company. Æschylus and Shakespeare alone stand for the soundness of Socrates' opinion, that it is within the province of the same writer to compose both tragedy and comedy. Lesser men would feel the intrusion of the comic into the tragic a fault against good taste, as witness all the critics who have suffered over the porter in *Macbeth*. But the great two, one surmises, were not concerned with good taste. They did what they pleased. A moment of tragic suspense, hardly to be equalled, is when the doors of Agamemnon's palace close upon the son who has come to kill his mother and has gained admission to her by pretending to be the bearer of the news of his own death. As he passes into the palace and the mind is full of the awful deed to be done, an old woman enters whom the chorus address as Orestes' nurse. She is crying:

> *Oh, I'm a wretched woman. I've known troubles enough but never any like this. Oh, Orestes, my darling! Oh, dear, he was the trouble of my life. His mother gave him to me to nurse, and the shrill screams at night that routed me out of bed, and all the useless bother of him. I had to put up with it. A child hasn't any sense, any more than a dumb beast. You've got to follow its whims. A baby can't tell you when it's hungry or thirsty or going to wet its clothes. And a child's stomach can do it all alone—and sometimes I knew what was coming, but often I didn't, and then all the clothes had to be washed. I wasn't only nurse, I was washerwoman too—*

And so exits the forerunner of Juliet's nurse and the play moves on to the murder of the mother by her son.

Shakespeare, it may be said, was above all a man of the theatre as Æschylus, it is the current opinion, was not. He is generally held to be a philosophic poet who strayed by some mischance upon the stage. So far is this from being true that he was first and foremost the born dramatist, a man who saw life so dramatically that to express himself he had to invent the drama. For that is what he did. Until he came there was only a chorus with a leader. He added a second actor, thus contriving the action of character upon character which is the essence of the drama. He was at least as much a man of the theatre as Shakespeare, not only the founder of it, but an actor and a practical producer as well. He designed the dress all Greek actors wore; he developed stage scenery and stage machinery; he laid down the lines for the Attic theatre.

Small wonder that with all this on his shoulders his technique was often faulty. No doubt he could write bad lines and bad scenes; he was a careless workman, negligent of detail. Sometimes he ignored legitimate minor interests; sometimes he dragged them out to a wearisome length, as in *The Libation-Bearers*, where Orestes' recognition by Electra is given briefly and tamely, while the discovery of the lock of hair on the tomb holds the stage for a hundred and fifty long lines. But he always realized the essential drama of the story he was dramatizing, and he always went straight to it. There he was not careless. The great central theme of each play he presented with consummate theatrical skill as well as dramatic power. The plays of his two great successors are often better theatre than his. They were more skillful craftsmen and had a far more developed technique, but there are scenes in his plays of a dramatic intensity which is beyond anything in Sophocles or Euripides. He not only invented the drama, he raised it to a height which has only once been equalled, and in the glory of that twofold achievement he stands alone.

One quotation to support the point must suffice, for the reason that only a fairly long passage can show this special power of

when ideas the world had never known before were stirring, but he soon left his followers far out of sight. That piercing intellect of his saw through false and foolish notions which were to hold the world enslaved for many a century to come. He was the forerunner of Euripides, the arch-rationalist. Long before Euripides had brought his terrible indictment against war in *The Trojan Women*, Æschylus, Marathon-warrior though he was, had stripped away its glory. He had fought in the ranks and he knew what war was like as only the man can who has seen it at close quarters. It is curious that he perceived how money and war are bound up together:

For all who sped
forth from Greece,
joining company,
such grief as passes power to bear
in each man's home,
plain to see.
Many things
there to pierce a heart through.
Women know whom they sent forth,
but instead of the living,
back there comes to every house
armor and dust from the burning.
And war who trades
men for gold,
living for dead,
and holds his scales
where the spear-points meet and clash,
to their beloved,
back from Troy
he sends them dust
from the flame,
heavy dust,
dust wet with tears,
filling urns in seemly wise,
freight well-stowed, the dust of men.

There are many passages like that in the *Agamemnon*.

In one brief sentence he dismisses a central—perhaps the central—dogma of the Greeks, that great prosperity is viewed jealously by heaven and ends in misery: "I hold my own mind and think apart from other men. Not prosperity but sin brings misery."

It is usually held that the radical and the religious temperaments are antagonistic, but in point of fact the greatest religious leaders have been radicals. Æschylus was profoundly religious and a radical, and so he pushed aside the outside trappings of religion to search into the thing itself. The gods come and go bewilderingly in his plays for the reason that they are only shadows to him, whose inconsistencies and incongruities do not interest him. He is looking past them, beyond the many to the one, "the Father, Ancient of Days, who fashioned us with his own hand." In Him, in God, he holds, rests the final and reconciling truth of this mystery that is human life, which is above all the mystery of undeserved suffering. The innocent suffer—how can that be and God be just? That is not only the central problem of tragedy, it is the great problem everywhere when men begin to think, and everywhere at the same stage of thought they devise the same explanation, the curse, which, caused by sin in the first instance, works on of itself through the generations—and lifts from God the awful burden of injustice. The haunted house, the accursed race, literature is full of them. "The sins of the fathers shall be visited upon the children." Œdipus and Agamemnon must pay for their forefathers' crimes. The stolen gold dooms the Volsungs. It is a kind of half-way house of explanation which satisfies for a time men's awakening moral sense. It did not satisfy Æschylus.

He was a lonely thinker when he began to think "those thoughts that wander through eternity." The Hebrew Ezekiel at about the same time perceived the injustice of this way of maintaining God's justice and protested against the intolerable wrong of children's suffering for their father's sins, but his way out was to deny that they did. As ever, the Jew was content with a "Thus saith the Lord," an attitude that leaves no place for tragedy in the world. He could accept the irrational and rest in it serenely; the actual fact before him did not confront him inescapably as it did the Greek.

Æschylus was conscious of his own isolation when he went beneath the accepted explanation. "I alone do not believe thus," he wrote. He took the problem at its worst, a wife driven to murder her husband, a son driven to kill his mother, and back of them an inheritance of black deed upon black deed. No easy way out that would "heal the hurt" of the world "slightly" would do for him. He saw the inexorable working out of the curse; he knew that the sins of the fathers are visited upon the children; he believed in the justice of God. The truth to reconcile these truths he found in the experience of men, which the men of his generation must have realized far beyond others, that pain and error have their purpose and their use: they are steps of the ladder of knowledge:

> *God, whose law it is that he who learns must suffer. And even in our sleep pain that cannot forget, falls drop by drop upon the heart, and in our own despite, against our will, comes wisdom to us by the awful grace of God.*

A great and lonely thinker. Only here and there in the very greatest have the depth and penetration of his thought been equalled, and his insight into the riddle of the world has not yet been superseded.

SOPHOCLES
Quintessence of the Greek

Tragic pleasure, Schopenhauer said, is in the last analysis a matter of acceptance. The great philosopher of gloom was defining all tragedy in terms of one tragedian. His definition applies to Sophocles alone, but it compresses into a single word the spirit of the Sophoclean drama. Acceptance is not acquiescence or resignation. To endure because there is no other way out is an attitude that has no commerce with tragedy. Acceptance is the temper of mind that says, "Thy will be done" in the sense of "Lo, I come to do thy will." It is active, not passive. Yet it is distinct from the spirit of the fighter, with which, indeed, it has nothing in common. It accepts life, seeing clearly that thus it must be and not otherwise. "We must endure our going hence even as our coming hither." To strive to understand the irresistible movement of events is illusory; still more so to set ourselves against what we can affect as little as the planets in their orbits. Even so, we are not mere spectators. There is nobility in the world, goodness, gentleness. Men are helpless so far as their fate is concerned, but they can ally themselves with the good, and in suffering and dying, die and suffer nobly. "Ripeness is all."

This is the spirit of Sophocles, as unlike that of Æschylus as the spirit of a man on a foundering vessel who stands aside to let the women and children fill the life-boats and accepts death calmly as his portion, is unlike that of the Elizabethan gentlemen who sailed the little *Revenge* against the Spanish Armada in that most glorious fight of history. There were scarcely two decades between the two tragedians, but the tremendous stream of the life of Athens flowed so swiftly that by the time Sophocles had reached manhood the outlook on life which had made Marathon, Thermopylæ, Salamis, possible had passed away. Their very names have power today to move us to great memories. "Gods then were men and walked upon the earth." Even today we can catch a glimpse of what it must have meant to watch the decline of that heroic endeavor and the failure of those high hopes. Athens had brought to birth freedom for the world, and then straightway turned to compass the destruction of her own glorious offspring. She grew powerful, imperial, tyrannical. She was for bringing all Greece beneath her yoke so that the rest of Greece turned upon her, and before Sophocles died, Sparta was at her gates and her sun was setting. As a very old man, when death the deliverer was close at hand, he wrote the well-known lines:

The long days store up many things nearer to grief than joy.
...Death at the last, the deliverer.
Not to be born is past all prizing best.
Next best by far when one has seen the light
Is to go thither swiftly whence he came.
When youth and its light carelessness are past,
What woes are not without, what griefs within,
Envy and faction, strife and sudden death.
And last of all, old age, despised,
Infirm, unfriended.

Sophocles

These words are not his creed. They were written when he was as full of grief as age, wretched in both. They are a record of his life: his youth in the bright day of Athens' hope; his manhood when war and party strife were assailing the city; and his old age when the enemy of beauty and tolerance and fair living, of all that Athens had stood for, was conqueror. An old man summing up his life after all the taste for life and all the reason for it, too, were gone, not the great poet's final judgment passed upon it. He gave that judgment in no uncertain words. Such times as those he lived in test the temper of men. To the weaker spirits they bring the despair of all things. The starry heavens are darkened and truth and justice are no more. But to men like Sophocles outside change does not bring the loss of inner steadfastness. The strong can keep the transient and the eternal separate. Sophocles despaired for the city he loved; to him himself evil had come and not good; but, as he saw life, outside circumstance was in the ultimate sense powerless; within himself, he held, no man is helpless. There is an inner citadel where we may rule our own spirits; live as free men; die without dishonoring humanity. A man can always live nobly or die nobly, Ajax says. Antigone goes to her death not uncomforted: death was her choice, and she dies, the chorus tell her, "mistress of her own fate." Sophocles saw life hard but he could bear it hard. When Deianira is being told of her husband's infidelity and her unwilling informant falters in his tale, she bids him, "Do not cheat me of the truth. Not to know the truth—that indeed would be my hurt." The last words of the second Œdipus strike the dominant note of all his plays: "Cease lamentation, for verily these things stand fast." He offers no refuge from things as they are except the refuge of suffering and death accepted in calm of mind, with strength unshaken.

For the rest, in the outside world nothing is sure and most things are sad. Sophocles is melancholy, not with a black or bitter melancholy; Milton's "pensive nun." "Friendship is often false" "Faith does not abide" "Human life is a shadow"—such sayings are on every page:

For never all days free from pain
are given mortals by the son of Kronos.
But joy and grief
the wheels of time
roll round to all,
even as the circling pathways of the stars.
Nothing abides for men, not bright-bespangled night,
not doom, not death.
Wealth comes and goes,
and grief and gladness.

The danger of this kind of moralizing is that it is easy and separated by a hair's-breadth only from the commonplace. Sophocles often grows sententious: "For all men it is appointed to die" "Before he sees it no man can read the future or his fate" "The honor of life lies not in words but in deeds." Not even the sweep of his mighty wing can lift this sort of thing into the realm of poetry, but here as in all else he is a Greek of the Greeks, lovers ever of antithesis and of a pithy saying. The wonder is not that Sophocles must draw the moral but that Æschylus signally does not. The point is only one of many that mark the fundamental difference between the two.

Sophocles was conservative, the upholder of an established order. In theology the conservative temper tends to formalism. Sophocles puts on the same level "to walk with no regard for justice" and to have "no reverence for images of gods." He took contentedly the orthodox view of the hierarchy of Olympus, but a mind and a spirit such as his could not rest there. His beatific vision has nothing to do with the fancies and fables of a childish mythology. The word forever on his lips is law and when he searched the heavens seeking to understand, what he found was, "Laws of purity and reverence which no forgetfulness shall ever put to sleep, and God through them is great and grows not old." He has substituted law for that proud word freedom which Æschylus so loved. Athens is to him the city which has "the perfect fear of Heaven in righteous laws." He loves "order" and "fair harmony" and "sobriety." Freedom, one suspects, looked to him a noisy, disorderly, intemperate business, not to be contained within decent limits. "And ever shall this law hold good," sing the chorus in the *Antigone*, "nothing that is vast enters into the life of mortals without a curse." That is the Greek speaking. All Greek words that mean literally *boundless, indefinite, unlimited,* have a bad connotation. The Greek liked what he could see clearly. The indefinite was unpleasant to him.

In every way Sophocles is the embodiment of what we know as Greek, so much so that all definitions of the Greek spirit and Greek art are first of all definitions of his spirit and his art. He has imposed himself upon the world as the quintessential Greek, and the qualities pre-eminently his are ascribed to all the rest. He is direct, lucid, simple, reasonable. Excess—the word is not to be mentioned in his presence. Restraint is his as no other writer's. Beauty to him does not inhere in color, or light and shade, or any method of adornment, but in structure, in line and proportion, or, from another point of view, it has its roots not in mystery but in clear truthfulness. This is the classic spirit as we have conceived it, and contrasted with Sophocles, Æschylus is a romanticist. How sober is Sophocles' utterance even in despair. His most desperate sayings have an air of reasonableness:

Only the base will long for length of life
that never turns another way from evil.
What joy is there in day that follows day,
now swift, now slow, and death the only goal.
I count as nothing him who feels within
the glow of empty hopes.

And how romantic is Æschylus' despair:

Black smoke I would be,
nearing the clouds of God.

All unseen, soaring aloft,
as dust without wings I would perish.
Oh, for a seat high in air,
where the dripping clouds turn snow,
a sheer, bare cliff, outranging sight,
brooding alone, aloft.
Down I would hurl myself, deep down,
and only the eagles would see.

The last words spoken by the two Antigones bring into clear relief the difference between the two men's temperaments. Sophocles' Antigone mourns:

Unwept, unfriended, without marriage song,
I pass on my last journey to my grave.
Behold me, what I suffer and from whom,
because I have upheld that which is high.

Not so Æschylus' heroine:

No one shall ever thus decree for me.
I am a woman and yet will I make
a grave, a burying for him... With my own hands!
Courage! For I will find the power to act.
Speak not to stay me.

Aristophanes in *The Frogs* gives a sketch of Sophocles which is in singular contrast to the mocking portraits of everybody else. The rest brawl like fishwives and fight like bad little boys, Æschylus and Euripides foremost. Sophocles stands aloof, gentle and courteous and ready to give place to others, "blameless in life and blameless, too, in death." Not even Aristophanes could then jeer at Sophocles to an Athenian audience.* There is no other proof so convincing of the general level of intelligence and cultivated understanding in Athens as the fact that Sophocles was the popular playwright. But however great and sad the difference between the taste of the theatre public then and now, in one respect they are the same: general popularity always means warmth of human sympathy. In Sophocles' plays one may catch a glimpse here and there of that tender and gentle spirit which so endeared him to the Athenians, and which is moving as only the tenderness and the gentleness of the very strong can be. The blinded Œdipus begging for his children:

> *Let me touch them—Oh, could I but touch them with my hands, I would think that they were with me as when once I could behold them. Do I hear weeping? My beloved near me? Come to me, my children. Come here to my hands.*

That is a new note. There is nothing like it in Æschylus.

Warmth of nature does not argue a passionate soul. Sophocles is warm, but underneath all he is passionless. A great tragedian and a supremely great poet, and yet a detached observer of life. Of another such it was said, "Thy soul was like a star and dwelt apart," and those who love Milton will always understand Sophocles best. The periods the two men lived in were as alike as the periods of Æschylus and Shakespeare were alike. Milton, too, passed through a time of exultant hope, when Cromwell put England on the map of Europe, and he, too, had to watch the failure of all he cared for and die at last, a very old man, seeing his country, to use his own words, "shamed and defiled." He, too, learned to accept life and view it as a thing apart from himself "in calm of mind, all passion spent." His world of lofty and solemn poetry is the world of the *Antigone* and the *Œdipus at Colonus*.

The supreme excellence of both men is the same. Alas for us, that it is one which for Sophocles was lost in its complete perfection when classic Greek ceased to be a spoken language. A great thought can live forever, passed on from tongue to tongue, but a great style lives only in one language. Of all English poets Milton is least read by non-English-speaking people. Shakespeare may almost be called German as well as English, but Milton is English alone. Sophocles and Milton are the two incomparable stylists. They are always artists of the great style. They maintain a continuous level of loveliness of word, of phrase, of musical sweep and pause. Compared to them Æschylus and Shakespeare are faulty workmen, capable of supreme felicity of expression side by side with grotesque distortion. Milton's poetry is typically English in its genius; it is poetry of magnificent opulence, of weighted phrase and gorgeous adjective, but there are times when he becomes so limpid, simple, clear, direct, that he is classic, and for one who cannot read Greek easily the surest way to catch a glimpse of that flawless perfection of utterance which is Sophocles, is to read Milton:

Sabrina fair,
Listen where thou art sitting
Under the glassy, cool, translucent wave...

While the still morn went out with sandals gray...

That is the way Sophocles can write.

And completely Sophoclean in substance and in style is:

Come, come; no time for lamentations now,
Nor much more cause. Samson hath quit himself
Like Samson and heroicly hath finished
A life heroic...
Nothing is here for tears, nothing to wail
Or knock the breast, no weakness, no contempt,
Dispraise or blame; nothing but well and fair,
And what may calm us in a death so noble.

It is hard to believe that Sophocles did not write that.

Milton was no dramatist. Thought was his great interest, not action. Sophocles turned naturally to the drama. He was a man of Periclean Athens where pre-eminently the play was the thing, but it is open to question whether his own bent would have led him that way. It is certain that he is a greater poet than dramatist. In dramatic power he stands below Æschylus. On the other hand, in good theatre, as distinguished from sheer drama, he is his superior, but that is only to say that he possessed in the highest degree the Athenian technical gift: in whatever direction he turned he was a consummate workman. If he wrote a play it would be done as well as it could be done from every point of view of theatrical craftsmanship. One imagines the young man watching a performance of Æschylus' *The Libation-Bearers* and noting every crude detail and the passing over of many a chance for a tense moment: that lock of Orestes' hair they will never have done talking about; the patent silliness of Electra's divining that her brother has arrived because the footprints she has found are like her own; the scene where she recognizes him, so quickly passed over when it held most admirable dramatic possibilities. And off he goes to do a really well-made play. Such is the *Electra*. So brief, but not a word wasted; Electra's character given in a moment by the sharp contrast to her sister; the intense, compressed dialogue, where every word means something different to the speakers and the spectators, and the effect is electric; that lock of hair relegated far to the background; the recognition scene worked to the full of all its possibilities; and in the end a thrilling moment. The son has come to avenge his father's death at the hands of his wife and her lover by murdering the two murderers. He has killed his mother, having gained admission to her by declaring that he is bringing her news of his own death. His sister waits at the palace door. To her comes their mother's lover, rejoicing that the one man they feared is dead:

ÆGISTHUS: Where are the strangers who have brought us news of Orestes slain?

ELECTRA: Within. They have found a way to the heart of their hostess.

ÆGISTHUS: Can I look upon the corpse with my own eyes?

ELECTRA: You can indeed.

(*The palace doors open. The shrouded corpse of* CLYTEMNESTRA *lies just within.* ORESTES *stands over it.*)

ÆGISTHUS: Uncover the face that I, who was his kinsman, may pay my due tribute of mourning.

ORESTES: Do you yourself lift the veil.

ÆGISTHUS: So be it—but you, Electra, call me Clytemnestra if she is near.

ORESTES: She is. Look no farther for her.

(ÆGISTHUS *lifts the face cloth.*)

ÆGISTHUS: What do I see—

ORESTES: Why so terrified? Is the face strange to you?

The lifting of that cloth is a supreme theatrical touch. It is the great moment in the play. But the story Sophocles was dramatizing centered around a situation which could not be surpassed for dramatic opportunity, the murder of a mother by her son. No attention is focused on this fact in the play. When the son comes out after killing his mother, he and his sister agree briefly that it is well done, and turn instantly to the real climax, the killing of Ægisthus. Sophocles deliberately avoided the horror of that first murder. He substituted for it the righteous punishment of a murderer, a death that could move no one to pity and awe. "Thoughts too great for man," he ever held, are not for man to utter. He had the sure instinct of the consummate artist: what was too tremendous ever to be done in finished perfection he would not attempt. The high passion that is needed for the very highest drama was not in him. He had a supreme gift of poetic expression, a great intellect, and an unsurpassed sureness of beautiful workmanship, but he did not rise to the heights where Æschylus and Shakespeare alone have walked.

* There is, of course, the comparison with Simonides in the play *Peace*, but that was many years earlier.

EURIPIDES
The Modern Mind

Euripides "with all his faults the most tragic of the poets," said Aristotle, supreme among critics, whose claim to pronounce ever the final verdict has only of late been called into question. His judgment here points the latter-day attitude toward him: the great critic was wrong; he confused sadness and tragedy. Euripides is the saddest of the poets and for that very reason not the most tragic. A very great tragedian, beyond all question, one of the world's four greatest, to all of whom belongs that strangest power, so to present the spectacle of pain that we are lifted to what we truly call the height of tragedy.

Euripides can indeed walk "those heights exalted" but the dark depths of pain are what he knows best. He is "the poet of the world's grief." He feels, as no other writer has felt, the pitifulness of human life, as of children suffering helplessly what they do not know and can never understand. No poet's ear has ever been so sensitively attuned as his to the still, sad music of humanity, a strain little heeded by that world of long ago. And together with that, something then even more unheeded, the sense of the value of each individual human being. He alone of all the classic world so felt. It is an amazing phenomenon. Out of the pages written more than twenty-three hundred years ago sound the two notes which we feel are the dominants in our world today, sympathy with suffering and the conviction of the worth of everyone alive. A poet of the antique world speaks to us and we hear what seems peculiarly our own.

There is an order of mind which is perpetually modern. All those possessed of it are akin, no matter how great the lapse of time that separates them. When Professor Murray's translations made Euripides popular in the early years of this century, what impressed people first of all was his astonishing modernity: he seemed to be speaking the very accent of 1900. Today another generation who have little care for the brightest stars of those years, George Meredith, Henry James, any or all of the great later Victorians, read Euripides as belonging to them. So the younger generation in 400 B.C. felt, and so will they feel in many a century to come. Always those in the vanguard of their time find in Euripides an expression of their own spirit. He is the great exponent of the forever recurring modern mind.

This spirit, always in the world and always the same, is primarily a destructive spirit, critical not creative. "The life without criticism," Plato says, "is not worthy to be lived." The modern minds in each generation are the critics who preserve us from a petrifying world, who will not leave us to walk undisturbed in the ways of our fathers. The established order is always wrong to them. But there is criticism and criticism. Cynical criticism is totally opposed to the temper of the modern mind. The wise king who looked upon all the works that his hands had wrought and on all the labor that he had labored to do, and beheld that all was vanity and vexation of spirit, was not a modern mind. To read Ecclesiastes is to feel, "This is what men have always thought at times and will always think" it never carries the conviction, "This, just this is modern. It is the new note of today." The same is true of Voltaire, that other wisest man and greatest critic, whose mighty pen shook the old unhappy things of his day until their foundations gave way. He is not a modern mind. His attitude, given in brief by his "*Je ne sais pas ce que c'est que la vie éternelle, mais celle-ci est une mauvaise plaisanterie*" is of another order. His is the critical intellect, directed upon human affairs but quite separated from "the human heart all ages live by," and that is a separation the modern-minded know nothing of.

Above all, they care for human life and human things and can never stand aloof from them. They suffer for mankind, and what preoccupies them is the problem of pain. They are peculiarly sensitized to "the giant agony of the world." What they see as needless misery around them and what they envisage as needless misery to come is intolerable to them. The world to them is made up of individuals, each with a terrible power to suffer, and the poignant pity of their own hearts precludes them from any philosophy in the face of this awful sum of pain and any capacity to detach themselves from it. They behold, first and foremost, that most sorrowful thing on earth, injustice, and they are driven by it to a passion of revolt. Convention, so often a mask for injustice, they will have none of, in their pursuit of justice at any cost they tear away veils that hide hateful things; they call into question all pleasant and comfortable things. They are not of those who take "all life as their province" what is good in the age they live in they do not regard; their eyes are fixed upon what is wrong. And yet they never despair. They are rebels, fighters. They will never accept defeat. It is this fact that gives them their profound influence, the fact that they who see so deep into wrong and misery and feel them so intolerable, never conclude the defeat of the mind of man.

Such a spirit, critical, subversive, destructive, is very rarely embodied in a poet. On the great secular scale of literature the modern minds for the most part are negligible. It is in the nature

Euripides

of things that it should be so. Genius moves to creation, not to destruction. Only a very few have combined both. Three hundred years before Euripides there was such a one, completely a modern mind, who felt, as no one has ever felt more, the pitifulness of human life and the intolerable wrong of human injustice, and whose eyes were keen to pierce beneath fair surfaces—the greatest prophet of Israel, Isaiah. A burning coal was placed upon his lips and he uttered the most magnificent indictment ever delivered against those who work evil, and, in words as beautifully tender as any ever spoken, the pity for those who suffer.

Isaiah stands with Euripides as the great example of the modern mind in literature. On every page he speaks his protest against the wrongdoing of men: "We look for judgment, but there is none; for salvation, but it is far off from us...and justice standeth afar off: for truth is fallen in the street, and equity cannot enter. Yea, truth faileth... Everyone followeth after rewards; they judge not for the fatherless, neither doth the cause of the widow come into them, which justify the wicked for reward and grind the faces of the poor,...which call evil good and good evil... If one look to the land, behold the light is darkened in the heavens, behold trouble and darkness and dimness of anguish."

Side by side with the burning of his anger appears the depth of his pity: "He hath sent me to bind up the broken-hearted... As one whom his mother comforteth, so will I comfort you... Can a woman forget her sucking child, that she should not have compassion on the son of her womb? Yea, they may forget, yet will I not forget thee... I, even I, am he that comforteth thee, to open the blind eyes, to bring out the prisoners from the prison, and them that sit in darkness out of the prison house... Oh, thou afflicted, tossed with tempest...in a little wrath I hid my face from thee but with everlasting kindness will I have mercy upon thee."

Parallel passages in Euripides must not be sought for, or even passages strictly comparable; the method of writing is too unlike. Euripides' indictment of evil is to be found not in this or that statement but in the entire body of his plays. The years of his manhood were the years of the great war between Athens and Sparta. His own country's victories at first, her immensely spreading power, never dazzled his eyes. He looked at war and he saw through all the sham glory to the awful evil beneath and he wrote *The Trojan Women*—war as it appears to a handful of captive women waiting for the victors to carry them away to all that slavery means for women. The fall of Troy, the theme of the most glorious martial poetry ever written, ends in his play with one old broken-hearted woman, sitting on the ground, holding a dead child in her arms.

So too it is impossible to show adequately by quotation his spirit of tender compassion for all the unfortunate and his sense of the worth of human life. He sets a poor ignorant peasant beside a royal princess and shows him at least her equal in nobility. Not Plato, the idealist, would have done that. Slaves, who, in the antique scale of human values were not persons any more but only goods and chattels, stand forth in his pages justified, men among men. Euripides has another standard to measure by: "A man without fear cannot be a slave." Old people, old women even and old slaves, completely negligible to the age he lived in, he touches with the deep pity of his perfect understanding. Hecuba remains with Lear the tenderest study in literature of desolate old age.

That spirit of compassionate love made him see deep into the human heart, deeper far than either of his two great predecessors. Not Æschylus, not Sophocles, nobody indeed but he himself, could have drawn the picture of utter pain so utterly human that closes *The Trojan Women*. The herald of the victorious Greeks comes to tell Andromache that her son is to be thrown from the wall of Troy. She speaks to the child:

Go, die, my best-beloved, my cherished one,
In fierce men's hands, leaving me here alone.
...Weepest thou?
Nay, why, my little one? Thou canst not know.

And Father will not come; he will not come;
Not once, the great spear flashing, and the tomb
Riven to set thee free!
How shall it be? One horrible spring...deep, deep
Down. And thy neck... Ah God, so cometh sleep?...
And none to pity thee! Thou little thing
That curlest in my arms, what sweet scents cling
All round thy neck! Belovéd; can it be
All nothing, that this bosom cradled thee
And fostered; all the weary nights, wherethrough
I watched upon thy sickness, till I grew
Wasted with watching? Kiss me. This one time;
Not ever again. Put up thine arms and climb
About my neck: now, kiss me, lips to lips...
Quick! take him: drag him: cast him from the wall,
If cast ye will! Tear him, ye beasts, be swift!
God hath undone me, and I cannot lift
One hand, one hand, to save my child from death.

When the little boy has been killed, his mother is gone, on her way to Greece in a Greek ship, and the dead body is brought to the grandmother, who holds it in her arms and speaks to it:

Ah, what a death hath found thee, little one.
...Poor little child!
Was it our ancient wall so savagely hath rent
Thy curls...here, where the bone-edge frayed
Grins white...Ah, God, I will not see!
Ye tender arms...how from the shoulder loose
Ye drop. And dear proud lips, so full of hope
And closed forever! What false words ye said
At daybreak, when he crept into my bed,
Called me kind names, and promised: "Grandmother,
When thou art dead I will cut close my hair,
And lead out all the captains to ride by
Thy tomb."...'Tis I—old, homeless, childless,
That for thee, must shed cold tears.

These are no austere figures, awfully remote, lifted to heights of tragedy inaccessible. The human heart was what Euripides cared about, and the mythical princess and queen of far-fabled Troy have become suffering women, who feel what women everywhere have felt, their only throne that which sorrows build. A supreme master in human nature added those slight touches that bring them close to us: the sweet smell of the baby's neck as the mother buried her face there for the last time; the old woman remembering the small boy climbing on to her bed of a morning to tell her how he would lead his captains out gloriously for her when she was dead. No tragic exaltation is here but the most poignant pain perhaps ever painted. Few passages in all the literature of pain can be set beside it.

The speculative side of the modern mind, the spirit that is forever examining and calling into question, is less easy to do justice to by quotation. In Isaiah it underlies all the denunciations, and the most cursory reading discovers it. Here and there, too, it finds expression in some isolated piece of acute critical judgment. His keen, questioning mind saw evils which even yet, after twenty-six hundred years, are not clearly seen as such: "Woe unto them that join field to field that they may be placed alone in the earth"—the evil of great landed estates given in brief, England's land question today. Euripides' well-known words about women in the *Medea*, familiar quotation to woman-suffragists so short a time ago, are a perfect parallel of farsighted criticism:

But we, they say, live a safe life at home,
While they, the men, go forth in arms to war.
Fools! Three times would I rather take my stand
With sword and shield than bring to birth one child.

But in truth the critical spirit is stamped upon Euripides as upon no other poet. He lived in a day when criticism was dominating more and more the thought in Athens. Life went at a rapid pace in that brilliant city, and the bare half century that separated Euripides from Æschylus saw astonishing changes. Signs of them are not to be sought for in Sophocles. Even though his long life did not end until a year or two after Euripides' death, he belonged to an earlier day. Or rather is it true that Sophocles was aloof from the spirit of his age and would always have been so no matter what the age. He was first and last the artist, who looked at human beings apart from himself as subjects for his art and who took life as he found it. Passionate protest in face of the facts of life would have seemed to him the action of a child. "Such was the pleasure of the gods, angry, haply, at my race of old," is the final comment of the innocent but blinded, blackened, ruined Œdipus. Questions where none could answer, Sophocles would not ask.

Over against him stand the other two, greatly different but akin. The spirit of inquiry dawning in Æschylus' day had moved him, too, to wonder and surmise. He was never one to acquiesce in what he found because it was there. He, too, saw war with clear eyes, and Sophocles' tranquil acceptance of "all Olympus' faded hierarchy" was never possible to him. Completely a modern mind he was not. He would never, under no circumstances, in no age, have seen mankind as chiefly pitiable. Indeed pity was not a major emotion with him. He had the soldier's temper which faces what is next to come with never a look back to mourn what is past. But even more than this, stamped upon his whole work is the conviction that human beings are capable of grandeur, and that calamity met greatly is justified. Passionate protest against the facts of life is no more to be found in him than in Sophocles, but for a totally different reason: a hero's death awakens neither pity nor indignation.

Completely unlike him in this point, Euripides is nevertheless his spiritual son; he inherits directly from him, passing over Sophocles as though he had never been. Æschylus disregarded the current religion; Euripides directly attacked it. Again and again he shows up the gods in accordance with the popular conception of them, as lustful, jealous, moved by meanest motives, utterly inferior to the human beings they bring disaster upon, and he will have none of them:

Say not there are adulterers in Heaven,
Long since my heart has known it false.
God if he be God lacks in nothing.
All these are dead unhappy tales.

His final rejection, "If gods do evil then they are not gods," is essentially a rejection of man's creating God in his own image, a practice that was to hold the world completely for centuries after him and is today more common than not. So can a master mind outstrip the ages. Of certainties he had few:

For who knows if the thing that we call death
Is life, and our life dying—who can know?
Save only that all we beneath the sun
Are sick and suffering, and those gone before
Not sick, not touched with evil.

Aristophanes' indictment of him in *The Frogs* is summed up in the charge that he taught the Athenians "to think, see, understand, suspect, question, everything."

He was, the stories that have come down about him say, an unhappy man. He withdrew from the world and lived the life of a recluse in his library; "gloomy, unsmiling, averse to society," runs an ancient description of him. A misanthrope, they said, who preferred books to men. Never was a judgment less true. He fled from the world of men because he cared for men too much. He could not bear the poignant pity of his own heart. His life had fallen on unhappy times. As final defeat drew ever nearer, Athens grew terrified, fierce, cruel. And Euripides had a double burden to carry, the sensitiveness of a great poet and the aching pity of a modern mind. How could such a one endure to come into contact with what his city had learned to tolerate and to commend? One thing alone to help her he had been fitted to do: he could so write as to show the hideousness of cruelty and men's fierce passions, and the piteousness of suffering, weak, and wicked human beings, and move men thereby to the compassion which they were learning to forget.

On these two scores it is easy to explain what at first sight seems puzzling, his great unpopularity in his lifetime and his unexampled popularity shortly after his death. Only five of his plays were awarded a first prize, whereas Sophocles gained over twenty. Aristophanes has good words for Æschylus and highest praise for Sophocles but nothing is too bad for him to say about Euripides. The modern mind is never popular in its own day. People hate being made to think, above all upon fundamental problems. Sophocles touched with the radiant glory of sublime poetry the figures of the ancient gods, and the Athenians went home from his plays with the pleasing conviction that old things were right. But Euripides was the arch-heretic, miserably disturbing, never willing to leave a man comfortably ensconced in his favorite convictions and prejudices. Prizes were not for such as he. And yet, very soon after his death, the verdict swung far to the other side and extraordinary tales of the way he was loved by all manner of men have come down to us.

The dogmatisms of each age wear out. Statements of absolute truth grow thin, show gaps, are discarded. The heterodoxy of one generation is the orthodoxy of the next. The ultimate critique of pure reason is that its results do not endure. Euripides' assaults upon the superstructure of religion were forgotten; what men remembered and came to him for was the pitying understanding of their own suffering selves in a strange world of pain, and the courage to tear down old wrongs and never give up seeking for new things that should be good. And generation after generation since have placed him securely with those very few great artists

Who feel the giant agony of the world,
And more, like slaves to poor humanity,
Labor for mortal good...

THE RELIGION OF THE GREEKS

What the Greeks did for religion is in general not highly esteemed. Their achievement in that field is usually described as unimportant, without any real significance. It has even been called paltry and trivial. The reason people think of it in this way is that Greek religion has got confused with Greek mythology. The Greek gods are certainly Homer's Olympians, and the jovial company of the *Iliad* who sit at the banqueting board in Olympus making heaven shake with their shouts of inextinguishable laughter are not a religious gathering. Their morality, even, is more than questionable and also their dignity. They deceive each other; they are shifty and tricky in their dealings with mortals; they act sometimes like rebellious subjects and sometimes like naughty children and are kept in order only by Father Zeus' threats. In Homer's pages they are delightful reading, but not in the very least edifying.

If Homer is really the Greek Bible and these stories of his are accepted as the Greek idea of spiritual truth, the only possible conclusion is that in the enormously important sphere of religion the Greeks were naïve, not to say childish, and quite indifferent to ethical conduct. Because Homer is far and away the best known of the Greeks, this really is the prevailing idea, absurd as it must appear in face of the Greek achievement. There is no truth whatever in it. Religion in Greece shows one of the greatest of what Schopenhauer calls the "singular swing to elevation" in the history of the human spirit. It marks a great stage on the long road that leads up from savagery, from senseless and horrible rites, toward a world still so very dim and far away that its outline can hardly be seen; a world in which no individual shall be sacrificed for an end, but in which each will be willing to sacrifice himself for the end of working for the good of others in the spirit of love with the God who is love.

It would be impossible to compress Greek religion into the compass of a single chapter, but it is perhaps possible to give an idea of the special Greek stamp which marked it out from the others. Greek religion was developed not by priests nor by prophets nor by saints nor by any set of men who were held to be removed from the ordinary run of life because of a superior degree of holiness; it was developed by poets and artists and philosophers, all of them people who instinctively leave thought and imagination free, and all of them, in Greece, men of practical affairs. The Greeks had no authoritative Sacred Book, no creed, no ten commandments, no dogmas. The very idea of orthodoxy was unknown to them. They had no theologians to draw up sacrosanct definitions of the eternal and infinite. They never tried to define it; only to express or suggest it. St. Paul was speaking as a Greek when he said the invisible must be understood by the visible. That is the basis of all great art, and in Greece great artists strove to make the visible express the invisible. They, not theologians, defined it for the Greeks. Phidias' statue of Zeus at Olympia was his definition of Zeus, the greatest ever achieved in terms of beauty. Phidias said, so Dion Chrysostom reports, that pure thought and spirit cannot be portrayed, but the artist has in the human body a true vessel of thought and spirit. So he made his statue of God, the sight of which drew the beholder away from himself to the contemplation of the divine. "I think," Dion Chrysostom writes, "that if a man heavy of heart, who had drunk often of the cup of adversity and sorrow should stand before it, he would remember no longer the bitter hardships of his life. Your work, O Phidias, is

Grief's cure,
Bringing forgetfulness of every care."

"The Zeus of Phidias," said the Roman Quintilian, "has added to our conception of religion."

That was one way the Greeks worked out their theology. Another way was the poet's, as when Æschylus used his power to suggest what is beyond categorical statement:

God—the pathways of his purpose
Are hard to find.
And yet it shines out through the gloom,
In the dark chance of human life.
Effortless and calm
He works his perfect will.

Words that define God clamp down walls before the mind, but words like these open out vistas. The door swings wide for a moment.

Socrates' way was the same. Nothing to him was important except finding the truth, the reality in all that is, which in another aspect is God. He spent his life in the search for it, but he never tried to put what he had seen into hard and fast statements. "To find the Father and Maker of all is hard," he said, "and having found him it is impossible to utter him."

The way of Greek religion could not but be different from the ways of religions dependent not upon each man's seeking the truth for himself, as an artist or a poet must seek it, but upon an absolute authority to which each man must submit himself. In Greece there was no dominating church or creed, but there was a dominating ideal which everyone would want to pursue if he caught sight of it. Different men saw it differently. It was one thing to the artist, another to the warrior. "Excellence" is the nearest equivalent we have to the word they commonly used for it, but it meant more than that. It was the utmost perfection possible, the very best and highest a man could attain to, which when perceived always has a compelling authority. A man must strive to attain it. We needs must love the highest when we see it. "No one," Socrates said, "is willingly deprived of the good." To win it required all that a man could give. Simonides wrote:

Not seen in visible presence by the eyes of men
Is Excellence, save his from whom in utmost toil
Heart-racking sweat comes, at his manhood's height.

Hesiod had already said the same:

Before the gates of Excellence the high gods have placed sweat
Long is the road thereto and steep and rough at the first.
But when the height is won, then is there ease,
Though grievously hard in the winning.

Aristotle summed up the search and struggle: "Excellence much labored for by the race of men." The long and steep and rough road to it was the road Greek religion took.

In the very earliest Greek records we have, a high stage has been reached. All things Greek begin for us with Homer, and in the *Iliad* and the *Odyssey* the Greeks have left far behind not only the bestialities of primitive worship, but the terrible and degrading rites the terror-stricken world around them was practicing. In

Homer

Homer, magic has been abolished. It is practically nonexistent in the *Iliad* and the *Odyssey*. The enormous spiritual advance this shows—and intellectual, no less—is hard for us to realize. Before Greece all religion was magical. Magic was of supreme importance. It was mankind's sole defense against fearful powers leagued against mankind. Myriads of malignant spirits were bent on bringing every kind of evil to it. They were omnipresent. A Chaldean inscription runs:

> *They lie in wait. They twine around the rafters. They take their way from house to house and the door cannot stop them. They separate the bride from the embraces of the bridegroom; they snatch the child from between his father's knees.*

Life was possible only because, fearful as they were, they could be appeased or weakened by magical means. These were often terrible as well as senseless. The human mind played no part at all in the whole business. It was enslaved by terror. A magical universe was so terrifying because it was so irrational, and therefore completely incalculable. There was no dependable relation anywhere between cause and effect. It will readily be seen what it did to the human intellect to live in such an atmosphere, and what it did to the human character, too. Fear is of all the emotions the most brutalizing.

In this terror-haunted world a strange thing came to pass. In one little country the terror was banished. For untold ages it had dominated mankind and stunted its growth. The Greeks dismissed it. They changed a world that was full of fear into a world full of beauty. We have not the least idea when or how this extraordinary change came about. We know only that in Homer men are free and fearless. There are no fearful powers to be propitiated in fearful ways. Very human-like gods inhabit a very delightful heaven. Strange and terrifying unrealities—shapes made up of bird and beast and human joined together by artists who thought only the unhuman could be divine—have no place in Greece. The universe has become rational. An early Greek philosopher wrote: "All things were in confusion until Mind came and set them in order." That mind was Greek, and the first exponent of it we know about was Homer. In the *Iliad* and the *Odyssey* mankind has been delivered from the terror of the unhuman supreme over the human.

Homer's universe is quite rational and well ordered and very well lit. When night comes on, the gods go to sleep. There are no mysterious doings that must shun the eye of day either in heaven or on the earth. If the worship of the powers of darkness still went on—and there are allusions to practices that point to it—at least literature takes no notice of it. Homer would have none of it, and no writer after him ever brought it back. Stories like that of the sacrifice of Iphigenia, which clearly point back to brutal rites, always represent what was done as evil.

An ancient writer says of Homer that he touched nothing without somehow honoring and glorifying it. He was not the Greek Bible; he was the representative and spokesman of the Greeks. He was quintessentially Greek. The stamp of the Greek genius is everywhere on his two epics, in the banishment of the ugly and the frightful and the senseless; in the conviction that gods were like men and men able to be godlike; in the courage and undaunted spirit with which the heroes faced any opponent, human or divine, even Fate herself; in the prevailing atmosphere of reason and good sense. The very essence of Greek rationality is in the passage in which Hector is advised to consult the flight of birds as an omen before going into battle and cries: "Obedience to long-winged birds, whether they fare to the right or to the left—nay; one omen is best, to fight for our country." Homer was the great molding force of Greece because he was so Greek himself. Plato says: "I have always from my earliest years had an awe of Homer and a love for him which even now [when he is about to criticize him] make the words falter on my lips. He is the great leader and teacher."

The Greeks never fell back from the height they had reached with him. They went further on, but not in the directions he had banned, away from reason to magic, and away from freedom to creeds and priests. His gods, however, could not continue long to be adequate to men fired by the desire for the best. They were unable to satisfy people who were thinking soberly of right and wrong, who were using their critical powers to speculate about the universe, who, above all, were trying to find religion, not the doubtful divinities of Olympus, but a solution of life's mystery and a conviction of its purpose and its end. Men began to ask for a loftier Zeus, and one who cared for all, not only, as in the *Iliad*, for the great and powerful. So in a passage in the *Odyssey* he has become the protector of the poor and helpless; and soon after, the peasant-poet Hesiod, who knew by experience what it was to be weak and have no defense against the strong, placed justice in Olympus as Zeus' companion: "Fishes and beasts and fowls of the air devour one another. But to men Zeus has given justice. Beside Zeus on his throne Justice has her seat."

Delphi, the oracle of oracles, took up this implied criticism of Homer and put it into plain words. Moral standards were applied to what went on in Homer's heaven. Pindar, Delphi's greatest spokesman, denounced Homer as speaking falsehoods about the gods. It was wicked and contrary to reason, he protested, to tell unedifying tales about divinities: "Hateful is the poet's lore that utters slander against the gods." Criticism of this kind came from all sides. The rationalizing spirit, which was Homer's own, turned against him. The idea of the truth had dawned, to which personal preferences had to give way; and in the sixth century one of the leaders in what was the beginning of scientific thinking, wrote:

One God there is, greatest of gods and mortals,
Not like to men in body or in mind.
All of him sees and hears and thinks.
We men have made our gods in our own image.
I think that horses, lions, oxen too,

Had they but hands would make their gods like them,
Horse-gods for horses, oxen-gods for oxen.

Homer's Olympians were being attacked by the same love for the rational which had brought them to birth in a mad and magical world. Not only new ideas but new needs were awakening. Greece needed a religion for the heart, as Homer's signally was not, which could satisfy the hunger in men's souls, as the cool morality of Delphi could not.

Such a need is always met sooner or later. A new god came to Greece who for a time did very strange things to the Greek spirit. He was Dionysus, the god of wine, the latest comer among the gods. Homer never admitted him to Olympus. He was alien to the bright company there, a god of earth not heaven. The power wine has to uplift a man, to give him an exultant sense of mastery, to carry him out of himself, was finally transformed into the idea of the god of wine freeing men from themselves and revealing to them that they too could become divine, an idea really implicit in Homer's picture of human gods and godlike men, but never developed until Dionysus came.

His worship must have begun in a great religious revival, a revolt very probably against the powerful center of worship Delphi had become. At any rate, it was the very antipodes to Delphi, the shrine of Apollo the most Greek of all the gods, the artist-god, the poet and musician, who ever brought fair order and harmony out of confusion, who stood for moderation and sobriety, upon whose temple was graven the great Delphic saying, "Nothing in excess." The new religion was marked by everything in excess—drunkenness, bloody feasts, people acting like mad creatures, shrieking and shouting and dancing wildly, rushing over the land in fierce ecstasy. Elsewhere, when the desire to find liberation has arisen, it has very often led men to asceticism and its excesses, to exaggerated cults bent on punishing the body for corrupting the soul. This did not happen in Greece. It could not happen to a people who knew better than any other that liberty depends on self-restraint, who knew that freedom is freedom only when controlled and limited. The Greeks could never wander very far from the spirit of Apollo. In the end, we do not know when or how, the worship of Apollo and the worship of Dionysus came together. All we are told of this momentous meeting is that Orpheus, the master musician, Apollo's pupil, reformed the violent Bacchic rites and brought them into order.

It must have been after this transformation that Dionysus was admitted to the Eleusinian mysteries, the great solemnity of Greece, and took his place beside Demeter in whose honor they had been founded. It was natural to associate the two—the goddess of the corn and the god of the vine, both deities of earth, the benefactors of mankind from whom came the bread and the wine that sustain life. Their mysteries, the Eleusinian, always chiefly Demeter's, and the Orphic, centering in Dionysus, were an enormously important force for religion throughout the Greek and Roman world. Cicero, clearly an initiate, says: "Nothing is higher than these mysteries... They have not only shown us how to live joyfully, but they have taught us how to die with a better hope." In view of their great importance, it is extraordinary that we know almost nothing about them. Everyone initiated had to take an oath not to reveal them, and their influence was so strong that apparently no one ever did. All we are sure of is that they awakened a deep sense of reverence and awe, that they offered purification from sin, and that they promised immortality. Plutarch, in a letter to his wife about the death of a little daughter during his absence from home, writes her that he knows she gives no credence to assertions that the soul once departed from the body vanishes and feels nothing, "because of those sacred and faithful promises given in the mysteries of Bacchus... We hold it firmly for an undoubted truth that our soul is incorruptible and immortal... Let us behave ourselves accordingly, outwardly ordering our lives, while within all should be purer, wiser, incorruptible."

A fragment of Plutarch's apparently describes the initiation ceremonies. "When a man dies he is like those who are initiated into the mysteries. Our whole life is a journey by tortuous ways without outlet. At the moment of quitting it come terrors, shuddering fear, amazement. Then a light that moves to meet you, pure meadows that receive you, songs and dances and holy apparitions." Plutarch lived in the last half of the first century A.D. There is no possible way of telling how much of all that carefully arranged appeal to the emotions belonged to the mysteries of the Periclean age, but some great appeal there was, as Aristophanes shows beyond question in *The Frogs*:

HERACLES: Then you will find a breath about your ears
Of music, and a light about your eyes
Most beautiful—like this—and myrtle groves,
And joyous throngs of women and of men—
The Initiated.

At first sight, this whole matter of an ecstatic religion of salvation, wrapped in mystery and highly emotional, is foreign to our idea of the Greek. Delphi and Pindar, teaching practical morality and forever emphasizing moderation, seem the true representatives of Greece. But they would never by themselves have reached the loftiest and the deepest expression of the Greek spirit. Noble self-restraint must have something to restrain. Apollo needed Dionysus, as Greeks could be trusted to perceive. "He who not being inspired," Plato says, "and having no touch of madness in his soul, comes to the door and thinks he will get into the temple by the help of art—he, I say, and his poetry are not admitted."

The Delphic way and the way of Dionysus reached their perfect union in the fifth-century theatre. There the great mystery, human life, was presented through the power of great art. Poet and actors and audience were conscious of a higher presence.

They were gathered there in an act of worship, all sharing in the same experience. The poet and the actors did not speak to the audience; they spoke for them. Their task and their power was to interpret and express the great communal emotion. That is what Aristotle meant when he said tragedy purified through pity and awe. Men were set free from themselves when they all realized together the universal suffering of life. For a moment they were lifted above their own griefs and cares. They ceased to be shut-in, lonely individuals as they were swept away in a great onrush of emotion which extraordinarily united instead of isolating. Plato said the perfect state was one in which the citizens wept and rejoiced over the same things. That deep community of feeling came to pass in the theatre of Dionysus. Men lost their sense of isolation.

The religion of the mysteries was individual, the search for personal purity and salvation. It pointed men toward union with God. The religion of the drama brought men into union with one another. Personal preoccupations fell away before the soul-shaking spectacle of pain presented on the stage, and the dammed-up flood within was released as the audience wept their hearts out over Œdipus and Hecuba.

But in the long and terrible struggle of the Peloponnesian War, ideals grew dim. Safety, not salvation, was in men's thoughts, the spirit of getting what one could while one could in a world where nothing seemed certain; nothing indeed, for the gods and the old morality were failing. Euripides had succeeded to Æschylus, and a new criticism of all things was in the air. In Pericles' Athens a noted teacher was declaring that "whether there are gods or not we cannot say, and life is too short to find out." The state took alarm and there was a persecution, so slight in comparison with mediæval and later times that it would not deserve notice if it were not for the last victim of it who was Socrates.

One form of religion perpetually gives way to another; if religion did not change it would be dead. In the long history of man's search for God and a basis for right living, the changes almost always come as something better. Each time the new ideas appear they are seen at first as a deadly foe threatening to make religion perish from the earth; but in the end there is a deeper insight and a better life with ancient follies and prejudices gone. Then other follies and prejudices come in, and the whole process has to be gone over again. So it was at this time in Greece, when the supports of all belief seemed to be giving way. Socrates taught and died because of his teaching. In the bitter disillusion caused by the long-drawn-out suffering of the endless war, and even more by the defeat of the Athenian spirit before the hard, narrow, intolerant Spartan spirit, Athens needed above all to be brought back to a fresh realization of the old ideal which her three tragedians had presented so magnificently. She needed a restatement of excellence, and that is what Socrates did for her and all the world to come.

He can never be separated from Plato. Almost all Plato wrote professes to be a report of what Socrates said, a faithful pupil's record of his master's words; and it is impossible to decide just what part belongs to each. Together they shaped the idea of the excellent which the classical world lived by for hundreds of years and which the modern world has never forgotten.

Socrates believed that goodness and truth were the fundamental realities, and that they were attainable. Every man would strive to attain them if he could be shown them. No one would pursue evil except through ignorance. Once let him see what evil was and he would fly from it. His own mission, Socrates believed, was to open men's eyes to their ignorance and to lead them on to where they could catch a glimpse of the eternal truth and goodness beneath life's confusions and futilities, when they would inevitably, irresistibly, seek for a fuller and fuller vision of it. He had no dogma, no set of beliefs to implant in men's minds. He wanted to awaken in them the realization that they did not know what was good, and to arouse in them the longing to discover it. Each one, he was sure, must seek and find it for himself. He never set himself up as a guide. "Although my mind is far from wise," he said, "some of those who come to me make astonishing progress. They discover for themselves, not from me—and yet I am an instrument in the hands of God."

He was always the seeker, asking, not teaching; but his questions upset men's confidence in themselves and in all the comfortable conventions they lived by. The result at first was only perplexity, and sometimes extreme distress. Alcibiades told the company at Agathon's dinner table:

> *I have heard Pericles and other great orators, but they never stirred my soul or made me angry at living in a way that was no better than a slave. But this man has often brought me to such a pass that I felt I could hardly endure the life I was leading, neglecting the needs of my soul. I have sometimes wished that he was dead!*

Aristotle says happiness is activity of soul. That defines precisely Socrates' way of making men happy. He believed that the unexamined life, the life of those who knew nothing of themselves or their real needs and desires, was not worthy to be lived by a human being. So he would sting into activity the souls of men to test their lives, confident that when they found them utterly unsatisfying they would be driven to seek what would satisfy.

His own life did as much to arouse the divine discontent as his words did. He was aware of a counsellor within him which guided him in all his dealings and enabled him to maintain a perfect serenity of spirit always. When he was taken to court on a life-and-death charge of corrupting young men—and no pupil of Socrates could take seriously Homer's gods, still the state religion—he jested with his accusers in a spirit of perfect good will, refused with complete courtesy to save his life by a promise to give up teaching—and ended by comforting his judges for condemning him to death! "Be of good cheer," he told them, "and know of a certainty that no evil can happen to a good man either in life or after death. I see clearly that the time has come when it is better for me to die and my accusers have done me no harm. Still, they did not mean to do me good—and for this I may gently blame them. And now we go our ways, you to live and I to die. Which is better God only knows."

In the prison cell when the time had come to drink the hemlock, he had a kind word for the jailor who brought him the cup, and he broke off his discourse with his friends when he was telling them that nothing was surer than that beauty and goodness have a most real and actual existence, by exclaiming: "But I really had better go bathe so that the women may not have the trouble of washing my body when I am dead." One of those present, suddenly recalled from the charm of his talk to the stark facts, cried: "How shall we bury you?" "Any way you like," was the amused answer. "Only be sure you get hold of me and see that I do not run away." And turning to the rest of the company: "I cannot make this fellow believe that the dead body will not be me. Don't let him talk about burying Socrates, for false words infect the soul. Dear Crito, say only that you are burying my body."

No one who knew of Socrates could fail to believe that "goodness has a most real and actual existence." He exemplified in himself that excellence of which Greece from the beginning had had a vision. Four hundred years before Christ the world took courage from him and from the conviction which underlay all he said and did, that in the confusion and darkness and seeming futility of life there is a purpose which is good and that men can find it and help work it out. Aristotle, through Plato a pupil of Socrates, wrote some fifty years after Socrates died:

> *There is a life which is higher than the measure of humanity: men will live it not by virtue of their humanity, but by virtue of something in them that is divine. We ought not to listen to those who exhort a man to keep to man's thoughts, but to live according to the highest thing that is in him, for small though it be, in power and worth it is far above the rest.*

THE WAY OF THE GREEKS

Character is a Greek word, but it did not mean to the Greeks what it means to us. To them it stood first for the mark stamped upon the coin, and then for the impress of this or that quality upon a man, as Euripides speaks of the stamp—character—of valor upon Hercules, man the coin, valor the mark imprinted on him. To us a man's character is that which is peculiarly his own; it distinguishes each one from the rest. To the Greeks it was a man's share in qualities all men partake of; it united each one to the rest. We are interested in people's special characteristics, the things in this or that person which are different from the general. The Greeks, on the contrary, thought what was important in a man were precisely the qualities he shared with all mankind.

The distinction is a vital one. Our way is to consider each separate thing alone by itself; the Greeks always saw things as parts of a whole, and this habit of mind is stamped upon everything they did. It is the underlying cause of the difference between their art and ours. Architecture, perhaps, is the clearest illustration. The greatest buildings since Greek days, the cathedrals of the Middle Ages, were built, it would seem, without any regard to their situation, placed haphazard, wherever it was convenient. Almost invariably a cathedral stands low down in the midst of a huddle of little houses, often as old or older, where it is marked by its incongruity with the surroundings. The situation of the building did not enter into the architects' plans. They were concerned only with the cathedral itself. The idea never occurred to them to think of it in relation to what was around it. It was not part of a whole to them; it was the whole. But to the Greek architect the setting of his temple was all-important. He planned it, seeing it in clear outline against sea or sky, determining its size by its situation on plain hilltop or the wide plateau of an acropolis. It dominated the scene, indeed; it became through his genius the most important feature in it, but it was always a part of it. He did not think of it in and for itself, as just the building he was making; he conceived of it in relation to the hills and the seas and the arch of the sky.

To see anything in relation to other things is to see it simplified. A house is a very complicated matter considered by itself: plan, decoration, furnishings; each room, indeed, made up of many things; but, if it is considered as part of a block or part of a city, the details sink out of sight. Just as a city in itself is a mass of complexity but is reduced to a few essentials when it is thought of as belonging to a country. The earth shows an infinite diversity, but in relation to the universe it is a sphere swinging in space, nothing more.

So the Greek temple, conceived of as a part of its setting, was simplified, the simplest of all the great buildings of the world, and the Gothic cathedral, seen as a complete whole in itself, unrelated to anything beyond itself, was of all buildings the most elaborated in detail.

This necessity of the Greek mind to see everything in relation to a whole made the Greek drama what it is just as it made the

Greek temple. The characters in a Greek play are not like the characters in any other drama. The Greek tragedians' way of drawing a human being belongs to them alone of all playwrights. They saw people simplified, because, just as in the case of their temples, they saw them as part of a whole. As they looked at human life, the protagonist was not human; the chief role was played by that which underlies the riddle of the world, that Necessity which brings us here and takes us hence, which gives good to one and evil to another, which visits the sins of the fathers upon the children and sweeps away innocent and guilty in fire and pestilence and earthquake shock. "Shall the thing formed say to him that formed it, Why hast thou made me thus? Hath not the potter power over the clay to make one vessel unto honor and another unto dishonor?" To St. Paul the puzzle was easy to solve. To the Greek tragedians it was the enigma never to be answered and they thought of human beings first and foremost in relation to that mystery. So placed against "the background of infinity," part of an immeasurable whole, human complexities are simplified. The accidental and the trivial, from the point of view of the whole, drop out of sight, as in a wide landscape figures can be seen only in outline, or as the innumerable lines on one of Rembrandt's old women's faces would disappear if she were placed in a spacious setting.

For us it is the other way about. Each human being fills an entire canvas. We have dismissed from our scheme of things fate that spins the thread and cuts it. Human nature is the great enigma to us; the mystery of life is the mystery of a man's own self and the conflict we care about goes on within. A man's life is seen not as what is done to him but as what he does to himself, the fault not in our stars but in ourselves, and there is a stage where each one of us is the only actor. We differ from the Greeks in nothing so much as in the way we look at the individual, isolated, in and for himself. Our drama, all our art, is the very reverse of simplified. It is a work of most subtle individualization.

But to the Greek, human beings were not chiefly different but chiefly alike. The Greek dramatists, placing their characters on the tremendous stage whose drama is the conflict between man and the power that shapes him, man "created sick, commanded to be whole," saw as important in them only the dominant traits, the great emotions, the terrors and desires and sorrows and hatreds, that belong to all mankind and to all generations and make the unchanging pattern of human life. Put any character from a Greek tragedy beside one of Shakespeare's and the difference that results from the different points of view is clearly to be seen. One is simple and uncomplicated; the other complex and contradictory too.

An obvious comparison is that between the Clytemnestra of Æschylus and Lady Macbeth, the two outstanding examples of splendid evil embodied in a woman. The greatest poet of classic times drew the one; the greatest poet of modern times the other; the two characters point the way their creators looked at the world of men.

Clytemnestra in the Greek play is magnificent from beginning to end. When she enters, we have been prepared for her hatred of her husband and her determination to kill him as soon as he comes back from Troy; we have heard most pitifully told the tale of how, ten years before, her young daughter was killed by her own father when the gods demanded a human life to speed the ships to Troy. There is one sentence in her first speech which hints at what she has felt:

> *Even though the victors wend their way securely home, what those dead suffered yet may work them ill—that pain which never sleeps.*

It has never slept for her throughout the years—that pain which one dead girl suffered. So much to win our sympathy the poet allows himself, but in all that follows he draws boldly in clear, firm outline the picture of a strong woman without a single weakness; calm and proud and sure of herself; scornful of opposition; never doubting that what she determines she can carry through alone, with help from no one. So does she do; she murders her husband and coming out through the palace doors, she proclaims her deed:

Lies, endless lies I spoke to serve my purpose.
Now I gainsay them all and feel no shame.
Long years ago I planned. Now it is done.
Old hatred ended. It was slow in coming,
but it came—
I stand here where I struck. So did I.
Nothing do I deny. I flung around him
a cloak, full folds, deadly folds. I caught him,
fish in a net. No way to fly or fight.
Twice did I strike him and he cried out twice
and his limbs failed him and he fell. Then—then
I gave him the third stroke—
So there he lay and as he gasped, his blood
spouted and splashed me with black spray—a dew
of death, sweet to me as heaven's sweet raindrops
When the cornland buds... Oh, if such a thing might be
over the dead to pour thank-offerings,
over this dead it would be meet and more,
who caring not, as if a beast should die
when flocks are plenty in the fleecy folds,
slew his own daughter—dearest anguish borne
by me in travail—slew her for a charm
against the Thracian winds.

CHORUS: Loud words of boasting—and the man your husband.

CLYTEMNESTRA: Call me to trial, like any silly woman? Curse me or bless—all one to me.
Look: this is Agamemnon,
my husband, dead, struck down by my right hand,
a righteous workman. So the matter stands.

Here lies the man who scorned me, me, his wife,
the fool and tool of every shameless woman
beneath Troy's walls.

Her last words, addressed to her lover angered at the people's outcry, and the last words of the play,* are:

Dogs will bark. Who cares to listen? What avails this empty talk? You and I are lords here. We two now will order all things well.

Lady Macbeth is a second Clytemnestra through the earlier acts, as sure of her purpose, as resolute, as untroubled by a doubt. When Macbeth wavers she has strength enough to make him strong. Would he, she asks him, by failing to carry through his determination, live a coward in his own esteem? The words have the very ring of Clytemnestra's. So too in her great speech she is one with the Grecian queen exulting in the stains upon her from her husband's blood:

I have given suck, and know
How tender 'tis to love the babe that milks me:
I would, while it was smiling in my face,
Have plucked my nipple from his boneless gums,
And dash'd the brains out, had I so sworn as you
Have done to this.

When Duncan is dead and Macbeth comes to her with the daggers that should have been left by the attendants as proof they were guilty, she bids him carry them back and smear the men with blood, and to his horrified refusal:

I am afraid to think what I have done;
Look on't again I dare not.

she answers scornfully,

Infirm of purpose!
Give me the daggers. The sleeping and the dead
Are but as pictures...

Even so would Clytemnestra have spoken and have done. The portrait of Lady Macbeth is drawn up to her last appearance as simply, in as clear outline, as Æschylus could have done it, with only one slight and yet significant exception. While she is waiting for Macbeth to kill the king, and fearing that his purpose will not hold, she speaks to herself:

Had he [i.e. the king] not resembled
My father as he slept, I had done't.

That sentence blurs the clear outline. Did Clytemnestra have a moment of anguish, a sharp memory to stab her, when her husband rose from the bath for her to throw the cloak around him? Be sure if she had, Æschylus would never have put it in his picture. Clytemnestra's inmost personal life was not his concern. To him her significance, her importance, lay in what was clear for all to see, outstanding, uncomplicated, a great and powerful nature brought to ruin by a hatred within her she could not resist because it was the instrument of fate. When death at her own son's hand came upon her she met it as unflinchingly as she had dealt it. Lady Macbeth at the end, broken, pitiful, forever washing the hands which all the perfumes of Araby will never sweeten, shows a contradiction completely foreign to the Greek stage. She is the victim of her own most individual reaction to the murder she had planned and desired above all things. Her tragedy is within. Shakespeare was looking at what was deepest and what was loneliest in her.

Clytemnestra's tragedy was without; her adversary was fate. Æschylus, like the Greek architect building his temple, was not looking at her alone; he did not see her isolated with her fate in her own hands, or rather, within her own self, as Shakespeare saw Lady Macbeth. He had in view much else besides; he saw her against the background of the past, terrible deeds of old that must work out in evil for her and hers; the thread of her web of life spun far back in dim years of old; she herself, for all her great spirit, doomed before ever she began. Crime upon crime through the generations behind her; the Trojan War brought about by her sister; because of it her daughter made to die, and she, killing her husband, killed in turn by her son. That is life, said the Greek tragedian, human beings each weaving a bit of the web of sorrow and sin and suffering, and the pattern made by a power before which the heart stands still. Against that background an individual vagary or inconsistency does not stand out. Only a clear outline can be discerned, simplified down to the dominating, the essential, that which past all question stamps a man for what he is.

Hecuba in Euripides' *The Trojan Women* is in all outside circumstances comparable to Lear. She too is old and royal and most miserable. She was queen of Troy; now Troy has fallen, husband, sons, are dead; she and her daughters wait beside the ruined walls while the Greek princes draw lots for them. Hecuba's opening speech shows her complete. All the rest of the drama only confirms that first impression of a woman able to suffer to the uttermost, in misery and helpless old age, unbroken. When the play begins she wakes from her bed on the ground and speaks:

Up from the earth, O weary head!
This is not Troy, about, above—
Not Troy, nor we the lords thereof.
Thou breaking neck, be strengthenèd!
Endure and chafe not...
Who am I that I sit
Here at a Greek king's door,
Yea, in the dust of it...
A woman that hath no home.
Weeping alone for her dead—

All kings we were,
And I must wed a king. And sons I brought
My lord King, many sons...all, all are gone.
And no hope left that I shall look upon
Their faces any more, nor they on mine.
And now my feet tread on the utmost line:
An old, slave woman...

The Greek herald tells her one of her daughters has been sacrificed on Achilles' Tomb; the Greek soldiers carry off her other daughters one by one; they cry to her,

Mother, see'st then what things are here?

She answers:

I see God's hand that buildeth a great crown
For littleness and hath cast the mighty down.

The last to go, Andromache, her son Hector's wife, she counsels:

Lo, yonder ships: I ne'er set foot on one,
But tales and pictures tell when over them
Too strong breaks the o'erwhelming sea: lo, then
All cease and yield them up as broken men
To fate and the wild waters. Even so
I in my many sorrows bear me low,
Nor curse, nor strive that other things may be.
The great wave rolled from God hath conquered me.
Thou—thou—let Hector and the fate that fell
On Hector, sleep. Weep for him ne'er so well,
Thy weeping shall not wake him. Honor thou
The master that is set above thee now,
And make of thine own gentle piety
A prize to lure his heart.

Such is Hecuba from first to last, placed by the mysterious workings of fate, through no fault of her own, upon the height of misery, and able to remain there; outside, a pitiful old woman, but within, no variableness nor shadow of turning; raised above human weakness even though completely human in her power to suffer.

The contrast Lear shows is obvious the moment one thinks of him, his passionate temper, his unreasoning folly, that brought him to such a pass; the Trojan War and all that followed it, could do no worse to Hecuba. As Goneril and Regan carelessly comment to each other:

> *'Tis the infirmity of his age; yet he hath ever but slenderly known himself.*
> *The best and soundest of his time hath been but rash.*

Yet so lovable, a high and careless spirit, slow to mark a slight:

KNIGHT: —to my judgment, your highness is not entertained with that ceremonious affection as you were wont...for my duty cannot be silent when I think you highness wronged.

LEAR: I have perceived a most faint neglect of late; which I have rather blamed as mine own jealous curiosity than as a very pretense and purpose of unkindness. I will look further into 't—But where's my fool?

All the little touches that bring him near us. His struggle to control his rage when terror is at his heart:

LEAR: Deny to speak with me? They are sick? They are weary?... Fetch me a better answer.

GLOUCESTER: My dear lord,
You know the fiery quality of the duke...

LEAR: The king would speak with Cornwall; the dear father
Would with his daughter speak, commands her service;
Are they informed of this? My breath and blood!—
Fiery? The fiery duke?—Tell the hot duke, that—
No, but not yet—may be he is not well—

And most endearing, most moving of all, his weakness:

No, you unnatural hags,
I will have such revenges on you both
That all the world shall—I will do such things—
What they are, yet I know not; but they shall be
The terrors of the earth. You think I'll weep;
No, I'll not weep—
I have full cause of weeping—

Toward the end those most piteous words that strip him bare:

I am a very foolish fond old man,
Four score and upward, not an hour more nor less;
And, to deal plainly,
I fear I am not in my perfect mind.

So, just as Clytemnestra and Lady Macbeth, the old queen and the old king stand over against each other, she the victim of fate, he of his own self; her character given broadly without detail, simplified down to the dominant; his individual composition, like no one's else, given to us unanalyzed. Lear has the whole stage to himself; Hecuba only a part. We have no need to question what she stands for; we look past her; her pain and her ruin point us to that which no one ever shall understand, what Ajax saw when he was driven innocent to death:

All strangest things the multitudinous years
bring forth and shadow from us all we know.

Falter alike great oath and steeled resolve,
and none shall say of aught, This cannot be.

A Greek temple makes the spectator aware of the wideness and the wonder of sea and sky and mountain range as he could not be if that shining marvel of white stone were not there in sharp relief against them, and, in the same way, a Greek tragedy brings before us the strangeness that surrounds us, the dark unknown our life is bounded by, through the suffering of a great soul given to us so simply and so powerfully, we know in it all human anguish and the mystery of pain.

But simplicity of characterization is not the same thing as lack of characterization. It is true in fact that characters simply drawn are almost never distinctly individualized, but Greek tragedy is the great example of how it can be done. The personages of a Greek play are clearly characterized. Hecuba is not in any respect one with Clytemnestra; each of them has her own way of meeting the determined things of destiny. Shift about the scene for them and Hecuba would never have avenged her daughter's death upon her husband; with Clytemnestra in Hecuba's place the Greek soldiers would have found their task less easy. Their portraits have been simplified; much is omitted from them, but all is there that is necessary to make each live, her own self and no one's copy. An artist can make an outline of a face which shows the individual as unmistakably as a minutely detailed portrait could, and in the same way the Greek tragedian while simplifying could individualize.

The point is one that must be stressed because it is generally held that the personages of the Greek drama were not people at all but only types, abstractions of humanity. This is not true in fact and it could not be true in theory. As regards the fact, an example of individualization more easily perceived than either Hecuba or Clytemnestra, is Electra as each of the three tragedians saw her. They all left dramas in which she is a chief figure, and they all conceived her in a completely different way.

She is Clytemnestra's daughter who has continued to live on in the palace after her father's death, with one hope only, that her brother Orestes will come back from exile and avenge the murder. All three plays open when Orestes returns to find her living in utter wretchedness, refusing to make terms with her father's murderers and insulted and ill-treated by them.

In Æschylus' play when she enters, she is carrying offerings to her father's grave, sent by her mother, who is terrified because of a dream. Her first words, addressed to the chorus, slave-women of the household and devoted to her, show her troubled and uncertain:

Women, who order well all in our house,
be my advisers.
These offerings of sorrow—while I pour them
upon the grave, tell me the words to say.
What can I speak of good? How voice my prayer?
Say that I bring this from a loving wife
to a loved husband—sent by my own mother?
Not that—I have not courage. What then? Speak.
Shall I in shame and silence, as he died,
pour out the offering for the earth to drink?

The chorus bid her pray for "one to come who shall take life for life," but she shrinks back:

Can it be righteous for me to make prayer to
God for such a gift?

Assured by them it is her very duty, she prays, but in veiled words. She cannot ask for her brother to come and take vengeance upon her mother:

My father, pity me, and dear Orestes.
I pray, may he come home with happy fortune.
And I—O grant that I may be more pure

of heart, more innocent of hand, than she,
my mother. For your enemies, my father,
may retribution come, the slayers slain.

That is the utmost she can say. No passionate reproaches against her mother, no crying out for revenge. She is not passionate but very quiet, self-contained in all her sorrow, and yet when Orestes appears and she knows him, she is eagerly, warmly loving. She calls him:

My joy, my four loves, father, mother, sister,
so pitilessly killed—my brother, trusted, reverenced,
you are them all to me.

And in the dialogue that follows while the chorus cry exultantly that they will shout in triumph when the murderers are killed, and Orestes says:

Let me but take her life, then let me die.

she wishes only that her father's murderers had been slain in some far-off land. Her final prayer is that no mortal hand but Zeus himself would bring down justice on the murderers. So she passes from the scene. From first to last she never speaks of her brother's killing her mother, and she has no share in the deed. As Æschylus has drawn her, she could not have.

Completely different is Sophocles' Electra. She is burning with resentment for every wrong that she has ever suffered. She tells the chorus that she lives like a servant in her father's halls:

Clad in mean clothing, eating a slave's food,

taunted and insulted by "that woman," her mother, and "that abject dastard," Ægisthus, her mother's lover. When her sister tells her they have decided to imprison her in a dungeon as soon as he returns from his journey, she cries:

If that be all, then may he come with speed
that I may be removed far from you, every one.

To her mother who reproaches her for perpetually insulting her and thinking only of her father, never of her sister whom her father killed, she retorts:

Call me disloyal, insolent, outrageous.
If I am so accomplished, then be sure
I am your very child.

But now and again there is something pitiful in her. At the beginning of the play she prays:

Send me my brother, for I have no more
The strength to bear alone my load of grief—

To the chorus who reproach her gently for her "sullen soul" that must "forever be breeding conflicts," she answers:

I know my passion—it escapes me not—
I am ashamed before your chiding.

And when Orestes arriving speaks kindly to her before they recognize each other, she says:

Know this, you are the first to pity me.

But when he goes within to kill their mother and a shriek is heard:

Oh, I am struck down—smitten.

she cries to him:

Smite if you can once more!

As he comes out from the murder she greets him exultantly:

The guilty now is dead—is dead...

At the end when her mother's lover pleads for his life, she bids her brother:

No—slay him and forthwith, and cast him dead
Far from our sight, to dogs—to birds of prey.

They are her last words.

Euripides' Electra is unlike both of the others. In his play she has been married to a peasant so that her children might never have power to work harm to Clytemnestra and Ægisthus. Her first words are addressed to him as she comes out from their hut. Tenderness and gratitude are in them:

O friend, my friend, as God might be my friend,
Thou only hast not trampled on my tears.
Life scarce can be so hard, 'mid many fears
And many shames, when mortal heart can find
Somewhere one healing touch, as my sick mind
Finds thee.

He bids her gently not to work so hard for him:

So soft thy nurture was—

but she answers as a generous nature would:

Not pour
My strength out in thy toiling fellowship?

Thou hast enough with fields and kine to keep.
'Tis mine to make all bright within the door.

But when he departs she speaks to herself what she really feels:

Onward, O laboring tread,
As on move the years;
Onward amid thy tears,
O happier dead!
Let me remember: I am she,
Agamemnon's child, and the mother of me
Clytemnestra, the evil queen... My name
Electra...God protect my shame.
Oh, toil, toil is a weary thing,
And life is heavy.

She cannot endure the peasant's life of squalor and unending work, she who was once a princess. When Orestes comes and tells her at first that her brother has sent him to find out how matters are, she speaks with fierce passion. If he will but come back she will stand with him and kill her mother:

Yea—with the selfsame axe that slew my father.
Let me shed my mother's blood and I die happy—

And then she pours out all her misery and her humiliation and her hatred:

Tell him this grime and reek of toil that choke
My breathing; this low roof that bows my head
After a king's. This raiment—thread by thread
'Tis I must weave it or go bare...
And she—she! The spoils
Of Troy gleam round her throne, and by each hand
Queens of the East, my father's prisoners, stand,
A cloud of Orient webs and tangling gold.

And there upon the floor, the blood, the old
Black blood, yet crawls and cankers, like a rot
In the stone.

When Orestes has revealed himself to her, she is passionate with him to kill their mother and never spare. He sees Clytemnestra coming from afar and memory stirs in him:

My mother comes, my mother, my own
That bare me.

But she is exultant:

Straight into the snare!
Aye, there she comes—

And then that ever-present wrong of her rough clothing that she loathes, and her mother's soft Eastern gold-embroidered stuffs, stings her again. She says:

All in her brave array—

Orestes is thinking only of one thing:

What would we with our mother? Didst thou say
Kill her?

ELECTRA: What? Pity? Is it pity?

ORESTES: She gave me suck. How can I strike her?

ELECTRA: Strike her as she struck Our father!

When her mother arrives she goes with her into the house so that she can help in the murder, with never a hesitation, never a thought to hold her back. But after it is done and brother and sister re-enter, all her passion has gone. She is horror-struck, but her thought is for Orestes, not herself. She wants to take all the guilt and spare him, warm and generous as in the first scene with the peasant:

Brother, mine is the blame—
And I was the child at her knee—
"Mother," I named her name.
What clime shall hold
My evil or roof it above?
I cried in my heart for love—
What love shall kiss my brow
Nor blench at the brand stamped there?

Orestes cries that the deed was his:

I lifted over mine eyes
My mantle: blinded I smote
As one smiteth a sacrifice,
And the sword found her throat.

But she will have it the guilt is hers who planned and urged him on:

I gave thee the sign and the word.
I touched with mine hand the sword—

Then she kneels to cover the body:

Her that I loved of yore,
Her that I hated sore—

her last words, except at the end to bid her brother farewell.

The three women have nothing in common but their situation. Æschylus' Electra is gentle and loving and dutiful, driven on against her own nature by the duty so all-important in antiquity, to exact vengeance for a father's death; but not only completely incapable herself of carrying it out, not even equal to facing her brother's doing so.

To Sophocles she is an embittered, stern, strong woman, who lives for one thing only, vengeance. Completely brave, never stooping to submit to those who have absolute power over her; resolved if Orestes does not return, to try to kill her father's murderers herself or die; knowing no least hesitation before killing her mother or shadow of regret when she is dead; and yet touched here and there with something of pathos.

Euripides' picture is by far the most carefully studied. He too draws an embittered woman, but one in whom the lesser insults rankle as much as the great wrongs done her. She hates her poverty and her grimy hut and her poor clothes, along with her father's murderers. She is as determined as Sophocles' heroine that her mother shall be killed, indeed she helps in the murder, as Sophocles does not have her do, but the moment the deed is done she turns upon herself with a passion of loathing and remorse, and at the end, covering her mother's body, she remembers that she loved her.

Each of the three is an individual woman different from the other two but all are drawn with complete clarity. There is nothing complicated in them, nothing to be doubtfully analyzed. There they stand, unmistakably outlined, each herself, a person, greatly suffering and able to exalt us by the passion of her pain, but simple, direct, easy to understand, an example of "the plain reporting of the significant." Our attention is to be directed elsewhere, to matters of a wider scope than the inner conflicts of a complex nature.

If types were what the Greek drama had centered in, bloodless representatives of humanity, and all three Electras were essentially the same—a woman, any woman, possessed by the spirit of vengeance—the plays so written would not have been tragedies. The idea of the type is as indefensible theoretically as it is false actually. A tragedy cannot take place around a type. There is no such thing as typical suffering except in the mind, a pallid image of the philosopher's making, not the artist's. Pain is the most individualizing thing on earth. It is true that it is the great common bond as well but that realization comes only when it is over. To suffer is to be alone; to watch another suffer is to know the barrier that shuts each of us away by himself. Only individuals can suffer and only individuals have a place in tragedy. The personages of the Greek drama show first and foremost what suffering is in a great soul, and therefore they move us to pity and awe. Emotions are not aroused by an abstraction of the mind, but Hecuba is forever something to us to stir the feelings and quicken the spirit. Tragedy belongs to the domain of poetry which has nothing to do with the type.

The type belongs to comedy, intellectual comedy, the comedy of wit and satire. According as an art is strongly intellectual or not, the balance is tipped toward the type or toward the individual. In modern days the art which is inclined toward the typical, which is centered in what the mind and the eye perceive, is best exemplified by the French. The individualizing tendency, the preoccupation with the deep and lonely life of each human being, marks the English. The French are interested in what things are; the English in what things mean. They are the great poets of the modern world as the French are the great intellectualists.

In a Molière comedy the central character is a type, only slightly individualized. Tartuffe is not a hypocrite, he is the hypocrite. His creator has not only depicted his hypocrisy with such complete fidelity that the vice is stamped clearly forevermore, but he has at the same time so heightened it—*l'exagération juste* is the French phrase—that hypocrisy is embodied in Tartuffe. He is a great artistic creation; he is not a living human being. Like all Molière's characters he moves on the stage, not in real life. Molière is called by common consent a great comic poet but he has nothing of the poet in him unless the word is used to cover all creative genius. His comedy of wit, irony, and satire is the creation of the crystal-clear intellect, the farthest remove from that which allies the lunatic, the lover, and the poet. But to Shakespeare, the poet, types meant nothing at all. His characters are people in real life, never thought of as personages of the stage. Falstaff sits at his ease in his inn; he walks the London streets; always he moves against the background of life; it is inconceivable that he should be placed forever on the theatre boards. Is it a stage wood and moonlight of the electric arc that come to mind with Bottom and his crew? The green plot is their stage, the hawthorn brake their tiring house, the chaste beams of the wat'ry moon their light. To think of Beatrice and Benedict is to be transported to an orchard as inevitably as to think of Alceste and Célimène is to be in fancy seated before the footlights.

Life is what the spirit is concerned with, the individual. Abstractions from life are what the mind is concerned with, the classified, the type. The Greeks were concerned with both. They wanted to know what things are and what things mean. They did not lose the individual in the type nor the type in the individual, Tartuffe's universal truth or Falstaff's living reality. The most familiar of all the sayings that has come down to us from classic times was spoken indeed by a Roman but it is a purely Greek conception, the basic idea of one of the greatest of Greek philosophies, "I am a man and nothing in mankind do I hold alien to me."

In Greek tragedy the figures are seen very simply from afar, parts of a whole that has no beginning and no end, and yet in some strange fashion their remoteness does not diminish their profoundly tragic and individual appeal. They suffer greatly and passionately and therefore they are greatly, passionately alive.

There is only one other masterpiece that can help us to an understanding of this method, the life of Christ. It is the supreme tragedy but it is tragedy after the Greek model. The figure of Christ is outlined with complete simplicity, and yet by no possibility could He be thought of as a type. In a Shakespeare tragedy the moving power is that the characters are so shown to us, we can look deep into the mystery of the human soul, as we cannot even with our nearest and our dearest. And the result is that we identify ourselves with them; we ourselves become in our degree Hamlet or Lear. That is not the moving power of a Greek drama nor has it anything to do with what moves us in the Gospels. The Evangelists never let us know what went on within when the words they record were spoken and the deeds they tell of done. "And Peter said, Man, I know not what thou sayest. And immediately while he yet spake, the cock crew. And the Lord turned and looked upon Peter."

Our sense of the tragedy of the Gospels does not come from our identifying ourselves with Christ nor from any sense of deep personal knowledge. He is given to us more simply drawn than any other character anywhere, and more unmistakable in His individuality than any other. He stands upon the tremendous stage of the conflict of good and evil for mankind, and we are far removed; we can only watch. That agony is of another sort from ours. Yet never, by no other spectacle, has the human heart been so moved to pity and to awe. And after some such fashion the Greek dramatists worked.

It is an achievement possible only when mind and spirit are balanced. The mind simplifies, for it sees everything related, everything part of a whole, as Christ in the Gospel story is the mediator between God and man. The spirit individualizes. The figure of the Son of Man, so depicted that throughout the centuries a great multitude which no man could number, of all nations and kindreds and peoples and tongues, have suffered with Him and understood through Him, is the creation of the spirit.

So too the characters in Greek drama were the result of the Greek balance, individuals that showed a truth for all humanity in every human being, mankind in a man. The Greek mind that must see a thing never in and for itself but always connected with what was greater, and the Greek spirit that saw beauty and meaning in each separate thing, made Greek tragedy as they made Greek sculpture and Greek architecture, each an example of something completely individual at once simplified and given its significance by being always seen as connected with something universal, an expression of the Greek ideal, "beauty, absolute, simple, and everlasting...the irradiation of the particular by the general."

* i.e. of the Agamemnon, which is the first of the trilogy dealing with all that happened after Agamemnon's return, to Orestes' final acquittal for his mother's death.

THE WAY OF THE MODERN WORLD

In its ultimate analysis the balance between the particular and the general is that between the spirit and the mind. All that the Greeks achieved was stamped by that balance. In a sense, it was the cause of all they did. The flowering of genius in Greece was due to the immense impetus given when clarity and power of thought was added to great spiritual force. That union made the Greek temples, statues, writings, all the plain expression of the significant; the temple in its simplicity; the statue in its combination of reality and ideality; the poetry in its dependence upon ideas; the tragedy in its union of the spirit of inquiry with the spirit of poetry. It made the Athenians lovers of fact and of beauty; it enabled them to hold fast both to the things that are seen and to the things that are not seen, in all they have left behind for us, science, philosophy, religion, art.

But since the days of Greece that balanced view has been the rarest of achievements. The Western world has not taken outright the way of the spirit, nor the way of the mind, but wavered between the two, giving adherence now to one, now to the other, never able finally to discard either yet powerless to reconcile their claims.

When the Greek city-state came to an end, in the bewilderment and insecurity that followed, men turned away from the visible world of the mind to the Stoics and the unshakable security of their kingdom of the spirit. In like manner, during the first centuries after Christ the trend of the Church, poor and weak and persecuted, was strongly away from the visible. Those were the years that saw the anchorites of the desert; the saint who lived upon a pillar; they saw self-torture and self-mutilation exalted. The things that are seen began to be viewed not only as negligible but as evil, drawing men away from the pure contemplation of the invisible. With the coming of the great monastic orders, that extreme tendency was checked; learning and art had a place and austerities were moderated, but the misery that underlay the lovely superstructure of the Middle Ages worked as misery has always done, turning men against the bitter reality of life, and freedom of thought was as unknown as if Greece had never lived. With the Renaissance and the rediscovery of Greece the pendulum swung far over to the other side. Grim wretchedness had ceased to be a matter of course in the Italian cities. People had begun to enjoy themselves and they were using their minds. They demanded liberty to think and to love life and the beauty of earth, but in their turn they ended by regarding as negligible the things that are not seen and they made their gain finally at the cost of morality and ethics. The Reformation asserted both morality and man's right to think for himself, but denied beauty and the right of enjoyment. The last great swing of the pendulum was in the late nineteenth century when the battle was fought for scientific truth, and in the victory religion and art and the claims of the spirit were all slighted or discarded.

Never since Greek days has the balance been maintained throughout; only very seldom has it been achieved even in a single field. Here and there through the ages, however, it has come to pass in this matter or in that, and always, even when so circumscribed, it has accomplished something great and of lasting good. When the wisest of Roman lawgivers said that the enforcement of an absolutely just law without any exceptions, irrespective of particular differences, worked absolute injustice, he was declaring in effect that Rome had been able in this one matter to perceive the balance between the individual and the general, between the claims of the single man and the majority, between men's sympathy and their reason. In this one field Rome reached the balance Greece reached in every field she entered, and Rome has been the lawmaker for the world.

The only balance we can see with any degree of clearness that we are struggling toward today is in some sort like that achieved by Rome. The opposition between the spirit and the mind which we are chiefly conscious of is that between the individual and the community. Our great achievement, that which our age will stand for above all, is Science, but modern science, unlike that of Greece, has kept to the mind alone, and the balance there between the law and the exception, the particular and the general, is only intellectual; the spiritual does not enter in. As regards our art and our literature nothing certain can be perceived. The trend toward the individual reached its height in Shakespeare and the Renaissance painters; nothing since has approached in greatness what was then done, but the individual has continued to be the focus of all our art.

At the moment, there seems to be discernible a turning away from this extreme individualization, but the movement is too new for us to know whether it has any real importance or promise for the future. The balance we are seeing more and more distinctly before us will be, if ever it is achieved, a new one, because we are directing our chief energies toward new fields of social and economic forces, and, most of all, because we have a knowledge and a point of view about the individual which have never been in the world before.

For nineteen hundred years the West has been undergoing a process of education in the particular versus the general. We have been in school to the foremost individualist of all time who declared that the very hairs of each man's head were numbered. That intense individualization has molded our spirit, and it has brought to us problems new in the history of mankind, together with trouble of mind and bitter disagreement where once there was ease and unanimity. It is not men's greed, nor their ambition, nor yet their machines, it is not even the removal of their ancient landmarks, that is filling our present world with turmoil and dissension, but our new vision of the individual's claim against the majority's claim.

Things were simple in days of old when the single man had no right at all if a common good conflicted, his life taken for any purpose that served the public welfare, his blood sprinkled over the fields to make the harvest plentiful. Then a new idea, the most disturbing ever conceived, dawned, that every human being had rights. Men began to question what had been unquestioned since the world began: a father's authority, a king's, a slave-holder's. Perplexity and division came where all had been plain and simple. The individual had made his appearance and nothing was to be plain and simple again; no clear distinction could be drawn any more between what was just and unjust. Today we see, fitfully and dimly, but more constantly and clearly, the individual sacrificed to the greatest good of the greatest number—the coal miner, the criminal in the death-house. Everywhere we are distracted by the claim of the single man against the common welfare.

Along with this realization of each unit in the mass has come an over-realization of ourselves. We are burdened with over-realization. Not that we can perceive too clearly the rights and wrongs of every human being but that we feel too deeply our own, to find in the end that what has meaning only for each one alone has no real meaning at all.

Greek scientists in their century or two of life remade the universe. They leaped to the truth by an intuition, they saw a whole made up of related parts, and with the sweep of their vision the old world of hodge-podge and magic fell away and a world of order took its place. They could only begin the detailed investigation of the parts, but, ever since, Science has by an infinite labor confirmed their intuition of the whole. Greek artists found a disorganized world of human beings, a complex mass made up of units unrelated and disordered, and they too had an intuition of parts all belonging to a whole. They saw what is permanently important in a man and unites him to the rest.

We cannot recapture the Greek point of view; the simplicity and directness of their vision are not for us. The wheels of time never turn backward, and fortunately so. The deep integration of the idea of the individual gained through the centuries since Greece can never be lost. But modern science has made generalizations of greater truth than the Greeks could reach through a greater knowledge of individual facts. If we can follow that method and through our own intense realization of ourselves reach a unity with all men, seeing as deeply as the great tragic poets of old saw, that what is of any importance in us is what we share with all, then there will be a new distribution in the scales and the balance held so evenly in those great days of Greece may be ours as well. The goal which we see ourselves committed to struggle toward without method or any clear hope, can be attained in no other way: a world where no one shall be sacrificed against his will, where general expediency which is the mind of mankind, and the feeling for each human being which is the spirit and the heart of mankind, shall be reconciled.

"For we war not against flesh and blood," wrote St. Paul, "but against principalities and powers..." The bitterest conflicts that have divided the minds of men and set family against family, and brother against brother, have not been waged for emperor or king, but for one side of the truth to the suppression of the other side. And yet, as our struggle today is again proving, there is something within us that will not let us rest in the divided truth. Even though the way of the West since Greece has been always to set mind against spirit, never to grasp the twofold aspect of all human beings, yet we are not able to give ourselves wholly up to one and let the other drop from our consciousness. Each generation in turn is constrained to try to reconcile the truth the spirit knows with the truth the mind knows, to make the inner world fit into the ever-changing frame of the outer world. To each in turn it appears impossible; either the picture or the frame must go, but the struggle toward adjustment never ends, for the necessity to achieve it is in our nature.

The East can let the frame go and give up the struggle. We of the West, slaves to the reason, cannot. For brief periods we have thought that we could let the picture go, but that negation of the things each man knows most surely for himself is always partial and of short duration. In our present effort after adjustment which not only seems to us, but is, more difficult than any before because we are aware of so much more, it is worth our while to consider the adjustments achieved in the past. Of them all, the Greek was the most complete. The Greeks did not abstract away the outside world to prefer the claims of the world within; neither did they deny the spirit in favor of its incarnation. To them the frame and the picture fitted; the things that are seen and the things that are not seen harmonized.

For a hundred years Athens was a city where the great spiritual forces that war in men's minds flowed along together in peace; law and freedom, truth and religion, beauty and goodness, the objective and the subjective—there was a truce to their eternal warfare, and the result was the balance and clarity, the harmony and completeness, the word Greek has come to stand for. They saw both sides of the paradox of truth, giving predominance to neither, and in all Greek art there is an absence of struggle, a reconciling power, something of calm and serenity, the world has yet to see again.

IMAGE COPYRIGHT INFORMATION

Page 9: Serato/Shutterstock.com;
Page 59, 79, 225: Wikimedia Commons/Public Domain;
Page 99, 123, 140, 162, 200, 213: Shutterstock.com;
Page 183: Wikimedia Commons/Public Domain–US.

BOOKS BY EDITH HAMILTON IN THE HACHETTE BLACKJACKET SERIES

The Roman Way

Mythology

UPCOMING TITLES IN THE HACHETTE BLACKJACKET SERIES

- *A History of Western Philosophy* by Bertrand Russell
- *Ideas and Opinions* by Albert Einstein
- *Gandhi's Letters to a Disciple*
- *Out of Africa* by Karen Blixen
- *Phulmat of the Hills: A Tale of the Gonds* by Verrier Elwin
- *Ten Days That Shook the World* by John Reed
- *The Autobiography of Alice B. Toklas* by Gertrude Stein
- *The Hedgehog and the Fox* by Isaiah Berlin
- *The Idea of History* by R.G. Collingwood
- *The Richest Man in Babylon* by George Samuel Clason
- *The Thurber Carnival* by James Thurber

Hachette BlackJackets